Surviving the Bible

Surviving the Bible series:

Surviving the Bible:
A Devotional for the Church Year 2018

Surviving the Bible:
A Devotional for the Church Year 2019

Surviving the Bible:
A Devotional for the Church Year 2020

Christian Piatt

Surviving
the
Bible

A Devotional
for the
Church Year

2019

SURVIVING THE BIBLE
A Devotional for the Church Year 2019

Copyright © 2018 Fortress Press an imprint of 1517 Media. All rights reserved. Except for brief quotations in critical articles or reviews, no part of this book may be reproduced in any manner without prior written permission from the publisher. Email copyright@1517.media or write to Permissions, Fortress Press, PO Box 1209, Minneapolis, MN 55440-1209.

Cover design: Brad Norr
Design and Typesetting: PerfecType, Nashville, TN

Print ISBN: 978-1-5064-2067-7
eBook ISBN: 978-1-5064-2068-4

The paper used in this publication meets the minimum require-ments of American National Standard for Information Sci-ences—Permanence of Paper for Printed Library Materials, ANSI Z329.48-1984.

Manufactured in the U.S.A.

Contents

Series Introduction

The Bible clearly says . . .

We've all heard this phrase, usually in the middle of some ideological combat about "values." And yet, it seems like we tend to use the Bible to reinforce whatever we already believe. But when we see what we want to see in Scripture, it mutates from being a light and path to being a sword and shield.

As Anne Lamott says, "You can safely assume you've created God in your own image when it turns out that God hates all the same people you do."

That, or the Bible feels too big, complicated, beyond our reach. So many people understand it better than we do. At the same time, we have this need to connect, to find wisdom in its pages. We feel a pull back to it, over and again. And in a time of "alternative facts," when we long for something true, something real to offer us some deeper wisdom, we wonder what Scripture *really says* about climate change, war, sexuality, gender roles, and money. We would welcome its guidance, if we only knew how to get at it.

I have tried, more than once, to read the Bible from start to finish. Maybe you have too. I can't count how many times I started with Genesis and, by the time I get to the labyrinth of laws in Numbers (if not before), I give up. That's why I'm writing this three-book series called *Surviving the Bible*.

The Bible is the bestselling printed volume in world history. It was the very first thing printed after the printing press was created, and it's sold over 2.5 *billion* copies since. Over 100 million copies are sold or given away every year, or more than 190 every single minute. The entire Bible has been translated into more than 650 languages; the New Testament has been translated into more than 1,400. It's consistently at the top of the list of favorite books in America when people are surveyed.

And yet I'd argue it's also the most misunderstood text in our culture, partly because most of us have never read the whole thing. In fact, only about 9 percent of folks asked claim to have read it all.

My kids love what I call my "dad jokes," or at least I tell myself they love them so I have an excuse to keep telling them. And of course I can't resist sneaking some lessons in there when I can. One of my favorites is "How do you eat an elephant? One bite at a time." Yeah, they roll their eyes but I know they're laughing hysterically inside.

The point is that we don't have to read the Bible all at once. It's not a book written from start to finish, meant to be read like a novel either. It's a collection of laws, stories, history, poems, and predictions written by dozens of different people from multiple cultures and in several languages over thousands of years. It was written for different people with different needs at different times. But the reason we still consider it important today is because so much of the wisdom found, sometimes buried mysteriously like treasure, still rings true.

But who goes looking for treasure without a map? It would be a waste of time. The problem is that so many so-called maps to the wisdom in Scripture are more like instruction manuals, telling us what to think and how to believe. Maps, on the other hand, offer a way to find something without telling us what you have to do with it when we get there.

We crave meaning, grounding. We long to separate fact from opinion, to grab hold of something bigger than ourselves. We want to broaden our vision in a time when everyone seems so utterly blinded by the immediate reality, right in front of them. We want answers, but more than that, we want peace. We want to separate fact from opinion and to discern truths that transcend immediate facts, wisdom that has resonated across cultures and generations since we started asking questions as a species about why we're here and what our purpose is.

Fred Craddock was right when he claimed that the Bible can be used to make any point we want. But it's too important a resource to depend on others to tell us what it means. We can think for ourselves; all we need is a guide.

This book is set up like a weekly meditation, breaking down the Bible "elephant" into bite-sized pieces. It follows the church calendar in case you're a part of a church that observes it, but you don't have to be. In fact, you don't have to go to church at all to use this. You don't have to know what you believe either. You don't even have to be a Christian. Use it as a weekly study, or browse the glossary for themes you're curious about. It's an ideal resource to use with a friend or small group, but it's set up to be accessed by anyone who has enough curiosity, openness, and a desire to grow.

Start anywhere. Set it down and come back to it, over and over. There's no "wrong way" to use *Surviving the Bible*. Just open it up, grab a Bible, and take a bite.

Christian Piatt

All in
the Family

Lectionary Texts For
December 2, 2018 (First Sunday in Advent)

Texts In Brief
My dog ate my Bible!

FIRST READING
Jeremiah 33:14–16

The prophet speaks of a time in the future when a promise made by God will be fulfilled. A "branch" (i.e., person) will come along who will be born of David's lineage. He will be named "the Lord is our righteousness" and will save descendants of Judah and the citizens of Jerusalem.

PSALM
25:1–10

The psalmist asks God to have a short memory for their previous screw-ups, focusing instead on directing them toward a more righteous path in life. The ending shifts from speaking to God to addressing readers about God's wise and faithful nature.

Second Reading
Thessalonians 3:9–13

Paul is praying in this letter on behalf of his Christian colleagues in Thessalonica. From the tone of it, it sounds like they're getting discouraged and maybe even turning that negative energy in toward each other. But instead Paul asks God to reinvigorate them and strengthen their conviction to point them back toward their mission.

Gospel
Luke 21:25–36

There's going to be a time in the near future, Jesus says, when people will start freaking out because of all of the volatility around them. Some will take that distress and take it out on other people, but Jesus encourages his audience to look more closely at the signs all around them of what all of this means, and to what it is pointing. Finally, he offers a word of warning for them to stay alert for all of this as it comes rather than getting distracted by earthly preoccupations. It's not going to be easy to handle when it all goes down, Jesus says, so he urges them to pray for strength and endurance.

Bible, Decoded
Breaking down Scripture in plain language

Branch—Really, this is just another word for "descendant." It helps to solidify the impression that the line of David's descendants (going back to Abraham, both of whom were blessed by God) are all part of a bigger story, and that when this person comes, they too will be a part of that story playing out.

Judah—Judah was the fourth son of Jacob and Leah, and more important to this story, he was said to be a direct ancestor of Jesus. So again, the point is being driven home that all of these people and all of their stories are connected, part of a larger whole.

Points to Ponder

First Thoughts

One thing that can be lost on us today is the importance of ancestry and bloodlines in the times when these texts were written. Whereas we are better known these days for what we do, back then people were defined largely by who their ancestors were. We can tell in their names, like when we consider that Jesus's last name wasn't "Christ" or "of Nazareth"; it was Jesus-ben-Joseph. That means "Jesus, son of Joseph." His name is tied right to his father. Of course, we still have the tradition of passing on last names, and sometimes even first "family" names, but it's just that more than anything: tradition.

Most of us don't know much, if anything, about our ancestors just a few generations back. But these cultures held ancestry in tremendously higher regard, thus the great lengths undertaken to trace Jesus's lineage over thousands of years back to these particular people.

It might be easy enough for us to question why this really matters. After all, if we believe Jesus is directly from God, then what does the rest really matter? But more than the blood itself, it points to the importance of story—and history as revealed through story—to show that we're all part of something much, much bigger than just ourselves.

It's humbling if you think about it that way. Maybe this whole ancestry thing has some unrealized value that we've lost touch with.

Digging Deeper

Mining for what really matters . . . and gold

This Jeremiah text was authored around six hundred years before Jesus's birth, and yet it's pointing the way toward this yet-to-be-known event. But why? Or put another way, why now?

Consider that the Hebrews are a people without a place, without any sense of home at this point. They've been defeated by the invading Babylonians, sentenced to serve them as slaves. For those among them who know their ancestry, they're aware that this is all too familiar in their past as a people. Exile and enslavement have been a part of their story since their captivity in Egypt. So they're a people without place and without identity.

Jeremiah's prophecy, however, is meant to offer them some sense of rootedness by reminding them that they are a part of a much bigger, broader, and longer story. And while their present circumstances are really tough, it's a promise not only that they will endure (they have to, after all, for this promise from God to be fulfilled) but that they are an integral part of the most important story they've ever heard.

In Thessalonians, Paul is offering some similar relief, not by calling his fellow apostles back from the mission field, but by reorienting their focus back on something beyond the present difficulties. Jesus's foretelling is a little bit different because he's letting those listening know that the hard time hasn't come yet, but it will soon.

Talk about a buzzkill.

But he's paying attention to the signs he refers to. He sees them before they do. He knows that if he keeps at his current focus, he's not long for this world. Granted, this Gospel text can be interpreted as a foreshadowing of times further into the future, as later described in more (horrible, weird) detail in Revelation. But he also has enough common sense and self-awareness that there's only one outcome to his ministry, and it's not going to be pleasant.

It's kind of like when my dad would promise me that I could have Oreos if I'd let him cut my hair. It's not that the Oreos got me out of getting my hair cut, and I still hated it. But somehow, having those Oreos to focus on while he was cutting it made it a little bit easier to endure. There was a longer game at play, and when I had a reason to endure the yucky stuff, I was more capable of getting through it.

A trivial comparison, maybe, but the point remains that being afforded some vision of what's beyond the present challenges does make the difficulties more manageable. It makes me wonder if Jeremiah, Paul, and Jesus would have had an easier go of it if they'd only had some Oreos.

Heads Up

Connecting the text to our world

Raise your hand if you feel settled and grounded during Lent. And for you literalists, put your hands down; I'm just using this figure of speech to make a point.

Advent is—I think somewhat intentionally—a time of *not* feeling in balance or centered. We're headed toward this incredible miracle that's hard to make any sense of, but we're not there yet. And even when we get there, we're not sure we'll be ready for all it represents.

It's also this weird time of contradiction for those of us in the Northern hemisphere. While we've associated the secular season of Christmas and Advent with snow and evergreens, something about it doesn't seem to fit. Days are getting shorter, we're spending more time in darkness, and on top of that, it's *cold!* I know some of you may argue that you like to be half-frozen, but I'm not with you. There's nothing celebratory about being cold to me. It's more something to be endured.

Then again, maybe that's exactly what we should be wrestling with on the way to a miracle we still don't completely understand after all these years. Wandering in darkness is kind of fitting, actually. And yet we keep going toward Christmas, one tentative step at a time, not entirely sure we're doing it right, not sure we feel how we ought to feel, not sure how everyone else seems to at least pretend to be feeling.

Birth is messy, even violent. There's going to be friction, even conflict, on the way there. But if we don't get too caught up in all of the noise and frenzy and instead look a little more closely, maybe we'll see these subtle signs around us that keep saying to us—even inviting us, in a way . . .

> *Something is coming.*

Prayer for the Week

God, I get bogged down in the hard stuff right in front of me, to the point that I feel kind of lost and without direction. Help me make sense of it if I can, or at least give me the strength to handle it.

Popping Off

Art/music/video and other cool stuff that relate to the text

Star Wars: Return of the Jedi (movie, 1983)

Black Panther (movie, 2018)

My God,
It's Full of Stars

Lectionary Texts For
December 9, 2018 (Second Sunday of Advent)

Texts in Brief
My dog ate my Bible!

First Reading
Malachi 3:1–4

The prophet talks of the time when someone will come to live among his people and speak of the soon-to-come messiah. He clarifies that it's not going to be easy, as there will be a lot of proverbial housecleaning to do. The ways in which people have strayed from their intended path will have to be made right, and they're cautioned against making empty rituals of whatever they offer to God. God will still look on God's people with a merciful heart, but there will be work to do in getting people fit for being in God's presence.

Second Reading
Philippians 1:3–11

Paul showers affection on his colleagues in Philippi and instills them with the confidence he has in them that they will have people ready when Jesus returns. He prays on their behalf that their divinely inspired love and wisdom would continue to grow so that they would be purified by it before God's work on earth is to be completed.

Gospel
Luke 1:68–79

A song offered by Zechariah that first praises God for giving them the fulfillment of God's promises for a Messiah. He also acknowledges that God has afforded the people of Israel a path to where they are in the present, having spared them from extinction at the hands of their many enemies over time. Then he sings to his son, John the Baptist, about his calling as a prophet—a speaker of truth—to help prepare people for the Messiah's imminent coming. John is to give people what they need to prepare for what is about to happen.

and

Luke 3:1–6

An account of John the Baptist being called to his ministry as the prophet, leading the way for the Messiah's entry into the world. It speaks of his ministry of preaching and baptism, and how his coming is the beginning of the fulfillment of Isaiah's foretelling of the emergence of a Chosen One who would set things right within God's much-loved creation.

Bible, Decoded

Breaking down Scripture in plain language

Zechariah—There are a couple of Zechariahs in the Bible, so we'll clarify who we're talking about. This one is not the prophet who has a book of the Hebrew Bible attributed to him. This one is a priest who wasn't expecting ever to have children, as he and his wife, Elizabeth, had never been able to conceive. But once when he was making an offering in the temple, Gabriel (the same angel who told Mary she would give birth to Jesus) told him he and Elizabeth would have a child who would fulfill the Scripture's predictions of a messenger being sent to precede the Messiah (as is talked about in Malachi).

Malachi—The name "Malachi" can be translated as "God's messenger," which is exactly what he is (yay for truth in advertising!). The book of Malachi is the final one of the prophetic books of the Hebrew Bible, which also makes it the last book of the Hebrew Bible, period. He's kind of the warm-up messenger or pre-messenger that tells people to be ready for John the Baptist (who will then tell people to get ready for Jesus). Guess we can't say God didn't warn us!

Though it's hard to say exactly, most biblical scholars agree that this book was written at least 400 to 450 years before Jesus's birth.

Points to Ponder

First Thoughts

As we know, if we've read ahead in the story to know what kind of Messiah he will be, Jesus catches a lot of people by surprise. And we're not just talking about the Roman occupiers or the so-called gentiles (anyone who wasn't Jewish). I suppose it's understandable since they likely wouldn't have read the sacred texts for another people. So maybe John the Baptist was kind of an insurance policy for anyone who wasn't the quickest study, or who had come from a different background and missed the prophets' many predictions.

And yet people are caught flat-footed by this Jesus guy. You've got to imagine there was more than one great, big divine head-smack when people were still surprised by what he was all about.

No, he didn't come to kick butt and take names, driving out the powers that be and letting his own people have a turn for a change. And that was a drag for a lot of them, but he had more important things to focus on.

I get it, though. If I lived in a culture where I was under the thumb of some oppressive government—yet again—and the person my people had waited on for centuries finally showed up, I'd have my own agenda too about how I expected things to go down. And it's not that all of these prophets had the message they did so God could drop an "I told you so" on them when they missed the point. It speaks to God's arguably unwarranted faith in humanity's willingness to change for the better.

Or maybe God has us right, and we're just slow on the uptake. Maybe this Advent we'll seize the opportunity to see Jesus a little bit more clearly, to get at what was worth all of these prophets shouting about his arrival for hundreds of years. It's worth a shot at least.

Digging Deeper

Mining for what really matters . . . and gold

It's interesting that we have both Luke 1 and Luke 3 in the same week. First of all, it's not very often we get two Gospel texts in the same week, so this must have been on purpose. Second, in the words of *Sesame Street*, one of these things is not like the other.

With respect to chronology, all of the texts except for Luke 3 make sense for Advent. They all have to do with the birth of John the Baptist, which effectively coincides with Jesus's birth (his cousin). But then we jump into Luke 3, and suddenly John is an adult, kick-starting his ministry. Sorry, lectionary boss guys, but that isn't a Christmas story.

Or is it?

The season of Advent is known as a time of waiting, but the word itself isn't so much about waiting as it is about arrival. And more than that, it refers specifically to the arrival either of someone really important or something that's a big deal. It can also be understood as describing an emergence or appearance, which is interesting, as John in the Luke 3 text is emerging from the wilderness of Judea to get busy with his fiery preaching and baptism work.

But we could also use this as a chance to reframe the entirety of John the Baptist's ministry. Yes, we see him as a prophet, but what if we saw the entirety of his ministry as an advent event? Imagine being born for a singular purpose, one in which you are not at the center. You simply are a way-maker, a path-clearer, a speaker of truth to all who will listen about what is coming, and about the signs all around us already.

In a way, this is a summation of what the Christian experience is. We are an Advent people. And if we look at John's example, preparing and waiting isn't an idle occupation. On the contrary, he's fairly obsessed with sharing what he sees so clearly. Something he feels to his bones. Something he feels is so important, so world-shifting, that it's worth throwing his whole self into.

Heads Up

Connecting the text to our world

If ever there was a character in popular culture that epitomized John the Baptist, it would be Commander David Bowman from the movie *2001: A Space Odyssey* and the follow-up movie, *2010*. In the story, Bowman is on a mission to Jupiter, where he and his skeleton crew (survivors of the rest of the treacherous mission) discover a large, black monolith hovering mysteriously in Jupiter's orbit. Bowman takes a small pod toward the monolith to investigate, and a small portal opens. As Bowman enters the opening, the last thing he says in his transmission back to his ship is, "My God, it's full of stars."

Fast-forward to a reconnaissance and rescue mission to find out what happened to Bowman's ship and crew (which never returned). For the sake of brevity, let's just say lots of inexplicable things start happening, and at a climactic moment, Dr. Heywood Floyd encounters Bowman (or some specter of him at least) on the deck of his ship.

Bowman offers a cryptic sort of warning and also a seductive invitation to Floyd. "You see," says Bowman, "something's going to happen. You must leave."

"What?" Floyd asks. "What's going to happen?"

"Something wonderful," Bowman says, wistfully.

"What?" Floyd urges, exasperation rising in his tone.

"I understand how you feel," says Bowman. "You see, it's all very clear to me now. The whole thing. It's wonderful."

For some, the scene—and even the entire series of films—was maddening. *Just tell us what the something is!* They raged. It all felt so loose, unresolved, vague.

But not to Bowman. For him, the anticipation of "the event" was so overwhelming that it consumed his entire existence. Words couldn't have encapsulated it even if he had tried. Either you saw it and got it, or you didn't.

But it was something so wonderful that Bowman felt compelled to share about it, imperfect as his message might be.

This event—this in-breaking—would change everything. It would utterly remake all we knew, and yet it was an object of awe. How could something so disruptive, so significant that creation never would be the same, be something to look forward to with fear and trembling, a degree of anticipation that made everything else seem trivial by comparison?

We couldn't grasp it all if we tried. The only way to really get it is to take a leap, throwing our whole selves into the mystery of it, releasing all misgivings and surrendering to the possibility that this event was worth giving everything to.

Something's going to happen. Something wonderful.

Prayer for the Week

God, I want to see this thing before I surrender to it. It's in my nature to try and feel in control, and yet, part of the point is to release control. It's Advent yet again. Help me wrap my heart and mind around it a little bit more this time around.

Popping Off

Art/music/video and other cool stuff that relate to the text

2001: A Space Odyssey (movie, 1968)

2010 (movie, 1984)

Two-for-One Reality

_____/\/\/_____

Lectionary Texts For

December 16, 2018 (Third Sunday of Advent)

Texts in Brief

My dog ate my Bible!

First Reading

Zephaniah 3:14–20

In a dramatic shift in tone for a prophet known for dark, fearsome imagery, Zephaniah shifts to a mood of joyful of celebration about his vision of God's return to dwell in humanity's midst. Mid-text, he shifts from speaking about God to speaking on God's behalf, assuring the people of Israel that God is on their side and that God's promises will be fulfilled.

and

Isaiah 12:2–6

Isaiah takes up a similar tone in this text, calling all to be joyful as God dwells among them. He encourages them not just to be personally joyful but to make it an outward proclamation so all others would know about the source of their joy.

SECOND READING
Philippians 4:4–7

This is a third text in which the apostle Paul calls on the Christians in Philippi to be joyful and to make this joy known to all who can and will hear them. Maybe in response to some anxiety he has sensed among them, he reminds them not to worry but rather just to bring all of their needs or concerns to God. He assures them that if they do, they'll be overcome with a sense of peace.

GOSPEL
Luke 3:7–18

Leave it to John the Baptist to flip the script! John calls the onlookers—specifically the Pharisees—who come to observe him and his unconventional ministry a bunch of snakes. He reprimands them for assuming they're taken care of simply because of their ancestry. He says that God can look on anyone God chooses with equal favor and that more is required of them. When the crowds ask what they need to do, he offers commands to be generous and fair to others. When they start to wonder if he is the Messiah, he clarifies that he's just setting the stage for the One who is coming.

Bible, Decoded

Breaking down Scripture in plain language

Brood of Vipers—It seems there are two reasons why John the Baptist referred to the Pharisees as a "brood of vipers," or a den of snakes. First, it's a clear reference to the many occurrences of snakes in Scripture, which represent temptation for humanity to stray. So he's clearly accusing them of false teaching. Worse than that, perhaps, is that vipers are deadly venomous. So he could be saying that their poisoning people with such false teaching leads them into death.

Exhortation—An old word that we don't use much these days, to exhort means to teach, urge, or even warn someone.

Points to Ponder

First Thoughts

The message from Paul to the Christians in Philippi reminds me of a couple of sayings about worrying that seem fitting here.

The first, "Worry is a mild form of agnosticism," is a contemporary saying whose roots are tough to trace, but it's interesting. I'm not saying that worrying is in itself a sin. But it's certainly a waste of time and energy. As for it implying agnosticism—or doubt about whether God exists—I think the point is that worry presumes that whatever is concerning us is ours to fix in the first place. It's putting ourselves at the center of any possible solution rather than moving out of the way and putting God at the center. So in this case, it seems that the best antidote for worry is recognition that, as the first step in the Twelve Steps states, we are powerless over our problem.

The second thing it reminds me of is a Buddhist saying that always makes me smile but also annoys me with how true it feels:

If there is a problem and there's something you can do about it, then don't worry about it.

If there is a problem and there's nothing you can do about it, then don't worry about it.

I'd say that pretty much speaks for itself.

Digging Deeper
Mining for what really matters . . . and gold

To combine this pretty ferocious Luke text with the celebratory Scriptures that precede it this week might seem weird if we don't realize the surrounding context of the Zephaniah text. As noted above, Zephaniah usually sounds more like John the Baptist does in the Gospel, so it seems to point to the necessary coexistence of many layers of meaning, feeling and understanding of what's going on.

Is the Messiah to be a savior of peace and love? Yes.

Is he to be a judge of those who lead people from the path intended for people by God? Yes.

Is his arrival something to celebrate? Absolutely.

Should we be checking ourselves and getting our hearts and behaviors in order? Probably not a bad idea.

John the Baptist likely didn't win a lot of "most popular" awards in high school, and I'm guessing the locust-eating made him a bit of a pariah in the cafeteria. But you can be sure that people were listening.

And we should be clear here that John isn't coming down so hard on the Pharisees because they're preparing for the coming Messiah incorrectly. It's because they're not doing anything at all about it. It's like they've forgotten this critical part of their own sacred texts. They seem to be self-righteous simply because they know the laws of their ancestors and because they come from the bloodline of Abraham.

John's warning is a call to our whole selves to be invested in this coming. It's not enough to feel justified based on who we are (i.e., calling ourselves a Christian) or what we know (like being able to recite Bible verses form memory). It's a turning of our hearts that he's calling for, which should be expressed outwardly by the natural actions to follow.

The very fact that they're asking him what they need to do suggests to him that they don't get it, which is why he caps off the text with another fiery (literally here) screed about how those who aren't trying to change from the inside-out will be separated out. Appearances don't impress God. Transformation does.

Heads Up

Connecting the text to our world

I've been learning a lot about love, and about how grief is intimately entwined with joy.

We got the call on a Thursday night and were on a plane from Portland to New Mexico Friday morning. Papa Russ was dying, and we needed to come soon to help care for him and say our goodbyes. Cancer was everywhere: in his bones, his one remaining kidney, and other organs throughout his frail body. My six-year-old daughter, Zoe, wailed at the news, fearful that she would never see her Papa again, but we assured her we wouldn't let that happen.

On the journey to their ranch on the Rio Grande, the reality of what we were journeying to witness began to sink in.

"What is he going to look like?" asked my twelve-year-old son, Mattias. We explained that he was very different than he was before. At six-foot-two, he was down to less than 130 pounds and dropping rapidly. He hadn't eaten in more than a week, and his difficulty swallowing kept him from taking in many fluids too. He had decided against an intensive hospital stay, opting instead for home hospice care. That meant no IV, no around-the-clock nurses, and no ambulances.

"But what will he look like if he dies?" Zoe asked. Her eyes started filling with sadness. "I don't want to see Papa die."

"None of us does," we said, "but being dead is very, very peaceful. It's just like a very long sleep."

"No," she wailed, "I don't want to see him die!"

His body had been largely devoured by the tumors, but his spirit had, in many ways, been liberated. Nothing but peace and grace remained. When he saw us arrive at his bedside, he looked like a little boy coming downstairs at Christmas.

"Your spirit," he beamed, holding his hands up, outlining what he saw that we did not, "glows all around you. It's so beautiful."

Zoe crawled up next to him and kissed him gently on the forehead. Papa closed his eyes and smiled. Mattias sat on the edge of the bed and read Papa a history of the Boston Tea Party he had written, dedicating it to him. Papa had been a history teacher for decades, and he had family members read it to him over and over again in his remaining days.

The days were hard, and the nights more so. His breathing became increasingly labored, and the intervals between any breaths at all became steadily longer. We took turns doing three-to-five-hour rotations, swabbing his lips, applying lotion, reminding him that he was not alone and that he was loved.

Coherence slipped from him like the air around him. His hands reached out to nothing as he fixed farm equipment, split wood, or did his post-surgery stretches that filtered through his gauzy imagination.

Finally one of the apnea episodes didn't let go of him and he released himself to the otherness of death. We gathered around him in the middle of the lingering darkness as I read some verses from Kahlil Gibran's *The Prophet* that he and my mom had read at their wedding. We joined hands and prayed our farewells, I applied precious oil from the Holy Land to his head, his face and hands, sang "Softly and Tenderly" to ease his passage, and we cried together. It was eerily silent without the chatter and sigh of the oxygen machine behind his gasping wheezes every several seconds. Somehow in only a couple of days we had grown used to them, attuned to them.

And now they had stopped.

That night, as people filtered in and out of the house, delivering meals, sharing stories, and participating in our own *goy* version of sitting *shiva*, I went away to be alone. In some ways I'm like a dog who is sick and leaves the pack to lick my wounds. Whereas the rest of the family found comfort in togetherness, I found solace in the silence—save for the crackles of the fire in the wood stove, warming my feet and casting a patient glow in the otherwise empty room.

Zoe peeked in around the corner with a slice of lemon meringue pie for me in her tiny hands. As I took a few bites, she crawled into my lap, resting her head against my shoulder.

"Daddy," she said, "how far away is Papa?" I paused, thinking for a moment before responding. She isn't like other children who toss out questions as if they were stones, skipping across a river, only to sink forever into the blackness.

She was forming her understanding of good and evil, life and death, and therefore my words needed to be careful and intentional.

"I think he's here and here, honey," I said, touching her forehead and chest. "He'll always be with us."

"No," she shook her head. She pointed out into the glowing, dancing room. "I mean where is he?"

"I see," I said. "Well, how far does he feel like he is to you?"

"Really far away," she sighed and turned her face toward me. "I don't like far away."

"Me either," I said, closing my eyes and kissing the top of her head. "Maybe heaven is where 'far away' doesn't exist anymore."

"Maybe so," she smiled, curling her feet underneath her. "I think that sounds nice."

Perhaps the love of God fully realized closes the gap between our suffering and our joy and makes us whole.

Kahlil Gibran writes in *The Prophet* (1923), "Your joy is your sorrow unmasked. And the selfsame well from which your laughter rises is oftentimes filled with your tears. And how else can it be? The deeper that sorrow carves into your being, the more joy you can contain.

"Is not the cup that holds your wine the very cup that was burned in the potter's oven? And is not the lute that soothes your spirit, the very wood that was hollowed with knives? When you are joyous, look deep into your heart and you shall find it is only that which has given you sorrow that is giving you joy. When you are sorrowful look again in your heart, and you shall see that in truth you are weeping for that which has been your delight.

"Some of you say, 'Joy is greater than sorrow,' and others say, 'Nay, sorrow is the greater.'

But I say unto you, they are inseparable. Together they come, and when one sits, alone with you at your board, remember that the other is asleep upon your bed. Verily you are suspended like scales between your sorrow and your joy. Only when you are empty are you at standstill and balanced."

Prayer for the Week

God, I struggle to find joy when things are hard and to see beauty in brokenness. Help me unmask my sorrow to reveal the joy within it.

Popping Off

Art/music/video and other cool stuff that relate to the text

The Prophet, by Kahlil Gibran (book, 1923)

Salvation Is an Inside Job

Lectionary Texts For
December 23, 2018 (Fourth Sunday in Advent)

Texts in Brief
My dog ate my Bible!

First Reading
Micah 5:2–5a

Micah predicts that a great leader will come from the land of Bethlehem, a minor territory within the larger nation of Israel. This leader will help heal the divisions among the different factions among them and will call for political and military leaders to come together in pushing back the anticipated attack from Assyria against the Israelites.

Psalm
Psalm 80:1–7

Things are not good for the Hebrews. They're undergoing suffering and are at odds with their enemies, and the psalmist suggests that God isn't providing for them. Overall, this is a call to God for restoration of many sorts.

and

Luke 1:46b–55

A pregnant Mary, mother of Jesus, bursts into a song of praise to God. She marvels at being a nobody and yet being chosen for such an important role in the story of her people. She sings that God is merciful to and provides for all who serve God well, but that God scatters and makes low those who are arrogant or obsessed with material wealth. Finally, she sings that God always keeps God's promises throughout the generations, all the way back to Abraham.

SECOND READING
Hebrews 10:5–10

The author of Hebrews revisits the notion put forward by Jesus that our offerings don't make up for our sin. They may serve as a reminder of our sin, and that we need to change our ways, but the offerings do nothing for God per se. Part of Jesus's role, Paul notes, is to put an end to this tradition of making atoning sacrifices just because the law says to. Rather, he models that the real sacrifice God seeks is for us to live lives of sacrificial selflessness, placing love for others above all else, as modeled by Jesus.

GOSPEL
Luke 1:39–45

Mary goes to visit her cousin, Elizabeth, wife of Zechariah. They're both pregnant (Elizabeth is pregnant with the child who will become known as John the Baptist), and when Mary comes, Elizabeth's baby leaps in her womb. She takes this as a sign that Mary's baby is indeed important and will be the fulfillment of the promises made to her (by way of the angel Gabriel) about her giving birth to the Messiah.

Bible, Decoded
Breaking down Scripture in plain language

Shepherds—In the context of this Micah text, the shepherds mentioned in 5:5 likely are actually military officers who will serve to recruit and gather together forces to repel the attack from Assyria. In the Psalm, "shepherd" means "one who feeds," which adds a sting right after that to the complaint that God is "feeding" his people with bread made of tears.

Manasseh—Manasseh was Joseph's oldest son and was later adopted by Jacob as his son, along with his brother, Ephraim. The "tribe of Manasseh" is an allusion to descendants of Ephraim and Benjamin in the time of wandering in exile in the desert. The name literally means "God has made me forget." So this Psalm is alluding to an apparent "desert time," or rootlessness. While it's a plaintive call to God for provision, it could also be implying that the Hebrews have lost their way.

Points to Ponder
First Thoughts

It seems like this unusual combination of texts this week seeks to respond to the larger question about why Jesus came and what his purpose was. It could be distilled down to suggest that the Hebrews—that is, the people of God, or us—have lost our way and need redirection. Some Christians would note that clearly things aren't right between God and God's people, so something has to be done. So God sends Jesus to make good once and for all for our collective sinfulness.

I tend to challenge this interpretation, however. Yes, I agree that we continue, over and over again, to lose our way and end up back in the desert, seeking our purpose, our place, and our identity. Like Manasseh, we have forgotten from where we came and by whom we are made. We've forgotten our purpose. Instead, we've lapsed into an obligatory cycle of conducting rituals without ours hearts being invested, simply because it's "what we do."

But without our hearts being given in the ritual act, there's no point. This is why Jesus is sent: to remind us where life's true meaning rests and what God requires of us: *everything*.

The notion of living sacrificially—putting all else second to what God desires of us and what others need from us—can easily be lost, especially in a time of year when our rituals of transactional offering are at their peak. Maybe your child, friend, or partner wants the latest gadget, but God wants more. Much more.

Digging Deeper

Mining for what really matters . . . and gold

This section in Hebrews is a shuffling of the priestly deck, of sorts. On the one hand, it criticizes the tradition of animal sacrifice to atone for sin, claiming that

Jesus came not just to establish a new order, a new relationship between humanity and God, but also to put an
end to the old system. This, of course, would be seen as
a direct threat to the religious order of the time, and by
some, it would even be seen as heresy.

Rather than divesting our shadow sides or past transgressions onto some scapegoat, biblical scholar Michael
Joseph Brown asserts in "Commentary on Hebrews
10:5–10" (workingpreacher.org) that Jesus (at least as
interpreted in this Hebrews text) is establishing the "perfection of conscience" at the heart of our worship of God.

Put simply, salvation is an inside job.

But why connect this text that is apparently about
the end of Jesus's life to these Gospel texts about
his birth? On the surface, it seems like this is a more
appropriate Scripture for Lent rather than right before
Christmas.

But in a flourish of poetic license, the author not
only speaks on Jesus's behalf but also claims that these
sentiments were established from the moment when
Jesus came into the world. Clearly, this doesn't mean
that Jesus popped out of the womb giving a speech
but that Jesus's mission was clear from the moment he
was born. He was sent here to show us, once and for all,
how to place the perfection of human conscience at the
heart of our worship.

And when I say "worship," I don't mean just one
hour on Sunday at church. Clearly, God isn't impressed
by our religious rituals in themselves. Rather, it is
incumbent on us to *live worshipfully*, by endeavoring to
orient our hearts and minds in the imitation of the One
we claim is our beginning and end: Jesus.

Heads Up

Connecting the text to our world

I've been a musician most of my life. When I was little, I would pick out harmonies to songs on the radio and sing along before even knowing what harmony was. When my mom played the piano (she was the church pianist for much of my young life), I would sit underneath the upright, resting my head on the wood of the instrument so I could feel the music throughout my body.

As I got older, I decided that I wanted to make music and not just appreciate it. So I started learning to play. My drum instructor, Tommy, has since gone on to play professionally for his entire life, and I always marveled at how fluid his motions were. It was like he was speaking through his instrument. He could even play with his eyes closed. I would whack my drumsticks together and was lucky to hit the drum I was aiming for at all.

"You're thinking too much about what you're trying to play," he'd say, which baffled me. *Of course I'm thinking about it!* I'd say to myself in exasperation.

"You have to go back and solidify your rudiments first," he said. I hated rudiment practice. It was the equivalent of playing scales on the piano. First I'd do fifty paradiddles starting with my left hand, then with my right. Then I'd do flam-taps, alternating hands until the sticks slipped from my sweaty hands. And on and on they went.

But if I'm honest, I'd tend to exaggerate how much I actually practiced my rudiments. I just wanted to get to the part where I was amazing like Tommy. But he always knew if I hadn't practiced.

"Put your sticks down," he said during one lesson, when it was clear (once again) that I hadn't put the time in. He handed me a magazine called *Modern Drummer* for me to read from. I rattled off some recent review of Rush's Neil Peart, who was my other idol, but Tommy stopped me before I finished the paragraph.

"How'd you do that?" he asked me. I wasn't sure what to say.

"You mean read it?" he nodded. "I dunno," I shrugged, "I just . . . read it."

"You didn't stop and sound out the words?" he asked.

"No."

"So how were you able to read it, just like you were talking?"

"I guess it's just because I've read enough that I know how it all works." Tommy took the magazine and set it down.

"Exactly," he said. "You wouldn't try to read a whole magazine before you learned all of the words and how they work first, right?" I nodded tentatively. He held up my rudiment sheet. "So think of this as your vocabulary or spelling homework. Take it home and work on these before you worry anymore about writing a book."

It took some time for me to entirely understand what he meant. I had to internalize the basic skill set so well that my hands would just know what to do without thinking about it. He showed me how all the stuff he did that wowed me was just adaptations of flams, para-diddles, and the other rudiments I was playing.

We were doing the same thing, but his music was coming from the inside out. He had burned the practice into his mind and hands until it flowed out of him. He couldn't have just practiced at it an hour a week and expected to master it. He'd practice on his legs in a waiting room. He'd drum on his steering wheel in traffic. He'd play instead of watching TV or playing video games.

He wanted to internalize the music so desperately, from the core of his being, that it wasn't even a "have to." All of it was part of a longer series of steps toward a goal he couldn't imagine living without. Each hour of practice got him that much closer.

That's probably why he's playing tonight with Robert Earl Keen, and I'm here in my office writing about him.

Prayer for the Week

God, I want the rewards of faithfulness without the work. I want to go through the motions, hoping it's good enough, but you know better. Help me see the destination, so all of this sacrificial living stuff doesn't feel so much like a "have to."

Popping Off

Art/music/video and other cool stuff that relate to the text

The Tipping Point, by Malcolm Gladwell (book, 2006)

"Merry Christmas from the Family," by Robert Earl Keen (song, 1994)

If Kids Ruled the World

⎯⎯⎯⎯⎯⎯⎯〜⋀〜⎯

Lectionary Texts For
December 30, 2018 (First Sunday after Christmas)

Texts in Brief
My dog ate my Bible!

First Reading
1 Samuel 2:18–20

This portrayal of Samuel as a child being very faithful to God stands in direct contrast to the way Eli's (the priest) sons are described just before this. Because of Eli's faithfulness, his parents (Hannah and Elkanah) are blessed by God with many more children. And although it doesn't happen until he is older, Eli ultimately becomes the priestly successor of Eli instead of his own sons. Eli serves as not only a high priest but also as the last Israelite judge.

Psalm
Psalm 148

This is a psalm of praise that calls for praise to God from both heaven and earth. This is meant to indicate that God is indeed a god of both heaven and earth. One interesting note is that non-human objects are called to praise God simply by acting as they are designed to. So although it isn't explicitly stated, one could construe that the psalmist is saying that our greatest praise of God is to live entirely as we were made and intended to. That in itself is an act of praise.

Second Reading
Colossians 3:12–17

This passage is the conclusion of a section in Colossians that makes a case for Jesus being another Adam. All who live as Christ lived are a part of this new heritage, not by blood relations anymore, but by the orientation of their hearts and minds. So the habits that should be embraced by those imitators of Christ seeking to be adopted into this new, divinely inspired lineage are explained: compassion, kindness, humility, patience, and, above all, unconditional love. This, it says, is the one, true, perfect bond that's stronger than blood relation.

Gospel
Luke 2:41–52

If my kids did what Jesus does in this passage, they'd be grounded for a year. Mary and Joseph travel to the temple in Jerusalem for Passover, but after they leave, they can't find Jesus. They look for him for three days and finally find him in the temple, conversing with the temple elders and other onlookers. Everyone is amazed by his wisdom, but his parents aren't happy. When they ask him why he disobeyed his parents, he says they should have known he had to be in his "Father's house," meaning God. He agrees after this to do as he is told, but as he grows in years and wisdom, Mary starts to realize how remarkable Jesus is.

Bible, Decoded

Breaking down Scripture in plain language

Three days—It's not insignificant that the author in Luke goes out of his way to say that Jesus's parents can't find him for three days. This, as we know from other passages, is a length of time that is considered directly related to major transformation. So although he is still probably only about twelve years old in this scene, Jesus is undergoing a transformation here, from little boy to legitimate prophet.

Adam—It's kind of cool that this letter to Colossae is suggesting that Jesus is the new Adam. The simple translation of "Adam" is "man," or even "human one." And as we recall from other passages, Jesus refers to himself as the Human One (Common English Bible). And to the extent this text is saying we all can be adopted descendants of the Human One and therefore become part of Adam/the Human One, this supports the notion that references to the Human One are not just referring to Jesus himself but rather to all parts of the greater body of Christ.

Points to Ponder

First Thoughts

It's noteworthy that there are some remarkable similarities between the story of Eli in the 1 Samuel text and the passage about Jesus in Luke. The original audience for the Gospel text likely would have known the Samuel passage and would have understood—at least with some guidance—that the implied point in Luke is that, like Eli, Jesus is to be held in a position of high priesthood. We could even take it a step further and construe that as Eli was the final judge of the Hebrews, so Jesus is to be the final judge of all of humanity.

So who would the naughty sons be if the author of Luke is drawing a parallel to this 1 Samuel passage? Look in the mirror! It seems to suggest that God gave the descendants of Adam (all of us) a chance to live into this honor of priest and judge ourselves. To manage this, we would have had to internalize the practices to which we are called in Colossians. But since we've fallen short, we need to start fresh, with a "new Adam" and with a new priest and judge to help us get on the proper path again.

Digging Deeper

Mining for what really matters . . . and gold

There's another point of significance about this Luke section. It's actually the only place in all four Gospels that offers any account of Jesus's life from when he was little to when he began his ministry in young adulthood (young today, but actually around thirty, which was middle age then). So why was this so important for this to be included?

One reason is because it demonstrates that he would have been a good Jew. His parents made the pilgrimage to Jerusalem every year for Passover, which wasn't an easy trek, especially with kids. I'm no ancient geography expert, but it's about ninety miles from present-day Nazareth to Jerusalem, so it wasn't like this was a day trip for them. It was really important to them, and because he grew up in such a home, Jesus would have been instilled with these kinds of values.

Second, we have stories of how miraculous Jesus's birth was, but nothing after that until he was an adult. But it was common in ancient literature to illustrate remarkable events about important figures during their childhood years. This served to show that they were inherently special and weren't just really astute at learning "Miracles 101."

This also, more specifically, establishes Jesus on his way to becoming a prophet. The temple wasn't really a place for children to hang around, and they certainly wouldn't have been allowed to teach. So this scene suggests not only that Jesus will be a great speaker of truth and teacher of divinely inspired wisdom but also that he will be chief among the prophets and teachers, upsetting the natural order of coming into the priesthood through proper training and inheritance.

Claiming the prophetic mantle for Jesus is one of the book of Luke's primary goals. He is the teacher from whom all other teachers should seek wisdom. And this authority wasn't given to him by birth; his parents were commoners. And he hadn't gone through any particular training to earn such respect. This authority was given to him solely by God, and the Lukan Gospel wants this to be made clear in no uncertain terms.

Heads Up

Connecting the text to our world

Alex was born with a form of cancer called neuroblastoma. It would in many ways define the rest of her short life. But no one could have imagined some of the incredible beauty that would come from it too.

When she was only four years old, having endured more medical procedures and hospital stays than any human being ever should, she announced to her mother that she wanted to start a lemonade stand. When asked why, she explained that she had seen other children using lemonade stands to raise money and that she wanted to as well.

The only difference was that Alex wanted to raise money to give to other children struggling with cancer who didn't have the same kinds of resources she did. She saw herself as lucky and wanted to afford others a small amount of the good fortune she enjoyed.

As people learned about her motivation, they started giving her more for her little cups of lemonade than she was asking for. They were inspired by her selflessness. Word spread quickly, and others came by to pitch in. By the time she closed down business, her lemonade stand had raised two thousand dollars.

In addition, some people who had connections in the nonprofit sector decided her mission was noble enough to formalize. What she started that day on the street became Alex's Lemonade Stand Foundation.

Over the next four years, her lemonade stands raised more than one million dollars.

Alex died four years later from the effects of neuroblastoma on her fragile little system. However, her work continues even today. The foundation sponsors a weekend every month of June that they call Lemonade Days, encouraging others to set up fundraising stands in their communities.

On average, more than ten thousand volunteers participate in over two thousand different lemonade stands, raising millions of dollars to help children living with cancer.

Alex wasn't Jesus. She wasn't a doctor or a politician. She was a little girl with a heart far bigger than her brief life could contain, and the simple gesture of selfless love she offered nearly twenty years ago continues to grow today.

Prayer for the Week

God, if Alex can think beyond her own problems and invest herself in the needs of others, what excuse could I possibly have? Help me find my inner Alex, because I don't have to be Jesus to do God's work in the world.

Popping Off

Art/music/video and other cool stuff that relate to the text

Alex's Lemonade Stand Foundation for Childhood Cancer: www.alexslemonade.org

Soft Power

Lectionary Texts For
January 6, 2019 (Epiphany of the Lord)

Texts in Brief
My dog ate my Bible!

FIRST READING
Isaiah 60:1–6

This is a proclamation about the nation of Israel, whose time of prominence has come. Israel is described as a woman, illuminated and drawing other nations to her. This is in stark contrast to the descriptions elsewhere throughout Isaiah about darkness. Israel is to become a nation among nations, and great wealth will follow.

PSALM
Psalm 72:1–7, 10–14

The psalmist is asking for God's blessing of discernment and good judgment to fall on the king. There are very poetic phrases about how wonderful the king is and how he should live "as long as the sun." In a parallel to the Isaiah text, the psalmist also asks that representatives of other regions would come to the king with offerings. He is described as a ruler both of great mercy and fearsome power. Sounds like the king had a poet on the payroll!

SECOND READING
Ephesians 3:1–12

This is powerful text on many levels. One important point is that Paul is placing God's power as revealed by the life of Jesus above all earthly power, or even any other heavenly authority—so basically, everything. While under foreign occupation, this would be more than a little bit dangerous to claim. Second, Paul asserts that God's power is expressed in two ways: unearned grace and radical inclusion. He claims that this has been a part of God's plan all along but that it's finally time for it to be fully realized—and that it's the church's job to help realize it.

GOSPEL
Matthew 2:1–12

This passage serves to fulfill the prophecy set out in Isaiah. Magi (kings, astrologers, or mystics, depending on the interpretation) come to King Herod's palace to ask about the birth of the new king of the Jews. Herod isn't a fan of this idea of another king in his territory, so he tells them to report back to him when they find this child. All he knows from the Jewish texts is that the baby should be in Bethlehem. The magi find Jesus, but they were warned in a dream not to tell Herod where he was. So they left without returning to Herod's palace.

Bible, Decoded

Breaking down Scripture in plain language

Gold, frankincense, and myrrh—If these sound like dumb baby gifts, you're right. That is, unless your baby is the fulfillment of prophecy. Matthew, who is fairly obsessed with making sure readers believe that Jesus is who the prophets claim the Messiah will be, lays out these three gifts very intentionally. The gold is to represent Jesus's coming role as king of his people. The frankincense is a type of incense that was used in worship of a deity, and the myrrh is an anointing oil used on a dead body. So not only is Matthew claiming here that Jesus will be king of the Jews and is the Son of God, but that part of his calling on earth will lead him to death.

Points to Ponder

First Thoughts

Pop quiz: how many magi were there in the Matthew text? It's a trick question sort of, because although we usually assume there were three (because there are three gifts described), the Scriptures don't say how many there were.

In the Ephesians text, this is unique in that Paul isn't writing to his early church leaders like he usually does. Here, he's writing directly to the "gentiles," or non-Jews. It's also interesting to note the contrast of how he says God's power is expressed (through free grace and by welcoming all into membership as God's people) against how the Roman occupation expresses power (through force and threat of violence). While it's a beautiful and almost feel-good kind of passage, there's also a not-so-subtle insurrectionist tone to it.

Finally, the referral in Matthew to the magi coming from various foreign lands is meant to show how this, once again, is the coming fulfillment of event prophesied back in the prophetic texts, like the one noted from Samuel this week. Like I said above, Matthew is all about driving this home. We'll keep an eye out for it elsewhere in coming weeks too.

Digging Deeper

Mining for what really matters . . . and gold

We might consider this letter in Ephesians to be a recruitment letter of sorts. He's not just inviting people into the newly enlarged tent as established by Jesus; he's going so far as to say that if he can be a minister of the gospel, so can they. We have to keep in mind that as part of Paul's job before his conversion, he killed early Christians for the state. So the profoundness of God calling on someone so violently opposed to the Christian message to become one of God's greatest emissaries is pretty staggering. Few, if any, who would hear this would dispute his claim that they were worthy, at least if they agree that Paul is worthy.

Also consider the strategic pivot of power that takes place with Paul. As described earlier, the Roman state's power and authority was expressed through military might and sheer force, or at least the threat of it.

Paul, as an assassin or executioner, was the proverbial iron fist of the powers that be. And now he's claiming to serve an even higher power, but one whose power is expressed in an entirely different way.

Shift over, then, to King Herod, a sort of governor ruling this territory on behalf of the Roman Empire. He's clearly rattled by news of the birth of this baby, and in fact if we read ahead in the story, we know that he will go to great and horrible lengths to keep this "King of the Jews" from having a chance to rise to power.

But consider the absurdity of that for a minute. Herod, a delegate of the most powerful government in the world at the time, is scared. *Of a baby.* So if such manifestations of power are so potent, why don't these mighty empires use them? Is it a lack of vision? A lack of faith? And if they're not actually effective, why are they so worried?

For some, the miracle stories about Jesus or the claims about his divinity are hard to wrap their minds or hearts around. I understand this. But at the very least, let's consider the impact that the gospel—and in Jesus's case, the coming gospel—has on the authorities who claim all of the real power. It's enough to drive a regional king half insane with paranoia. It's enough to turn the heart of a professional killer.

If it possesses such potency, maybe Paul is right. Maybe it is big enough, even for the rest of us.

Heads Up

Connecting the text to our world

Some people hear a phrase like "art saves lives" and roll their eyes. But it's true. And while authority backed up with a gun or sword might change behavior, art has the power to change hearts.

Hip-hop artist Macklemore was frustrated by how his musical genre of choice was perceived in the rest of culture. He grieved that sentiments like misogyny and homophobia we considered acceptable in his type of music. So he decided to do something about it.

On his debut album, called *The Heist*, Macklemore teamed up with Ryan Lewis to record a song called "Same Love." The rap ballad celebrated his belief that love is love, whether it's between a man and a woman or between people of the same sex or gender. The video that accompanied the music portrayed people of all backgrounds, races, and ages in "normal" relationship situations, helping to humanize them as real, complete people, not objects to be diminished or ridiculed.

It was a tremendous risk to take such a bold stand on a first record. But many critics listed it among their top songs released in 2012. As the song gained popular momentum, it was adopted as an unofficial anthem for advocates of marriage equality, playing at rallies and in advertisements for ballot measures across the country.

For some fans, particularly younger audiences, the affirmation of who they were was a life-saving affirmation during a potentially tenuous time in their lives. The blogosphere and social media were peppered with claims that the song had been the thing that kept them going in the face of relentless bullying, or that the words had been a salve during a dangerously dark time in their lives.

Beyond just affirming the humanity of all people, Macklemore goes one step further by calling out the church of his upbringing for reinforcing (likely with different language) the same sort of intolerance and bigotry reflected in hip hop.

Sometimes soft power comes from the church. Sometimes it needs to be used against the powers coming from within it.

Prayer for the Week

God, help me find the courage to trust that the "soft power" inspired by the gospel really can and does work. It might not work in the ways I imagine or how I want it to, but if Jesus serves as my example, it works.

Popping Off

Art/music/video and other cool stuff that relate to the text

"Same Love," by Macklemore and Ryan Lewis (song, 2012)

One Big
Family Tree

Lectionary Texts For
January 13, 2019 (First Sunday after Epiphany)

Texts in Brief
My dog ate my Bible!

First Reading
Isaiah 43:1–7

This lyrical passage is an assurance from God (by way of the prophet Isaiah) that all will be well with the people of Israel. There are indirect references to their safe exodus from Egypt, assuring them that because they are loved by God, all of the Hebrews will be gathered together once again and will remain unharmed.

Psalm
Psalm 29

This is an interesting psalm offered by David. While it's a fairly common sort of psalm of praise in many ways, it also refers to other "divine beings." This could either be taken as an allusion to the existence of many gods, though subordinate to the one God of Abraham, or it could be implying some sort of holy council that serves God. The remainder of the song points to God's might and power and how it is superior to the gods of other cultures.

SECOND READING
Acts 8:14–17

The Christian evangelists in Samaria have been successful in opening the hearts of the local people to the gospel, so the disciples John and Peter were sent to pray for them and baptize them. This, according to the Scripture, was because the Holy Spirit hadn't come to dwell with them without having been baptized. But when they laid their hands on the Samarians, the Holy Spirit filled them.

GOSPEL
Luke 3:15–17, 21–22

People observing John the Baptist start to speculate if he is the Messiah, which he rejects. He isn't worthy of such a title, he says, and while he baptizes with water, the Messiah baptizes with the Spirit. The final two verses depict Jesus being baptized in the Jordan by John, followed by the descent of the Holy Spirit, during which Jesus is proclaimed to be the beloved Son of God.

Bible, Decoded
Breaking down Scripture in plain language

Samaria—While in Jesus's time Samaria was an area that was divided from Judea by the Romans, it had served as the capital of Israel in the past. So the act of Peter and John evangelizing there is a sort of reconciliation of the territory and its people with Judea, much like the Isaiah text claims will happen.

Fire—In more recent history, references to fire in Christianity are usually used to scare people. And it wouldn't be hard to imagine John the Baptist freaking some people out with his intensity. But when Paul talks about fire, he refers to it as something used to refine or purify. Now, in a moment of purification, one could see getting "burned" if we held on too tightly to whatever was being filtered out or burned away. But if we're able to keep perspective and set free those things that should be burned off or sifted out, what we're left with is essentially the "good stuff."

Points to Ponder

First Thoughts

When I read all of the texts this week, I picture one big family tree with God at the top. Of course, the longer we're here on this planet, the bigger and more complex the tree gets. But it's all still connected back to that one original taproot. It's the source from which all the others after it came.

Kind of like our own ancestry, it's easy to forget where we came from, especially with our fast-paced lives and our constant mobility. If you're like me, you probably can't name too many people in your own family tree beyond three, or maybe four, generations back. And while knowing all of the names, dates, and other facts might be interesting, what really matters is the recognition that we're all part of something so much bigger than ourselves.

On the one hand, when you consider this, it's easy to feel small and insignificant. But on the other hand, being a part of something that is so rich, broad, and deep is pretty amazing. It helps put everything else in perspective if you take a minute to really consider it.

Just a few passing thoughts from your forty-sixth cousin, six times removed.

Digging Deeper

Mining for what really matters . . . and gold

Many biblical scholars believe that the book of Acts is actually a continuation of Luke and is written by the same author. This is particularly interesting, given the other texts we're working with this week. In Luke we have an important contrast being drawn between how John baptizes before the coming Messiah and how baptism takes place afterward. It is no longer a physical ritual but rather a spiritual union with the earthly, a convergence and a consuming from the inside out.

This is demonstrated in how the people of Samaria are baptized by Peter and John. Notice that they don't dunk people in a river like John did. All they do is lay their (anointed) hands on believers, and the Holy Spirit takes it from there. Now, this doesn't mean that we can't baptize with water or that there's anything wrong with it. It just means that the ritual itself isn't the point. It's a reconciliation between flesh and spirit that takes hold, likely "burning off" or sifting out the false identities and values of the past. This takes place only after the hearts of the Samarians are open to it to be begin with, so they've tilled the soil; the holy seeds only have to be planted.

But this idea that this is a spiritual realization of Samuel's prophecy is interesting too. It suggests, at least to me, that the author of Luke-Acts really gets what Jesus is about. The geopolitical boundaries aren't what matter. What nationality with which we identify—or which church we belong to—is secondary to the new identity we embrace in the embrace of God. It's beautiful and mysterious but also pretty radical. It's something that no government can control.

I guess it stands to reason that the presiding powers, which had made a point of dividing up these territories to keep them weak and unable to rise against Rome, would ultimately seek to snuff out this divinely inspired fire that burns through such false constructs, revealing their true weakness.

Heads Up

Connecting the text to our world

In 1938 a study at Harvard began tracking a cohort of 268 people with the bold intention of revealing what the secret to happiness was. The "Harvard Study of Adult Development" remains one of the longest studies ever conducted about human behavior and development, and the data it yielded changed the way sociologists and other scientists think about how we work as individuals and as a society.

The study, which went on to track more than 1,300 children and grandchildren of the initial study subjects, found that the degree to which we have strong, long-lasting relationships is the single greatest predictor of how happy or joyful we will be in life; it also has a remarkable effect on our physical well-being and even longevity.

Nothing else was as strong of a determining factor in health, happiness, and long life. Not genetics, exercise, wealth, fame, where we lived, or what job we had. And the relationships that yielded these positive impacts weren't limited to familial bonds. Our friendships and our connections to our local community had an impact as well.

So maybe going to church is good for you after all, or volunteering, going to parties, spending time reading a book together, going on a family outing, or taking a class at the local college. If strengthening your relationships with others is a benefit of the activity, it's likely good for you.

So why do we spend so much time, energy, and emotion focusing on the other things? Maybe it's because relationships take work. They require vulnerability and compromise, and they may mean we have to change. Some days there may not feel like there are any real, tangible benefits, whereas going out and buying a fancy new car or getting that "wow" reaction from a stranger when they ask what you do might feel more immediate.

And sometimes we get so caught up in things like pursuit of esteem, wealth, or self-care that we sacrifice our relationships. It's one of the great ironies of human behavior that we'll do something in pursuit of a goal, only to have that very thing keep us from achieving what we think we want.

Connections matter. Relationships heal. Now all that's left for us to do is to lay down all of the things that don't get us what we want so we can get on with the work of being one together.

Prayer for the Week

God, sometimes I take the people in my life for granted, just like I take you for granted. Help me sift through what matters and what doesn't. Help pull me and my life back together again.

Popping Off

Art/music/video and other cool stuff that relate to the text

Life Is Beautiful (movie, 1997)

Happy (movie, 2011)

Harvard Study of Adult Development: www.adultdevelopmentstudy.org

People-to-Cake Ratio

Lectionary Texts For

January 20, 2019 (Second Sunday after Epiphany)

Texts in Brief

My dog ate my Bible!

First Reading

Isaiah 62:1–5

This is another prophetic text about the reconciliation of Jerusalem. The land is personified as a bride who will be remarried both to its people and also to God. It is meant to indicate the depth of intimacy of the connection between the land, its inhabitants, and their creator. It is to be a bastion of moral clarity for others and a symbol of pride and adoration for God.

Psalm

Psalm 36:5–10

This is a psalm about the extravagance of God's love and a request to God to offer that love to all whose hearts are set on righteousness. In this text God is depicted more as a mother bird gathering her faithful under her wings. Seen more broadly, this psalm could be seen as an example of God's relationship with all of creation.

SECOND READING

1 Corinthians 12:1–11

The author is speaking to recent converts about spiritual gifts and how we can see them manifest in our lives. God as expressed in Jesus is compared to the mute and removed former gods they followed. Although they might all possess different God-given spiritual gifts, they're all from the same source. The text lays out examples of spiritual gifts like knowledge, healing, speaking in tongues, and miracle performance. They all, however, are given for the same purpose of serving the common good.

GOSPEL

John 2:1–11

This is the story of Jesus's first miracle, when he turns water into wine at the wedding in Cana at the request of his mother. The servants fill six clay containers with water, each holding twenty to thirty gallons. After protesting that it wasn't time for him to reveal himself as one possessing gifts of the Spirit, he does it anyway. It's also noted that the wine is quality stuff.

Bible, Decoded

Breaking down Scripture in plain language

Three Days—Again in the Gospel we see a first happening after three days. Just like before, a three-day period is meant to demonstrate some sort of significant transformation. In this case, Jesus is going from being a teacher to a miracle-worker.

Wings—Any time wings are referenced with respect to God or Jesus in Scripture, it's in the context of affection or love. It tends to be like a parental sort of love.

Points to Ponder

First Thoughts

In some cases this week, God's love is compared to that between a husband and wife. Elsewhere it's more like the love between a parent and child. One way that love is expressed is in the giving of spiritual gifts. In another case, like in the Gospel, it's symbolized by overflowing, effusive generosity at a banquet (again, at a wedding).

But the question is: who is a part of God's family? In Isaiah, it's limited to the citizens of the nation of Israel. In the Psalm, though particularity may be implied, it could also be construed that God's love has a broader reach. In the Gospel story, the extravagant excess could not only be cause for celebration, but it could also be a reason to go out and invite others who hadn't been planned for at the banquet. After all, why waste such good wine when others have none?

Finally, the author of Corinthians lives this mandate—or at least an invitation—by reaching out among the non-Jews. And not only are they being invited to be a part of this growing body of Christ; they're told they'll be given special gifts, just like the ones Jesus himself and his disciples were given.

Imagine how stunning that must have sounded to them. These outsiders with whom the Jewish people had had so much conflict over so long are now being told they can be a part of something incredibly special, and in a way that puts them as equals with the greatest people in their new Gospel story. I'm a fan of great wine, but this sounds even more extravagant.

Digging Deeper

Mining for what really matters . . . and gold

In the Gospel text, there's a whole lot of great symbolism too about Jesus that helps foreshadow him ministry to come. One important symbol is in the receptacle used to hold the wine. They are previously used to hold water for the Jewish purification ritual, or *mikvot*. This points to two other texts. The first is the text from Jesus's baptism that we just studied, in which John the Baptist says that the Messiah's coming will result in a shift away from the need for rituals like purification with water (like water baptism). Instead, Jesus *is* to be the sacrifice that sets us right in God's eyes. We'll see the symbolism of the wine representing himself at the "last supper."

This is also a "coming of age" of sorts for Jesus, who is living into one of his spiritual gifts: miracle working. Clearly his mother already knows he can do this, so it may not be his first miracle. But it is apparently the first he has performed in public. He resists though, saying his time hasn't come. But we have to wonder if it's not so much about his own readiness and more about the people's readiness. After all, when he performs miracle later on, it's generally to make a greater point. The miracle itself isn't the endgame; they aren't special favors or party tricks. Rather they're meant to help point people toward God, not toward him.

Also, he does sneak a lesson in here. The act is an indication of how extravagant—even unnecessarily so—God's love and kingdom is. This wine clearly is good wine, as he contrasts it with the crappy stuff hosts usually pull out after guests have drunk through their premium stash. But he points out that *it's all good stuff* when it comes to God, even if you can tell the difference.

Finally, consider how much wine we're talking about here. If he made 180 gallons' worth, that's about nine hundred bottles by our measures, or about 4,500 glasses. And they've already been drinking! We could take this one of several ways. I've heard people interpret this as Jesus saying God's kingdom is a party, or a cause for celebration. Some more tongue-in-cheek suggestions have been that Jesus advocates getting hammered, though I don't really think so. What he's likely saying here, especially to people who have experienced plenty of scarcity in their lives, is that there's no longer any need for worry about there being enough anymore in God's presence.

There's enough of everything, including love. It's a liberation of sorts from this idea that they need to be God's only chosen people, as if God's love has limits. It's not unlike a parent explaining to a child who is about to have another sibling that having more people in the family to love doesn't diminish how much they are loved. On the contrary, it actually broadens and enriches that love, as it comes from more sources and gives us more opportunities to return that love.

Generally, human conflict comes from this sense of scarcity and the belief that we have to compete for what we need. Were we to get just this point—that there is and will always be enough in God's presence—I think we could be agents of God's coming kingdom so much more readily.

Heads Up

Connecting the text to our world

I realize as I write this that it will be the third time that cake has been at the center of one of my "Heads Up" stories. Honestly, I don't sit around obsessing about cake; it's purely coincidence. I think.

Anyway, this week's texts make me think of a scene from one of my favorite movies, *Office Space*. Milton is the quirkiest of any of the employees in his company, always getting relegated to worse and worse cubicles. Be the end of the movie, he's relocated to the boiler room in the basement, where he has a tiny table in the idle of stacks of boxes and other leftover items.

The scene I can't help but think of is at an office birthday party where, of course, they have the obligatory sheet cake. (If you're also a *Seinfeld* fan, you're probably also hearing Elaine railing about office party birthdays in your head right now.) Milton is next to the cake, eager for his piece, but he's told to keep passing the pieces to others next to him first.

As they pass out more pieces, Milton gets increasingly distressed. "Excuse me," he mumbles, "but the people-to-cake ratio is such that I will not have any cake." They brush him off and tell him to keep passing. Sure enough, by the time all of the cake is handed out, poor Milton is left empty handed. In his meek, mumbly voice, he grumbles something about how he'll burn the place to the ground as he shuffles off.

Scarcity leads to discontentment and resentment. The sense of inequity and deprivation leads to conflict, which often ends in violence. We see this in regions where there is not enough food, water, or medical care for everyone. Things get ugly fast. I can only imagine what I would do if there was a stockpile of food somewhere that I knew of while my children stood by starving.

God, however, is reckless and unilateral when it comes to generosity. This in itself is great news. However, we have to remember that in every act Jesus does, there's also usually a mandate to go and do likewise, even if it's not explicitly stated.

Being the recipient of extravagant generosity is one thing; having to be the source of that generosity is another. But if we really do want to help invoke God's kingdom here and now among us, we're called to keep passing without regard for the apparent people-to-cake ratio.

Prayer for the Week

God, I'd rather hold on to my cake. After all, you gave it to me, so it's mine, right? Deep down I know you gave me these things to allow me an opportunity to be a part of the common good, but to do it, I have to give away what was never mine to begin with.

Popping Off

Art/music/video and other cool stuff that relate to the text

"Office Parties" scene from *Seinfeld*, season 9, episode 18 (TV series, 1989–1998): tinyurl.com/y6vdt7bm

Office Space (movie, 1999)

Become a Badger

Lectionary Texts For

January 27, 2019 (Third Sunday after Epiphany)

Texts in Brief

My dog ate my Bible!

FIRST READING

Nehemiah 8:1–3, 5–6, 8–10

Ezra, the priest under the governorship of Nehemiah, gathers everyone together to hear teaching from the Torah as part of a renewal ceremony of their covenant with God. Ezra has the Levites (the other religious scholars) teach all who could understand. Following the teaching (likely two weeks later) was the Feast of Booths, which was shared with all, including the poor.

PSALM

Psalm 19

This psalm of David claims that everything in creation is a testament to the glory and perfection of God. This includes all that is of the natural world as well as all that is part of God's word. God's laws can give wisdom to those who lack it and can make things clear where they weren't before. David concludes by asking to be purified of all sin, including any sin of which he isn't even aware, and to be reconciled to wholeness with God, as imperfect as he is. So we go from the universality and elegance of God all the way down to the particular nature of God in covenant with one person.

SECOND READING

1 Corinthians 12:12–31a

This well-known passage describes the members of the body of Christ (as in all who identify with and follow in the way of Jesus) as respective parts of one larger body. As such, they are interdependent, and though they are distinct in their form, identity, and function, their individual nature is secondary to how they work in concert with the whole. In fact, this is why our individual identities, social orders, and hierarchies no longer matter: we all need each other, just like a brain needs a heart and a hand needs an eye, without one being better than the other. They all benefit and suffer together.

GOSPEL

Luke 4:14–21

Jesus reads from the scroll of Isaiah at the temple on the Sabbath. The Scripture speaks of a Messiah who will bring good news to the poor and marginalized. After reading this, Jesus claims that he is the fulfillment of this prophecy.

Bible, Decoded

Breaking down Scripture in plain language

Festival of Booths—In Hebrew, the *sukkot*, or Festival/ Feast of Booths, is also called the Feast of the Tabernacles. That it takes place in the middle of the seventh month of the year has a dual significance. First, it takes place at the end of the Hebrew harvest season, so it is a celebration of coming rest, and it also is a time of thanks for the harvest they have yielded. Second, the number seven is significant in religious texts because it represents religious perfection. So in holding the festival now and by bringing all together in an act of earthly reconciliation, it is done in the hope of achieving similar reconciliation with God.

Points to Ponder

First Thoughts

There's a lot of subtext to this Nehemiah text that is helpful to understand in order for it to make sense. First, this covenant renewal ceremony follows a long period when the Hebrews were ruled by the Babylonian occupying force. Nehemiah, the governor, and Ezra, the head priest, determine that this came upon them because the Hebrews has strayed for their fidelity to God, worshiping other gods instead.

This is a unique time of teaching when everyone is included rather than just the men or the elders. Women, children, and slaves can even come as long as they're able to grasp the messages. This, combined with the act of feeding everyone whether they contribute or not, is another gesture of leveling the traditional social hierarchy, placing all on equal ground for a moment.

In the psalm, David goes from the universal to the particular intentionally in order to show how he (and everyone else) is a part of this universal elegance, working in concert as a testament to the incredible wonder of God.

Then in 1 Corinthians, we go from the parts back out to the whole, but with the same sentiment we see in Nehemiah. The author is particularly intentional about emphasizing the importance of compassion and interdependence within the larger Christian community, far above any sense of title, status, or relative value.

Digging Deeper

Mining for what really matters . . . and gold

There are three Jewish holidays packed into the time in which this Nehemiah text takes place. While it sounds like it all went down in one day, it likely was over the course of two weeks, if the current Jewish calendar is reflective of the practices then. The teaching by Ezra took place on the first day of the seventh month, which is recognized as the fall new year, or *Rosh Hashanah*. On the tenth day of the seventh month, *Yom Kippur* is recognized, which is considered the holiest day of the Jewish year. Then finally on the fifteenth, we have *Sukkot*.

I'm only geeking out on this sort of detail because it's helpful to see all of these as related or interdependent, kind of like how Paul refers to the interdependence of the parts of the greater Christian body. *Rosh Hashannah* represents new beginnings. *Yom Kippur* is a time of intensive prayer in which we are to focus on repentance and atonement for wrongs we've done. Then we end with a celebration, but it is not just for a privileged few. After all, we've all atoned, so we're all equal in God's eyes. This is cause both for us to celebrate and also to do likewise.

Just as the text in 1 Corinthians says, we all celebrate together and suffer together. We need each other, and none of us is better or worse than another part. What matters now is not our individual identity or status but our value as part of the greater whole.

So why does Jesus—who stakes a claim both for himself in Luke as the fulfillment of the prophecies of a coming Messiah but also for the uplifting of the poor—apparently put this one group ahead of all others? This doesn't actually mean that Jesus loves poor people and not the rest of us; rather, he is making a point of saying to those who tend to go by unseen, "*I see you.*"

It's part of what we call throughout Luke Jesus's "great reversal," when the high are made low and the lowly are lifted up. It's not that he is intent on keeping imbalance in place and just shifting around who sits in what seats. The point is that we can't really be one body unless we feel and experience what everyone else does.

Pity is not enough. Sympathy falls short. Jesus wants compassion, and compassion happens when we suffer alongside our sisters and brothers who are suffering and when they have cause to celebrate when the rest of us celebrate. We have to see with one another's eyes and feel with one another's hearts.

Only then can the superficial distinctions and divisions we build up among us start to crumble, giving way to one overarching identity: the beloved creation of God.

Heads Up
Connecting the text to our world

Charles Foster used to watch a blackbird that would visit his backyard as a kid. But he wasn't watching it with the casual interest most of us might have in a bird in our yard. He saw his yard, and he saw the blackbird. But he wanted to see his backyard like the blackbird did. His obsession with animals led him to become a veterinarian as an adult, largely driven by this unquenchable desire to better understand animals.

He didn't want to just understand them as a human being; he wanted to *be* one of them.

He spent more and more time in the woods, endeavoring to get into the minds and lives of the creatures around him. At one point, he decided to take an intensive interest in what it was like to be a badger. He built a human-sized subterranean hideout. He crawled around on all fours, and he only foraged at night. He even blindfolded himself since badgers have very poor vision, forcing himself to depend on his sense of smell, touch, and hearing.

Charles did this for six weeks. As time went on, he learned his way around the forest by feel and smell. The longer the experiment went on, the more finely tuned those senses were. He learned to identify and track other animals by the smell of their urine and feces. He recognized the best soil for mushrooms by the taste of the soil. And he learned the calls of other forest animals at the signs of predators.

In the end, Charles Foster failed to become a badger, though his friends and family marveled at his efforts. But he did find that in going to such great lengths to experience the world through the mind and life of another creature, he learned incredible new things about himself and about how narrowly he had been perceiving the world up until that point.

Put simply, being a badger made Charles Foster a better human being.

Prayer for the Week

God, I give some of what I have away and hope that it will be enough. But I know you want more. Help take me where I need to go and experience what I need to experience in order to see with another person's eyes, whoever that person is.

Popping Off

Art/music/video and other cool stuff that relate to the text

"Becoming a Badger," from *This American Life*, episode 596 (podcast, 2016): tinyurl.com/y9a655q6

My Neighbor Totoro (movie, 1988)

When the Complete Comes

Lectionary Texts For
February 3, 2018 (Fourth Sunday after Epiphany)

Texts in Brief
My dog ate my Bible!

First Reading
Jeremiah 1:4–10

The prophet recounts his calling to speak on God's behalf from a young age. At first, he didn't think he could do it, but God dismissed that. God would give him the words he would need, and they would have the power both to create and destroy.

Psalm
Psalm 71:1–6

The author both praises God and asks God for protection from his enemies. He notes that he has known God and sought protection in God from birth, and he points to this as a testament to why God should honor his request.

Second Reading

1 Corinthians 13:1–13

In one of the most beautiful passages of Paul's letters, he reflects on the enduring nature and the importance above all else of love. Love is the only property that we possess that outlasts all else. It is pure and unwavering, and by living into an embodiment of love, we take on those same properties. He also offers, albeit sort of indirectly, a kind of warning or reminder that all other gifts—even those from God—are useless if they're not exercised in the spirit of love.

Gospel

Luke 4:21–30

After Jesus's proclamation in the temple to be the fulfillment of the prophecy about the coming Messiah, those in attendance ask him to perform miracles of healing like he has reportedly done in other regions. He says no, because it won't change any hearts, and he points out that this is in the tradition of many other prophets before him. They're not fans of this answer, so they take him to a cliff to throw him off. But he slips away.

Bible, Decoded

Breaking down Scripture in plain language

Jeremiah—Jeremiah is an important prophet not only in the Christian faith but also in Islam and Judaism. He is called the "weeping prophet" and (fittingly) is considered the author not only of his self-titled book in the Bible but also of Lamentations and 1–2 Kings. With respect to this week's texts, his importance might be more of an unstated one, given that his prophecies and other writings are considered to be foundational texts from which the new covenant later comes in the New Testament. This new covenant—or holy promise, or even marriage—is a relationship between humanity and God not based on written law and obedience to that law, but rather a relationship founded in love.

Capernaum—Capernaum would have been considered outsider territory to people in Jerusalem, so they resented the fact that Jesus would perform these miracles for "those people" while apparently neglecting his own. However, Capernaum actually ends up being pretty important in the story of the birth of the church, as it is believed to be where the disciple Peter is from. Peter, as we know by now, is the one on whom Jesus builds the larger church. So it seems that love of and care for "those people" is built into our very DNA as the Christian community.

Points to Ponder

First Thoughts

The prayer of protection in the psalm seems to be one that could have come in handy for Jesus at the end of this story in Luke. And in some ways it seems understandable. This is not the only time when Jesus shows apparent favoritism to others over his own; consider his renunciation of his own parents in the temple when he doesn't even acknowledge Mary and Joseph as his parents!

There are other times throughout the Gospels when even Jesus's disciples try to get him to stay closer to home, but time and again he presses the boundaries, going over to Galilee and elsewhere. If we consider this in the context of Paul's letter in 1 Corinthians, it seems to help answer the lingering question about why Jesus performs these miracles to begin with.

While those observing seem to see only the healing act itself, Jesus realizes that they're missing the point. The point is to reveal something much larger about the power and scope of God's love. And given that the people of Jerusalem already believe they are specially chosen and beloved by God, I think Jesus realizes they'll not get the point of the love behind the miracle.

Instead, he offers these miracles to those who believe they are forgotten, or even rejected, by God. For them, such a miraculous act would naturally lead them to ask the question: *why me?*

This is the response that opens the doors wide for the true message of the gospel to enter. If we already feel entitled to God's inclusion, grace, and love, then we're not the ones who need to hear about it. Rather, we're the ones who need to be embodying it for others who don't feel this way.

Digging Deeper

Mining for what really matters . . . and gold

Talk about tough love. Jeremiah is commissioned to speak truth to all nations, even where he isn't welcome, and to speak hard, discomforting truths sometimes. He's not called just to build up, encourage, and assure.

He's called to challenge, deconstruct, and push people beyond their false identities and preconceptions.

Imagine our reaction if some stranger came into our midst and started judging us.

Then let's imagine we have one of our own, someone clearly very special, who has gifts like no one else we've ever seen. And when they come into their own and begin to make these gifts manifest through outward acts, they announce to us that we're not meant to benefit from these God-given blessings.

Well that's just crappy. We get the criticism and the judgment, but not the good stuff? How in the world is that an act of love?

The Gospel of Luke, in particular, is intent on making sure we understand for whom Jesus was sent. And it's not that he wasn't sent for us but rather than he's sent primarily for those who need him most. He's sent for those who have not known love, compassion, health, or safety. He is sent to be the embodiment of the possibility of these things being accessible even to them.

But don't we need love too? Don't we deserve healing? The Gospels clearly claim that those who have found themselves already in the presence of God's grace are afforded with the very blessings that Jesus possesses. We are living, breathing miracles, here and now.

The question, then, is what we do with them. Too often we feel we've earned this position of privilege, which we may even mistakenly interpret as God's favor. In these cases, the greatest act of love that can be shown to us is a swift kick in the butt.

"Get going," God says. "None of these gifts I've given you matter at all unless you give them away, expressing them in the world as an ongoing, ever-growing gesture of my radical, boundary-smashing, world-changing love."

Tough love isn't always welcome, but sometimes it's the thing we need.

Heads Up

Connecting the text to our world

Typically only one-tenth of the volume of an iceberg is above water. That means 90 percent of it remains hidden from view under the ocean's surface. The part above the water represents what we think we know—about God, about love, about life, and about our purpose here on earth.

The part below the water is all the rest that we cannot see, cannot imagine exists. But it's there, and it is as real and all the more tremendous and extraordinary as we can even imagine.

Can't we see it? Can't we get a peek? It sure would make this faithfulness thing easier.

"Not yet," says Paul.

For now, we see only in part, but when the complete comes—when God's love is fully realized—then we will know fully, even as we have been fully known by God. It is this "not yet" quality of our faith that sets fire to hope within us. It's not a "No." It's a "Not yet."

So we will wait, not idly or fearfully, but hopefully, passionately, generously, and lovingly because we know that all of it is held together by something greater than we can comprehend.

What is the meaning of life? Love. To love. To be loved. To be fully known. What a promise! Now we know in part—but then we will know as we are known. To be known fully and loved fully—this is our greatest longing.

Theologian and scholar Paul Tillich was asked by a student after his lectures on eternal life to explain what all the notes he'd taken on his lectures meant. Tillich responded, "Look, all it means is God is going to win. We know only a portion of the truth, and what we say about God is always incomplete. But when the Complete arrives, our incompletes will be canceled."

And the love and mercy and grace of God we know now only in part will be fully known.

Prayer for the Week

God, sometimes I get comfortable with all that I have that is good in my life. It's even all too easy for me to start thinking I deserve this, while others don't share in the same kind of life I have. Help me remember that the reason I'm given what I have is to share it, and to do so not with the intent of getting recognition or feeling justified but rather to show that you are love and that all are worthy of that love.

Popping Off

Art/music/video and other cool stuff that relate to the text

Ink180: www.Ink180.com

Life after Hate: www.lifeafterhate.org

We're Not Worthy!

Lectionary Texts For
February 10, 2019 (Fifth Sunday after Epiphany)

Texts in Brief
My dog ate my Bible!

FIRST READING
Isaiah 6:1–8 (9–13)

King Uziah has just died, and Isaiah, who is there, has a vision of God. He is distressed by this arrival because he feels he is unworthy due to his sin. So an angel touches a coal to his lips and declares him purified of his sin. Then God asks who will go as God's messenger, to which Isaiah responds that he will. The optional text continues with a grave warning he is to share with the people of Judah about them being scattered soon from their homes because they haven't been faithful to God. And yet, even from among these, there is still something sacred that God can and will use.

Psalm

Psalm 138

This is a song of praise to God, who offers the psalm-ist strength and protection when he needs it. It's also noted that even though God is the holiest of all in creation, God still attends to even the lowliest in our midst. The psalm ends with a request never to be for-gotten by God.

Second Reading

1 Corinthians 15:1–11

Paul reminds his audience not to forget the essence of the good news of the gospel, which he reminds them of again. Then he proceeds to use himself as an illustra-tion of God's grace, as he isn't worthy to be in God's presence, and yet Jesus appeared to him after his res-urrection. Finally, he warns those who listen not to dis-miss the resurrection part of the story, because if there is no resurrection, then what Paul and the disciples are preaching is considered bearing false witness, which is a sin according to Mosaic law.

Gospel

Luke 5:1–11

Jesus takes Simon Peter's boat into the lake and teaches the crowds from the boat. After he's done he tells the Simon and the other fishermen to come out with him to fish. They grumble because they're tired and haven't caught anything all day, but they do it. They end up catching so much fish that they need the other boat to bring it in. Simon freaks out and tells Jesus he should leave because Simon Peter isn't worthy of being in Jesus's presence. Instead, Jesus offers him and his fellow fishermen a job as his disciples.

Bible, Decoded

Breaking down Scripture in plain language

Genessaret—Another name for the Sea of Galilee, where the fishermen (now the early disciples) are from. Jesus is also from nearby, and Galilee is a sort of dividing line between "us" and them" for many living on their side. The other side, however, populated by non-Jews, is where Jesus will spend a lot of time during his ministry.

Coal—The coal mentioned in Isaiah can also be translated as a glowing stone. Throughout Scripture this symbolizes divine good overcoming evil. Also interesting is that mineral-based coal isn't really available in Judah, where the Hebrews live at the time of this text. Mineral coal comes from Syria, which is actively in revolt against the king (formerly Uzziah, now Ahaz), whom Isaiah still follows. Though it may be a leap to conclude, it might be possible that this symbolizes that God can use something from the perceived enemy and make it into something for good.

Points to Ponder

First Thoughts

Paul says a lot of valuable things in this text, not just about resurrection, and not even just about being unworthy and still being of use. He points out that, because he knew he was perhaps the least worthy of all of the apostles (having killed Christians for a living), he worked harder than anyone else to earn his place at the proverbial table.

But, Paul says, God isn't wowed by his hard work. It's not like he finally filled in his apostle punch card and was redeemed. Paul wasn't made new from the outside in by his works; he was made new from the inside out by grace.

So while it's easy enough to miss, it seems there are two resurrection stories in this passage. Isaiah is made new in his texts as well. What this suggests isn't some one-time event that we simply passively witness and then talk about. We're supposed to take part in it. We're meant to live into an ongoing process of resurrection, both as individuals and collectively as all of humanity, every single day.

Want someone to believe in resurrection? Show them with your own life. Be resurrection.

Digging Deeper

Mining for what really matters . . . and gold

Generally, when we think of Gnosticism in the Bible, we think of John. The Gospel according to John is the most recent of the Gospel texts and is really different from the others. In fact, it almost didn't get included as part of the Bible—or canonized—by the early church because it was so different. But there are reasons why it's so unique.

One reason is because it's more of a response text to what's going on in the world in the region at the time. A form of mysticism known as Gnosticism was gaining traction, likely pulling Jews and/or Christians away from their previous faith. The thing about Gnosticism is that it's similar to more modern Calvinist versions of Christianity in its particularity. Like Calvinism, Gnostics believed you were either chosen at birth to possess God's favor, or you weren't. Nothing you could do about it.

In Gnosticism, the "divine spark" was inborn, but only in a select few. Yes, those elect could teach others, but they couldn't become enlightened like the masters. They simply weren't worthy.

John, then, adopts the "divine light" symbolism of Gnosticism but repurposes it, claiming that God is "the light that enlightens *everyone*." It's common practice throughout Scripture for religious leaders to borrow and repurpose symbolism and traditions from other religions to draw people in and teach them in their native context of understanding. This is why we have so many pagan symbols related to Easter and Christmas, for example.

Some scholars believe that some elements of Paul's writings, particularly the one this week, are also written at least in part as a response to the particularity of Gnosticism. His point is that if even he could be worthy of being in God's presence and then being commissioned to be an emissary of the early church, then anyone can be worthy. So he's using himself as an object lesson to confound the effects of Gnostic particularism and the possibility that any in his audience would dismiss themselves as eligible.

It's curious, then, that so many seem so intent on continuing to make Christianity a religion of particularity. Whether it's because of your past, how you were born, or even what party you vote for, we lapse into these bad habits of drawing lines of acceptance rather than doing just the opposite and endeavoring to erase them altogether.

We all do it; it's part of our nature. But God calls us to transcend our basic nature, submitting to the possibility that we are a part of something far greater and more inexplicably beautiful.

Heads Up

Connecting the text to our world

You know you're a child of the '80s and '90s when the first thing that comes to your mind after reading these texts this week is the "We're not worthy" scene from *Wayne's World.* The scene takes place when Wayne and Garth find themselves backstage with rock legend Alice Cooper. They're just about to leave when Cooper invites them to hang out. They drop immediately to their knees, prostrating themselves on the ground and wailing, "We're not worthy! We suck!," to which Cooper extends his black leather-clad glove for them to genuflect to.

We all have these people in our lives. For me it happened when I was invited to hang out on Dave Matthews's tour bus after a show in Texas. Honestly, I don't remember a whole lot that happened after that, because everything else was drowned out by my inner monologue, saying, *Holy crap, I'm on Dave Matthews's tour bus!* over and over.

I get how these guys are feeling. I mean, God is even a step up from Alice Cooper and Dave Matthews, after all. But a couple of things are interesting in the Isaiah and Luke texts. One that we've already addressed is that God finds use in them anyway. God sees the holy seed, as the psalm speaks of, in the midst of all the yucky stuff. But maybe more important than this, at least to me, is that God doesn't spend time indulging this sort of negative self-talk. Yeah, we do bad stuff. But as my wife, Amy, tells my kids all the time, "Just because you did a bad thing doesn't mean you are a bad person. There's a difference between 'I made a mistake' and 'I am a mistake.'"

God doesn't need perfection. God needs faithfulness. When God calls, asking for hands and feet to carry out God's work, "I'm not worthy" isn't an acceptable answer. "Here I am; send me" is.

Prayer for the Week

God, help me remember the difference between making mistakes and being a mistake. Help me aspire not for perfection but for faithfulness.

Popping Off

Art/music/video and other cool stuff that relate to the text

"We're Not Worthy" scene from *Wayne's World* (movie, 1992): tinyurl.com/y9rwn2br

"When You Feel You're Not Good Enough for Somebody," from *Psychology Today* (article, 2010): tinyurl.com/y8o7camg

Cover Girl (movie, 1944)

Cut This Down

Lectionary Texts For
February 17, 2019 (Sixth Sunday after Epiphany)

Texts in Brief
My dog ate my Bible!

First Reading
Jeremiah 17:5–10

Jeremiah speaks of the futility in depending only on the wisdom and sustenance provided by the physical world. He compares this to trying to survive in a barren desert, whereas trusting God's spirit is more like a tree being planted by a river that nourishes its roots. There is no need to worry about the future because the volatility of the world around it doesn't keep the tree from its source of life. Jeremiah ends by warning us not to lean too much on just what our hearts tell us, as they heart can lie and mislead us.

Psalm
Psalm 1

The psalmist draws a remarkably similar comparison to the one offered in Elijah between those who depend on God for life, identity, and wisdom and those who allow themselves to be misled by those who don't have their best interests at heart.

Second Reading
1 Corinthians 15:12–20

The first four verses here actually are a repeat of last week's, with Paul asserting how important it is that those listening or reading believe Jesus was resurrected. If he didn't, after all, he says that they are offering false teaching in God's name, and bearing false witness is a sin according to Moses's commandments. He goes on to argue that if Jesus couldn't overcome death, then no one else can either. Death has the final word.

Gospel
Luke 6:17–26

After offering healing to many in a large crowd, Jesus speaks of the so-called "blessings and woes." Those who are poor, sorrowful, or hungry now will experience just the opposite in the future because they are not leaning on the things of this world for their well-being. Those who are rich and comfortable and rejoice in earthly things, however, will experience in the future what their poor and hungry counterparts wrestle with now on earth. His final warning is to those about whom everyone speaks with admiration, because they will find themselves in good company among other false prophets.

Bible, Decoded

Breaking down Scripture in plain language

Fruit—Fruit is a symbol often used in Scripture to represent the byproduct of the nature of a person's heart. If they draw nourishment from deadly sources, the fruit will also be deadly, or it will just wither and die. It's by the type of byproducts our lives yield that God will determine the nature of our hearts rather than what we say. We're experts at lying to ourselves, but God sees clearly.

Points to Ponder

First Thoughts

When I hear these texts contrasting life and death, I tend to think about how both apply to this life, here and now. I think there's much more to these than some propositional claim like, "If you do _____, then _____ will happen to you when you die." I think it has more to do with living a life of meaning and purpose, driven by the desire to do and be more for the common good rather than dwelling in the death-dealing ways of obsessive worry, consumed by a mentality of scarcity.

As one who was a grade-A worrier as a kid, I can tell you that a life consumed with worry is hardly any life at all. It's a waste. I spent days in bed, wracked with abdominal pains from worrying about having to perform in my second-grade school play. Those are days I never get back. I might as well have tossed them onto the garbage heap.

In fact, Jesus talks about this very thing. He talks about the risk of people ending up "in the pit," or in a place called Gehenna that often wrongly gets translated as "hell." Actually, Gehenna was the name for the trash pit in the valley of Hinnom, where people discarded all of their junk. Put another way, anything lost in the pit, or in Gehenna, was waste. Trash.

Don't throw your lives away, Jesus implores us. We only have one that we know of, so why waste away precious days and the equally precious gifts we're given in worry or consumed by self-interest? We shouldn't relegate ourselves to the garbage heap of life when God sees so much more value in us. It would be like driving a new Tesla to the junk yard to scrap.

A life of self-service is no life at all.

Digging Deeper

Mining for what really matters . . . and gold

One of the most interesting things I found in looking for research into the backgrounds of these texts is how much people seem to avoid analyzing. It's as if this week's Scriptures were just carved out of the lectionary, and everyone decided to take a nap! But there's plenty here for us to mine if we look closely enough.

This metaphor of comparing lives to trees is not an infrequent one in the Bible. And much like when metaphors or symbols occur elsewhere, we should be mindful about why these particular images were chosen.

While we can apply the tree symbolism to our individual lives, we also have to consider its collective meaning. The Hebrews are a people of ongoing upheaval, conquered, colonized, and divided up like the spoils of war. As in the Psalm here, they are hewn down like a tree, felled for timber.

When they are faithful to God, the Hebrews are compared to the great cedars of Lebanon, which are sturdy, enormous, and seem to live on forever. And when they are invaded or exiled, the prophets tend to attribute this to a lack of faith in the Abrahamic God. They are, thus, chopped down to the stump.

The beautiful thing about this metaphor is what happens when a tree is cut down. If it is not well-rooted, it will die. It can't endure the trauma that life has dealt it. But if the roots are firmly in place and run deep, even though it may take some time and may appear dead to the unknowing eye, there is still life within.

From the stump of Jesse, a new sprig of life for the Hebrews grows, says Isaiah. From the remains of a well-rooted tree, a sacred seed can and will come.

It's a resurrection story. In fact it's *the* resurrection story. Jesus recognizes his fate transcends death as we know it because his roots run deep, all the way to the original source from which all life comes. That same source is available to all who go deep enough to find it and who trust what Jesus saw: that the power of death we have come to believe is an illusion.

The only tree that dies when cut down is one whose roots aren't properly nourished, in which case it's effectively dead already. We worry about our fruit when the thing that determines what the yield of our lives will be is actually the roots.

Heads Up

Connecting the text to our world

I'll admit that I struggle with this week's texts somewhat, although what I came to after some reflection is that my struggle is with the way they've been interpreted for me in the past. What I've tended to hear is two-fold. First, these Scriptures (especially the Luke text) have been used to suggest that Christianity is little more than a deferred benefit plan. Do the hard stuff now so you'll get all the goodies later. And what's more, you'll get to enjoy all your rewards while all the bad guys have to sit by and suffer.

Second, I've heard them used to justify fire-breathing hate speech disguised as preaching, simply because *it says right there in the Gospels* that speaking God's word in the world shouldn't be a popularity context. While this is true, it doesn't justify making people feel lesser than and basically acting like an a-hole as long as you say "Amen" at the end.

The Luke text is a continuation of what we call this book's "great reversals." The point of this is both to remind those who are well off in this life that it's not necessarily a sign of God's blessing or favor, and also to place central in the Gospel mandate a call to serve the poor and marginalized.

These who get trampled underfoot and are rejected by society are made in the image of God, Jesus says. Therefore they are where you should be doing God's work. And we should do so not with regard for protecting our privilege and power but rather with the intent of disrupting the whole system that is hell-bent on keeping wealth and power right where it already is.

Even the greatest empires will die. Even the richest, most powerful people among us will become worm dirt. We all end up the same once our hearts stop beating, and we shouldn't fool ourselves otherwise.

Finally, our work to disrupt and dismantle these systems of oppression and maintenance of the status quo shouldn't be done just because we think there will be *another* system like it after death, where we will end up on top. If God's kingdom is one that is meant to be sought after, I can't personally accept the idea that anyone would be left out.

While one suffers, we all fall. If one thirsts, we all have work left to do. That's the only way that God's love can be fully realized. Once compassion is the universal human currency, we might have some real hope that God's kingdom will come.

Prayer for the Week

God, when I hunger for more, let it be for more justice.

Popping Off

Art/music/video and other cool stuff that relate to the text

In & Out (movie, 1997)

"Roots," by Imagine Dragons (song, 2015)

Marcia, Marcia, Marcia!

Lectionary Texts For
February 24, 2019 (Seventh Sunday after Epiphany)

Texts in Brief
My dog ate my Bible!

First Reading
Genesis 45:3–11, 15

Joseph reveals his identity to his brothers, and they're scared. Joseph is now an Egyptian ruler, and they sold him into bondage there. But he explains that God used him for good and welcomes his brothers to bring their families there and live in safety and prosperity with them. Rather than punishing them, he cries and kisses them, filled with joy to see them again.

Psalm
Psalm 37:1–11, 39–40

This is a teaching psalm, telling us not to hold grudges or invest energy into enemies, as they will fade away anyway. Even if someone else's deceit leads them to success, we're reminded to stay faithful to God, acting in fairness and doing what is right. We are called on to release anger and trust that doing right pays off in the long run. Plus, this is the real path to peace, which is more important than personal gain.

SECOND READING

1 Corinthians 15:35–38, 42–50

Paul explains the difference between a physical body and the spirit that lives within it. He compares our bodily death and spiritual renewal to that of a seed placed in the ground. As it grows into something new, the seed is no longer a seed. It was more of a container for what would become the next thing. This, he says, is what it's like to undergo a spiritual rebirth with God. In fact, the physical body ultimately has to give way to spirit in order for us to be fully reconciled with God as part of God's larger kingdom.

GOSPEL

Luke 6:27–38

Jesus's teaching is about doing good for the sake of itself alone, not because we expect good in return or to be praised for our moral uprightness. It's also not our place to judge whether others are doing as they should or not, but rather to focus on our own practice of what is right, trusting that God will take care of us. In fact, the good we give to the world will be reflected in the good that comes back to us.

Bible, Decoded

Breaking down Scripture in plain language

Joseph—Joseph was the firstborn son of Jacob and therefore was admired by many in Israel. His brothers resented him for this and for his position of favor in his family, so they plotted to kill him. Ultimately, they sold him as a slave to the Egyptians instead, and he was adopted by the Egyptian king. Eventually he became the king of Egypt, and when he encountered his brothers again, he responded to them with love, mercy, and overflowing generosity instead of repaying their cruelty with more cruelty.

Children of the most high—Another way to say "children of God," or those who follow in the path that God has set out for them to live.

Points to Ponder

First Thoughts

All of this sounds good in theory, but it's so much harder to put into practice. We'd all like to think we'd be Joseph in these situations, but how often do we fall short?

Then I think of the unearned—arguably unfair, by all accounts—mercy God extends to us, and I feel a little bit stupid for keeping score. If God acted the way I did—the way we do—we'd all be screwed. Thankfully God is God, and we're not. And yet we're expected to resemble God in our own little ways and in moments when they present themselves. Like these.

I'm not saying I have anything near a 100 percent success rate, but I try to hit a mental and emotional pause button when I feel the impulse to jump to retribution. Instead, I try to breathe and to think to myself, *What is the universe trying to teach me right now?* The other thing I try to keep in mind is how I would hope God would respond to me if I were on the other side.

Then, even if I'm not feeling entirely merciful and loving, I try to act as if I were. I keep hoping that if I do it enough, it will become second nature. After all, it's in my best interest, as well as in the interest of those around me, to do so. But man, these impulses run deep.

Digging Deeper

Mining for what really matters . . . and gold

Is Joseph as good in this story as we want to believe? Let's consider a few things that might suggest he's more complicated than we think.

First, Joseph doesn't welcome his brothers with open arms at first. Initially he accuses them of spying and throws them in jail. Second, when he sends them back home but wants them to return, he holds Benjamin in bondage as a sort of insurance policy that they'll come back. Third, he controls all of the food supplies in the region and therefore controls how much people pay to eat—or if they eat at all. And finally, his job before being second in command to Pharaoh was to be in charge of all of his fellow slaves, of which he was one just moments before.

On one hand, we know from many other stories that God can do beautiful things with less-than-perfect people. But let's consider for a moment that Joseph's response might have been an intentional sort of disruption, exposing the cruelty of his brothers specifically by *not responding in kind*.

This brings to mind Walter Wink's interpretation of the "Walk the Second Mile" text, suggesting that Jesus's responses actually are intentional acts of subversion. Each has their own way in which it's potentially an act of nonviolent resistance, but let's just take walking the second mile for now.

It was the law of the land then that Roman soldiers could require Jewish people they came across to carry their stuff for them. It was not so much because they were tired and needed a break as it was an act of dominance, kind of like a dog lying down on top of another dog. However, in order to keep it from getting out of hand, the Roman state only allowed them to force the Jews to carry their packs for one mile (or whatever unit they used at the time that's translated as a mile).

By refusing to surrender the pack and continuing forward after the mile is complete, the oppressed person actually is forcing the dominant person into a violation of their own code. They are in a situation where they either have to beg the oppressed for their stuff back, which makes them look ridiculous, or they have to take it by force. And good luck explaining doing harm to someone you forced to do what they were doing in the first place. Their only other option is to stand in violation of their own law.

The point here is that the person who has been done wrong to exposes the cruelty of the law being used against them without resorting to violence to do so. It's an act of creative, subversive, nonviolent engagement, as Wink calls it in *Jesus and Nonviolence* (2003). And for those who seek to confront the corrupt powers in our world in the path of Christ, this is a hopeful illustration.

We resort to violence in the face of violence due to a lack of divinely inspired imagination. We are called to be as wise as serpents, Jesus says, not as aggressive as bulls.

Heads Up

Connecting the text to our world

My first thought after reading this story about Joseph in Genesis is to imagine how Jesus's siblings must have felt about him. We don't really hear about them, but just think about how jealous they must have been sometimes. It makes me think of that episode of *The Brady Bunch* when Jan throws her sister Marcia's trophies away. When her parents question her about it, she's seething with jealousy about all the attention and praise Marcia gets.

"It's always 'Marcia, Marcia, Marcia,'" complains Jan, clearly resentful of feeling like a distant second to her sister.

I suppose selling your brother into slavery is a little bit harsher than throwing his trophies in the trash, but hey, maybe they tossed Joseph's first-place shepherding award in the garbage heap too. The point is that we can all relate to this sort of resentment whether or not we have siblings, and likely we've been on the receiving end of it at one time or another too. If so, imagine being Marcia in that situation, after being done wrong at no fault of your own. On top of that, you have to be the bigger person and extend the sort of kindness you wish you had received—and quite possibly the kindness you felt you deserved—in the first place.

It's unfair according to the standards set by our baser impulses. And if I had a dime for every time one of my kids protested that something wasn't fair, I'd be retired by now. But what we talk to them about, which I think is fitting here, is that what is fair and what is right aren't always the same thing.

What's fair always changes, it seems, because it's tied to some basis of comparison to others. We see this when professional athletes suddenly are dissatisfied with their $25 million contract for playing football. While the payday was perfectly fine yesterday, now that their peer on another team got $40 million, they simply have to have similar treatment.

But does that make any of it right?

And while much of the biblical teachings are hardly fit for a self-help guide, there's some personal benefit to be found in emulating what's talked about and modeled this week. As Anne Lamott says in *Traveling Mercies* (2000), holding on to resentment is like drinking poison and waiting for your enemy to die. The harm we do largely ends up being to ourselves. The resentment is like a toxin that pulses through us, coloring everything we do with a pall of anger and mistrust.

Release of such notions of what's fair and responding to cruelty with mercy also contributes to the greater good. Not only do we liberate ourselves from the burden of carrying unnecessary resentment, we also contribute to breaking the cycle of retribution. And if we take anything away from the Bible, it's that retribution only leads to even more of the same.

The cycle is only broken once someone is willing to interrupt the cycle, revealing the absurdity of the transactional sense of justice at the heart of the whole thing.

Prayer for the Week

God, it's so easy for me to compare myself to someone else, and when I do, I never feel better for it. And I'm always inclined to respond to unfairness in ways I know aren't right. Help me be Joseph in the moments when I'd rather be his brothers.

Popping Off

Art/music/video and other cool stuff that relate to the text

"Marcia, Marcia, Marcia" scene from *The Brady Bunch*, season 3, episode 10 (TV series, 1969–1974): tinyurl. com/guutrub

Up to the Mountain

Lectionary Texts For
March 3, 2019 (Transfiguration Sunday)

Texts in Brief
My dog ate my Bible!

First Reading
Exodus 34:29–35

Moses comes down from Mount Sinai with the tablets containing the commandments he has been given by God. He doesn't know he's glowing from talking with God, but it freaks out his people. He explains to Aaron and the other leaders what happened on the mountain, and then they and the other people aren't afraid. After that, Moses keeps his face covered except when he goes to speak with God.

Psalm
Psalm 99

This is a poem of awe about the power and might of God. The psalm also recalls how God spoke directly to

Moses, Aaron, and Samuel, and from them came the commandments by which people are supposed to live. Finally, God is portrayed as an arbiter of fairness and forgiveness, and it concludes with a reaffirmation of the mightiness of God and how all should bow down in God's presence.

SECOND READING
2 Corinthians 3:12–4:2

Like Jesus, Moses, and Elijah, Paul explains, we are likewise transformed when we find ourselves in God's presence. However, unlike Moses, who covered his face, we aren't meant to hide how we are changed because of our connection with God. In fact, when we're truly in union with God, it should be as if people are looking at Jesus himself when they see us. Our faith should not be a source of shame or secrecy, but rather being a living, breathing example of our faith is an essential part of our respective ministries.

GOSPEL
Luke 9:28–36 (37–43a)

Jesus took Peter, John, and James up a mountain to pray with him. While there, Moses and Elijah appeared next to Jesus, and all of them were glowing, kind of like Moses was in Exodus. Peter is amazed and wants to stay there on this holy site, so he suggests building shelters to the three can stay there with the disciples. But Jesus explains, and God affirms, that the point is to take what they've witnessed and to bring similar transformation to the rest of the world.

Bible, Decoded

Breaking down Scripture in plain language

Veil—It's symbolically important to note that the word *veil* in the Exodus text is the same as the one referenced right after Jesus's death. The veil in the temple tears right when he dies, which serves as a boundary that is supposed to keep humanity and God separate. So in 2 Corinthians, Paul is effectively tearing up the veil between God and humanity, much like Jesus's death causes the one in the temple to rip. There is to be no more division between us and God anymore.

Elijah—Considered by many to be the greatest of the prophets, Elijah possess many qualities like those of Jesus. He speaks directly with God often, he is given the power to resurrect, and he is prophesied to raise from the dead before God's ultimate return. One of his greatest goals in his ministry was to convince people of the sovereignty of the God of Israel over other pagan gods.

Points to Ponder

First Thoughts

It's interesting that, while Peter is the one who wants to cloister everyone at the top of the mountain to be with God, even building little church-like structures there, Jesus calls on him to be the foundation of the church to come. From this we construe that Peter is the foundation of our religious structure. It is ironic that establishing set-apart structures for worship was precisely what Peter got reprimanded for!

But we have to bear in mind that Jesus didn't proclaim that Peter would be the founder of churches. He wasn't the first worldwide church planter per se. He was to be the foundation of the church itself. No, this doesn't mean people back then were supposed to cover him with cement and build things on top of him. It means his ministry and his faith are to be foundational to what all who follow after him do.

God's transforming work in our lives is explicitly not supposed to be contained in worship, kept in a building and hidden away, even if there's a sign out front that says *"All Are Welcome!"* Neither is the point to go out and get people to come to church. It's to be our transformed selves every day, out in the world, and to let that stand as an example of what God's nature is.

It shouldn't even really take much talking about it if we do it right, it seems. It's mostly in how we live, and where we live it out.

Digging Deeper

Mining for what really matters . . . and gold

When we consider the implications of Paul's message in 2 Corinthians, it can feel overwhelming. After all, I can hardly imagine the burden of trying to be Jesus in the world. I can try not to be a jerk, yes, and even occasionally do some good. But there's a lot to Jesus's ministry and his nature where I fall woefully short, and not for lack of trying (at least some of the time).

But we have to consider here that the "you" he's talking to could well be a collective "you." After all, he told us not long ago that we only had to try to be a *part* of the body of Jesus in the world. This brings some degree of relief but also other complications. This requires us to be interdependent, which means we're not only responsible for ourselves; we're accountable to each other too.

Maybe the idea of trying to go it alone wasn't so bad after all.

But even Jesus depended on others. It wasn't just that he was being nice to them and letting them hang around. On the contrary, his ministry wouldn't have worked if he had just retreated to a hilltop and meditated his whole life. Yes, in some ways what Jesus accomplished was impossible to replicate. And the good news is that we don't have to. Jesus took care of the heavy lifting.

Much of the rest of Jesus's ministry was pretty unremarkable when compared with the "wow" moments featured in the Gospel highlight reel. Most of the time he shared ideas, shared time and meals with people, walked around, and noticed and addressed needs. When asked why he did these things, he told people.

We don't have to do it all, but we're an integral part of the greater whole. And if one part declines to live into the fullness of his or her God-given potential, resorting instead to hiding away and keeping what they have to themselves, the rest of the greater body suffers, as do those who the body would endeavor to serve.

Heads Up

Connecting the text to our world

At age seventeen, I was kicked out of church. My doubts, questions, and heretical ideas were dragging other kids down into dangerous territory, my youth leaders said, so it was time for me to go. In the moment, I was certain that I was of no use to God. In fact, if the folks in church were right, I was practically God's enemy. But I couldn't change the fact that I couldn't believe the things they were telling me, so I accepted the label.

I've been a musician and writer for as long as I can remember, so I decided to put myself into those activities instead. I had one band after another, each with varying degrees of modest success, to put it generously. I wrote hundreds upon hundreds of pages; ideas continued to flow from me without any apparent end. And yet when I tried to get published, or when I'd send my music out to record labels, I was met with silence.

Ten years after the youth group incident, I met Amy, who was a minister at a new church in Denver. I had no idea how anything could come of a relationship between a black-sheep apostate and a church employee, but I gave it a try. I even went to church once to prove to her that I'd hate it. To my surprise, I didn't: in fact, the people were remarkably open, welcoming and . . . *real*.

When they asked me to bring my guitar and share something in worship a few weeks later, I balked. After all, I was this former metal head who fit better in smoky bars than in church. But after some persistence on their part, I relented. When I started playing, it was both familiar and foreign at the same time. The song was the same, but something else didn't seem right.

Actually, it turned out that it was the first time the song and I really felt right together, which was the foreign part.

Before I reached the bridge of the song, something broke open in me. I wept so much that I had to stop, but no one seemed to mind. In fact, once I got over my embarrassment, I realized that half of them were crying with me.

To make a very long story short, I ended up becoming a music minister at several churches, even helping Amy (now my wife of eighteen years) start a church in Colorado. Assuming that there might be something to this "giving my gifts over to God" thing, I tried something similar with my writing. Since then I've written hundreds of articles and stories for various newspapers and magazines, and this is my eleventh book.

I'm not one to say that God "blessed" me with the success I've had in putting my inborn gifts to work in my daily life. I think the gifts themselves were the blessing, and I had to transform in how I related to them and where I saw value in them for everything to take root.

I've been trying, imperfectly, to reflect the likeness of that grace I experienced in that small body of Christ in the new church in Denver ever since. I've never seen God face-to-face that I know of, but I like to think that I've come close. And just like they didn't show up at church that day with the aim of converting me or saving me, something beautiful happened.

So I keep singing, writing, and doing what gives me joy, in the spirit that those moments happen all the time. We just have to do our part.

Prayer for the Week

God, it's so much easier sometimes to stick with what I know and depend on the routine of worship, a little bit of charity, and maybe inviting people to church now and then. But help remind me that living a Christ-reflecting life is a twenty-four-seven deal. Help me communicate that without words.

Popping Off

Art/music/video and other cool stuff that relate to the text

"Up to the Mountain (MLK Song)," by Patty Griffin (song, 2007)

Give It Away, Now

Lectionary Texts For
March 10, 2019 (First Sunday in Lent)

Texts in Brief
My dog ate my Bible!

First Reading
Deuteronomy 26:1–11

The text where we get the ideas about giving "first fruits" and tithing from. The Scripture is addressing the Jewish people coming out of exile to settle after forty years of wandering. They're to take the best from their property's yield and bring it to the temple. There they give it to the priest and acknowledge that all of this was given to them by God. Their gift back to the temple is an act of celebration of that fact.

Psalm
Psalm 91:1–2, 9–16

A promise offered by God to those who seek protection and comfort in God that no harm will come to them.

They'll be able to prevail over things that would have hurt or killed them in the past. They'll live long lives and will be saved from danger.

Second Reading
Romans 10:8b–13

In the eyes of God, all who hold faith or claim that Jesus has overcome death are indistinguishable. While we're set on dividing and drawing distinctions and values among ourselves, all who cling to faith in God are equally loved and worthy of being in God's presence.

Gospel
Luke 4:1–13

After being baptized, Jesus goes out into the desert on a spiritual retreat for forty days. He fasts the whole time, and afterward he is overcome by temptation. The voice of temptation encourages him to turn the stones at his feet to bread, to worship a false god in exchange for material comfort, and to prove his divinity in a miraculous act. Jesus refuses all three, quoting several Scriptures, including the psalm noted above. Temptation retreated from him, but not forever.

Bible, Decoded
Breaking down Scripture in plain language

Adder—In the psalm, we could take this reference literally or figuratively. In one way, it refers to when Moses has the "magic staff" in the desert while the Hebrews wander that keeps them from dying by snakebite. But the snake/adder/serpent also is a symbol for temptation, or "the devil." So we could also take this to mean that anyone who seeks refuge in God's presence won't suffer the consequences of temptation. Hey, just like Jesus in Luke!

Forty days—Jesus retreating to the desert for forty days is no accident here. Whether he literally spent that long alone doesn't matter as much as *why* the author of Luke says it. It's meant to refer back to the forty years the Hebrews spent wandering the desert, during which time they too confronted many temptations and opportunities to stray from God's path.

Tithe—This is a practice that wouldn't have been new to most people hearing it, given that anyone who lived in a feudal system was probably expected to tithe (or something similar) to the king. Historically it's been understood to mean "tenth," or 10 percent of whatever someone earns, but today people tend to be much looser with it, using it to mean any donation at all to the church. I think the point of it being a symbol of celebration is sometimes lost.

Points to Ponder

First Thoughts

I couldn't help but wonder if the author of this Deuteronomy text was a priest. It definitely works to their advantage to have this as part of their people's sacred text. Or maybe it's more about reshuffling the order of things, placing God as "king" rather than some other ruler, many of whom often claimed to be gods in their own right.

It's interesting that the psalm explicitly states that people who seek God out will live long and well. It's a promise that's comforting, for sure, but it also sets up an interesting precedent for anyone whose family suffers misfortune, or even a premature death. It seems as if such tragedies are inherently compounded by the assumption that they did something to deserve it. Is this the God we believe in?

If you consider the temptations Jesus faced in the wilderness, a couple of them really don't seem so bad. Whipping up some miracle bread after weeks fasting in solitude wouldn't be an act anyone would blame him for. And if he were to throw himself off a cliff and pop back to life in front of an audience, I'm guessing his whole ministry thing might have been a little easier. The devil-worshiping part . . . yeah, you could say that one is bad. But we'll revisit this temptation idea in a minute.

Digging Deeper

Mining for what really matters . . . and gold

There's a lot to this Deuteronomy text that we can miss if we don't consider the background. First, let's consider the stark contrast here to what the Hebrews have just gone through. For more than a generation, they've been a people without a place, and they've barely been scraping by. They've managed a hand-to-mouth daily existence until they finally settle in this new land afforded to them by God. It not only provides for them but also yields more than they could possibly need.

It makes me think of my grandparents, who came from the Depression culture. They lived through way more scarcity than my children or I have ever known. They saved and lived frugally in ways that seemed strange to us, but at the same time, they were the most generous people I knew. When they gave something away, it was with great intention and done with real joy. Put another way, it meant more to them because they had come to value having enough to be able to share what they had.

Also, this act in Deuteronomy of giving the first tenth of their bounty away sets important precedent. It establishes what will become annual harvest festivals—curiously pagan in some ways, but done both as a gesture of gratitude to God and also as a way to care for their own poor. Finally, the Hebrews who wandered for more than a generation suffered in exile so that their descendants wouldn't have to. It's a blessing they're passing on to their children and grandchildren. But they're also setting an example with their generosity that both hands down a tradition of compassion and also serves as a reminder of what they've been through and where they've come from.

In spending his own time of want, solitude, and temptation in the desert, Jesus not only is kicking off what will become his ministry in earnest. He is also reasserting that, along with being something radically new, he is still deeply, utterly Jewish. He has not forgotten who he is or where he is from, and in fact, it is this past that will help contextualize his own work. The Hebrews were tempted in their exile, but (despite some hiccups) they were ultimately rewarded for their obedience. Jesus experiences similar temptation and emerges better for it. Having endured his first challenges in his new calling, he has earned the right, in a sense, to claim his place as the Messiah.

Past, present, and future all work in concert to birth something entirely, unexpectedly new. What this new thing will be is yet to be known entirely at the time, but evidently it's something worth giving his life over to for Jesus.

Then Paul takes us a step further toward that vision of what the "new thing" might be by breaking the divine blessing open and making it available to all. Consider how much the Hebrews have gone through to "earn" God's blessing. They've endured generations of suffering, homelessness, conflict, and starvation, remaining faithful (again, with some divergences along the way) to God through it all.

And now Paul comes along, who is new to the faith as it is, and claims that *anyone* can earn this abundance of grace simply by orienting their hearts toward the example set by Jesus. Once again we have an example of the unfair breadth and scope of unconditional love. Yes, we owe a debt of thanks for those who struggled to get us to this point. For that we should offer at least some gesture of gratitude, be it in the form of a material tithe or by giving of our entire lives.

But although we're called to the hard work of living by Jesus's example, it's not in order to earn God's love. That's already a given. We do it because it changes us and sets our hearts on a course for joyful, selfless generosity. It's not about what's fair; it's about what's right.

Heads Up
Connecting the text to our world

We all want credit for what we've been through or for the hard work we've done. It's part of our egoist nature to want that kind of recognition. But it doesn't always work that way.

My wife, Amy, has seen some examples first-hand of people pushing back against the blessings of one generation's hard work, skipping ahead and falling on the heads of those who follow them. She has talked with women from mixed generations and heard, far more than once, the phrase, "When I was a woman in the workforce, I didn't get . . ." with respect to the desire for more pay, time off for maternity leave, or some other benefit. The women's empowerment movement that took hold largely in the '60s and '70s didn't see the full realization of its desire for gender equity and female empowerment for years, or even decades. In fact, we're still a long way from reaching a point where women are represented, recognized, and compensated on par with male peers.

And while most women who struggled to earn such equality celebrate on one level the progress being made, there's also a tinge of hard feelings on occasion. After all, who wouldn't feel at least a slight grudge toward someone who benefitted from your own hard work?

We've seen similar reactions within the movement for racial equality, like when Jesse Jackson was caught on tape speaking ill of soon-to-be President Barack Obama. Jackson had invested his life in the civil rights movement, but it wasn't until Obama's generation that we saw a man that looked like Jackson in the Oval Office.

It's an understandably human response. But fortunately we're called to transcend some of our baser human tendencies. How? With God's help and through

Jesus's example. It's not fair by our modern, personal standards, but unconditional love never is. However, working together to realize the God-inspired vision for "Your kingdom come" here in our midst certainly is worth it.

Prayer for the Week

God, I don't always feel joyful in my acts of selflessness or generosity. As I "fake it 'til I make it," give me the strength to keep at it, and help me see the bigger vision that sometimes feels so far beyond my own line of sight.

Popping Off

Art/music/video and other cool stuff that relate to the text

The Giving Tree, by Shel Silverstein (book, 1964)

Pay It Forward (movie, 2000)

Get Growing,
Seeds!

Lectionary Texts For

March 17, 2019 (Second Sunday in Lent)

Texts in Brief

My dog ate my Bible!

First Reading

Genesis 15:1–12, 17–18

God visits Abram (who later will be renamed Abraham by God) and tells him he will have lots of children, and that his family tree will be enormous. Abram questions this, having never had a son, and assuming that a boy borne by one of his slaves would end up being his heir. God assures him not only that he'll have descendants as numerous as the stars but that he'll also own all of the land he can see. Abram questions this too, but God orders him to gather several animals to sacrifice. After he does, Abram falls asleep as night comes.

PSALM

Psalm 27

King David is clearly feeling threatened from many sides by enemies, so he composes a song of praise to remind himself of the promises of protection God has given him. And just as a sort of insurance policy, even though he claims in the song that God will never give up on him, he asks again to make sure God won't let him down, even if his own parents turn on him.

SECOND READING

Philippians 3:17–4:1

Paul writes a letter of encouragement to the early Christians in Philippi, as it sounds like they're not the most popular kids on the block at the time. In fact, it sounds from the tone of his letter like they may be at risk of persecution. He reminds them that those who are enemies of the ways of Christ are driven by earthly desire, and that they're missing out on the true community that transcends politics, human wants, and frailties. He ends by reminding them that he loves them and appreciates their faithfulness.

GOSPEL

Luke 13:1–35

This wide-ranging (and pretty weird) Gospel text starts with Jesus explaining there is no such thing as being better or worse off if you haven't turned your life toward the way Jesus calls people to. Failure to repent—or turn around—results in the same bad news. Then he tells a parable of a fig tree that doesn't bear fruit, which the landlord wants to cut down. But the gardener (likely Jesus in this parable) begs for mercy for the tree for another year, hopeful it will finally yield. He then uses another parable to explain that it only takes a tiny bit of faith for God to do amazing things, and another to illustrate that an existence in God's presence gives everything real meaning. He explains, however, that the doorway into heaven is narrow and hard to get through. Finally he is warned that Herod wants to kill him, so he laments having to leave the town where he is doing important work. He expresses a maternal sort of longing to care for Jerusalem's people but mourns for the fact that they resist.

Bible, Decoded

Breaking down Scripture in plain language

Yeast—This is an important symbol in understanding the kingdom of God as Jesus explains it, for a few reasons. First, it's clear from this that the kingdom is something that informs our present lives and isn't just something to long for after we die. Second, it isn't the be all, end all of creation. Rather it's the secret sauce, so to speak, that gives existence its flavor and richness, and makes it worthwhile.

Abram—Just because Abram has some reservations about the promises God is making doesn't make him unrighteous in God's eyes. In fact, God blesses him because he is obedient and sticks with God's promises, even when he doesn't entirely understand them. After all, he and his wife Sarai have lived their lives together under the assumption that they would have two children and likely little to pass on as an inheritance anyway. It wasn't that they were complaining about this, though. On the contrary, Abram was faithful to God despite things not exactly going his way to this point.

Mustard seed—This is not exactly a symbol many of us can relate to today, but a mustard seed is really tiny, hardly bigger than a big speck of dust. In Jesus's time, everyone would have been familiar with them, and the bushes that grew from mustard seeds were really big. The idea was that God could work with even a dust-speck of faith and make it into something great.

Points to Ponder

First Thoughts

There are lots of binaries, or absolutes, this week, which is tough for a postmodernist like me. Jesus stakes the claim that there's no real merit in having more faith than someone else, since even the tiniest bit does the job. He also argues that there's no "halfway saved" in God's eyes: you got it, or you don't got it.

It's kind of like the idea that there's no such thing as being "kind of pregnant," which would ring true for Abram and Sarai. And now they're going to go from being totally childless to having more offspring than they can ever imagine.

For David, it feels like it's him against the rest of the world, and the same goes for the small, struggling church in Philippi.

However, there is one other common thread that's important to recognize throughout these Scriptures.

Despite the circumstances, Paul is on the side of the Philippian Christians, and insofar as Jesus is referring to himself when he speaks of the gardener in the fig tree parable, he is on the side of those he is reaching out to in Jerusalem as well. And in the case of Abram and David, they have God in their corner.

Is it just me, or does anyone else have James Taylor's "You've Got a Friend" going through their head right now?

Digging Deeper

Mining for what really matters . . . and gold

There are a few interesting things to know about the Genesis text, some of which we can get from reading backward and more by reading forward (like way forward, to the prophets). Looking back in Genesis, we can see that this isn't the first time God has made such a promise to Abram about giving him children and land. So this isn't news to Abram, though he's yet to see any evidence of the fulfillment of the promise. This is, however, the first time that Abram responds to God after being given the promise. More important than this, though, is how he says what he says.

The particular words (from the original Hebrew) he uses to question God about this covenant are found later in the prophetic writings, like in those attributed to Amos. And each time they're employed as a direct plea to God for something. So rather than considering this a "Oh yeah? How would you know?" moment between Abram and God, we should think of it more like a wistful, longing, "Oh, that it might be so" kind of expression.

We see similar words from David in the psalm, though he first offers thanks to God for offering him protection from his enemies thus far, followed by confidence that it will continue. But then he follows up this "confidence" with a kind of pleading for God to make it so.

Though there's a lot in the Gospel text, the little gem in the fig tree parable is critical. The gardener pleads directly to the landlord on the tree's behalf—an allegory for Jesus pleading to God on behalf of the citizens of Jerusalem. So in this case, the pleas now shift to being for someone else rather than on someone's own behalf.

Finally, in the Philippians letter, Paul pleads with the fledgling Christians to hang in there. He's rooting for them both as a partner in ministry and as their leader. They know, without a doubt, that they are included in his prayers all the time.

It's almost as if there came a time along the way when we needed an intercessor, someone to mediate for us to God on our behalf. Did God lose faith in us? Did God grow tired of our screw ups, generation after generation? Maybe God considered reneging on the promise not to destroy the world again and had second thoughts about this whole humanity thing.

Or maybe the departure was more on the side of the people. In the beginning of Scripture, people like Abram, and later David, spoke directly to God and maintained faith in God even when events around them hardly reflected what they believed God had promised them. Their faithfulness *in spite of circumstances* are central to these stories.

But by the New Testament, it seems the very same blessings offered by God to God's people not only went unrecognized, they were utterly rejected. In fact, those who represented such a God were perceived as enemies, threats to the people's way of life. And yet God, as expressed by the faith in Jesus and Paul, clings to the mustard seed of hope that we could still see the light.

It's sobering to consider God nurturing this barely visible, utterly fragile speck of hope in humanity. But thank God for people like Jesus, Paul, the handful of early disciples, and the Christians in Philippi for nurturing that little seed, trusting that someday, somehow, it could yield the kind of fruit they had been promised.

Heads Up

Connecting the text to our world

My brain works in weird ways. When I think of the story of Abram, where he makes a sacrifice and then falls asleep before any of God's promises are fulfilled, and then combine that with the fig tree and mustard seed parables in the Gospel, I immediately thing of the *Frog and Toad* children's story called "The Garden."

Weird, right?

In the story, Toad thinks Frog's garden is pretty great, so Frog gives Toad some seeds to plant his own garden. Not entirely sure how the process works, Toad sticks the seeds in the ground, waters them, and then sits and stares at the ground, waiting for them to grow. Toad gets impatient after a while and start yelling at the seeds, "Now seeds, start growing!"

After some harsh words aimed at the poor seeds, Frog suggests that Toad is freaking them out. So instead he plays music for them and reads them poems. Still, no growth. Day after day, he tries this, but no results.

Finally, Toad loses hope and, having worn himself out one evening, falls asleep right there in the garden. When he wakes up, he's surrounded by little sprouts everywhere. Elated and proud, he shares the news with Frog, proclaiming that Frog was right; growing a garden is hard work.

Prayer for the Week

As Paul says, faithfulness is having hope for things we haven't seen yet. Thanks, Jesus, for having hope that I could become something I haven't even imagined yet.

Popping Off

Art/music/video and other cool stuff that relate to the text

"You've Got a Friend," by James Taylor (song, 1971)

"The Garden," from *Frog and Toad Together*, by Arnold Lobel (book, 1972)

A Prostitute Party

Lectionary Texts For

March 24, 2019 (Third Sunday in Lent)

Texts in Brief

My dog ate my Bible!

First Reading

Isaiah 55:1–9

The poetic text begins with an invitation to a feast, which seems to be a metaphor for spiritual nourishment rather than literal food, and a reminder to stay focused on the things that really matter. Isaiah, speaking on God's behalf, reminds the audience that they, King David's people, were part of the promise that bound David and God together. Because of this, they would be a people to whom others would come, seeking to be a part of the feast. Aware that not all of those who heard this would be able to make sense of it, Isaiah (speaking as God) concludes by reminding them that God's ways are different than their own human ways, and not always to be made rational sense of.

PSALM

Psalm 63:1–8

King David speaks of longing for God like someone who is desperate for water. He has found no other source of real nourishment like he has in staying faithful to God and God's commands. David also compares what he receives from God to the sense of fullness he has after a rich, expensive meal.

SECOND READING

1 Corinthians 10:1–13

Paul reminds the Christians in Corinth that they are descendants of Moses and the Hebrews who wandered in the desert. He says that their times of want came from their pursuit of things that weren't of God. He calls Jesus the rock from which the water that they longed for comes from. He wants them to remember the times when their predecessors struggled to survive and learn from their mistakes so they won't repeat them. He assures them that the temptations they face are normal, but although they're tempted, they don't have to succumb to whatever tempts them.

GOSPEL

Luke 13:1–9

People talk to Jesus—apparently with some disdain—about the Galileans who were killed by Pontius Pilate. But Jesus warns them not to feel superior to them because they could lose something even greater without changing their misdirected ways. We also find another telling of his parable about the fig tree that the landlord (aka God) wants to cut down for not bearing fruit. But the gardener (aka Jesus) asks him to hold off another year, to tend to it a little longer and trust that it will finally yield fruit. Essentially, while also chastising the audience, he's also reassuring them that he's on their side.

Bible, Decoded
Breaking down Scripture in plain language

Galilean—Most of the early disciples of Jesus (except for Judas) were from Galilee, so when people talk about "the Galileans" in the Gospels, we need to remember two things: first, they're referring to Jesus's disciples (not necessarily just the twelve we tend to think of), and second, it's a term of disparagement. Kind of like saying "those people."

Pontius Pilate—Pilate was like a governor of the Roman-occupied territory known as Judea. Ultimately, he and Jesus will have a sort of face-off that leads to Jesus's crucifixion, but at this point, Pilate is ordering the execution of those who are preaching Jesus's gospel. He sees this as a direct challenge to the Roman-enforced peace, which required all subjugated by Rome to recognize the Roman emperor as god.

Feast—In the Bible, a feast wasn't just a meal; it was a gesture of hospitality for those coming to the host's house. Hospitality—and specifically, extravagant hospitality—was important in the culture in which the

Scriptures were written. It was kind of like a party, a celebration of coming together, which is why we hear of feasts being thrown at important times—like when the "prodigal son" returns home, or at a wedding.

Points to Ponder

First Thoughts

I'm afraid that the symbolism of a feast loses some of its punch in our modern, Western culture, particularly since most of us are so surrounded by excess that we've never know real hunger. But being hungry, even starvation, was a common state of being in these times. So to pour out an excess of food or drink for someone would have been really special. Whereas sometimes now we roll our eyes at having to go to a banquet or party, the opportunity to have more than enough was very special. Further, it was likely a real sacrifice on the part of the host to offer it.

The warning Jesus offers to the people speaking with contempt to him about those being persecuted by Pilate reminds me of his warning another time about how to pray. He warns the Pharisees not to pray in the spirit of "Thank God I'm not like that guy." Essentially, his chastisement is meant to get them focused back on their own faults rather than feeling satisfied that they're better off than someone else.

Finally, the words of Isaiah reminding readers that they don't have to fully understand God's ways in order to heed them also echoes Jesus's words in the Gospels. Yet another reminder that we can't "think our way into salvation."

Digging Deeper
Mining for what really matters . . . and gold

Based on other historic accounts of brutal mass mur-ders by Pilate after apparent threats to Roman rule, we can assume that this account of death of religious pil-grims, who are making a trek to Jerusalem, was signifi-cant enough to rock people. It wasn't done so much to punish the religious pilgrims that he had killed as it's meant to strike fear in others who might follow their example.

Whereas in the Ten Commandments passage from a couple of weeks ago, Moses writes that God's first command is not to have any other gods before the God of Abraham, Pilate's message is not to have any other gods before Caesar . . . or else.

So people bringing up this event to Jesus wouldn't likely be doing so because they think he hasn't heard about it; everyone is talking about the bloodbath where the Galileans' blood comingled with the blood of their sacrifices. They wanted to see what he would do. Would he run? Would he condemn Pilate and risk immediate imprisonment?

Jesus, master of controlling his own message, stays on point. Rather than address the violence and engaging Pilate—who also might have done this as a provocation to see if Jesus would take the bait—he focuses on what we're to do, or not do, in the face of such tragedy.

First, he reminds us not to assume that God had anything to do with these untimely deaths. Considered more broadly, we might take this to presume that Jesus is reminding us not to blame God when bad things happen to good people. Contrary to what people may think, and even contrary to some texts in the Hebrew Bible, perhaps God doesn't work this way.

Second, he acknowledges that life is incredibly fragile. Along with this recognition, he wants to make sure people understand—as illustrated with the fig tree parable—that the fact that they are alive and others are dead doesn't automatically mean that they're doing the whole "faith thing" right any more than it means those who died were doing it wrong.

Instead, he suggests that the thing that's sparing them from what they deserve is grace, God's faith (perhaps as embodied in Jesus) in humanity to be able to turn it around.

How, if at all, does this tie back into the feast illustrations throughout the other texts? Again, we have to understand the culture from which these stories come. When a feast was held, there was no velvet rope or bouncer at the door. *Everyone* was welcome. In fact, sometimes servants would be sent out into the streets to invite strangers in to participate. No one was quizzed to determine their merit first. The doors were thrown open; you feasted not because you had earned it but because of the radical welcome and generosity of the master of the house.

So while we participate in the bounty before us, we should do so with full and thankful hearts rather than sitting on the high horse of self-satisfaction, thinking somehow that we deserved to be there while others didn't.

Heads Up

Connecting the text to our world

Author and pastor Tony Campolo has spoken all over the world in his long career. He didn't always get to go to glamorous places to speak, but on occasion there would be a conference somewhere like Hawaii where he got an invitation to talk. Unfortunately, because he lived on the east coast, Tony's body didn't easily acclimate to the five-hour shift in time zones. So when he woke up in Hawaii, with his body thinking it was 8:00 in the morning, the clock said 3:00 a.m.

No one else was awake, so he went out for a (very) early morning walk. He came across a diner, so he wandered in and ordered coffee and a donut.

Suddenly, a group of—let's say nontraditional—women wander in, all dressed in miniskirts and skin-tight tank tops or in dresses barely covering the parts that God gave them. They had lots of makeup on, and the language they threw around would suggest they didn't just come from a 3:00 a.m. worship service. Even Tony, the good Christian gentleman that he is, knew soon enough that he was surrounded by a group of prostitutes who had just called it quits for the night.

"You know," one woman sitting next to him at the counter said, looking his way, "tomorrow is my birthday. I'll be thirty-nine." Immediately the woman's "friends" start giving her a hard time. "What, you want a party?" they harassed her. "Want us to buy you a cake and sing to you?"

The soon-to-be birthday girl tried to hide her hurt, snapping back at them that she didn't want or expect anything from them. "I've never had a birthday party in my whole life," she said. "Why should I start now?"

Tony lingered until the women filed back out onto the street, then asked the man behind the counter if the ladies came in every night around the same time. The man nodded, and Tony leaned closer, a smile growing on his face.

"You think we could throw her a little party tomorrow night?"

Tony returned at 2:30 a.m. the next morning, weighed down with decorations to hang in the diner and a "Happy Birthday!" sign they put over the door. The cook had made her a cake and put the word out that Agnes (the birthday girl's name) was having a party.

By the time Agnes and her crew wandered in at 3:30 a.m., the place was packed. "Happy birthday, Agnes!" everyone yelled, to which Agnes nearly fainted on the spot. They brought out the cake, everyone sang, and they waited for her to cut her first-ever birthday cake.

"If it's okay with you," she said, staring at the cake, "I'd like to take it home and keep it for a while. I never got anything like this before." Everyone agrees; after all, it's her cake and her party. She can do what she wants!

"I'll be right back," she said, sliding off the stool, cake in hand. "Promise."

As she disappeared into the darkness, Tony invited everyone in the diner to pray together. Everyone awkwardly joined hands in a prayer for Agnes. After the prayer was over, the man behind the counter leaned toward Tony.

"You never told me you were a preacher," he said. "What kind of church do you belong to anyway?"

"A church that throws birthday parties for prostitutes at 3:30 in the morning," he said.

Prayer for the Week

When things are going well, God, it's all too easy for me to fall under the mistaken impression that I deserve it, kind of like I do when things are crappy. Help me give thanks for all things, even when they suck.

Popping Off

Art/music/video and other cool stuff that relate to the text

The Kingdom of God Is a Party, by Tony Campolo (book, 1992)

Our Daily Bread (movie, 1934)

Hotel Rwanda (movie, 2004)

Get It Together!

———⟋⋀⋁⋀⟍———

Lectionary Texts For
March 31, 2019 (Fourth Sunday in Lent)

Texts in Brief
My dog ate my Bible!

FIRST READING
Joshua 5:9–12

God announces to Joshua about removing the "disgrace of Egypt" from the Jews. Previously they have lived under a pall because of past sins. They celebrate Passover in Gilgal surrounded by plenty. The land finally fields crops to them again and they no longer have to eat manna.

PSALM
Psalm 32

The psalmist implores those who have sinned to go to God and ask for forgiveness. The claim is that, while we live under the burden of our unforgiven sin, there is real joy in having that burden removed by God, but only if we ask for it.

SECOND READING
2 Corinthians 5:16–21

We don't recognize people by human standards anymore, even though we all first understand Jesus in human terms. God reconciled the world to God through Christ, and now we have our own ministry of reconciliation as ambassadors of Christ. We represent God in the world, so long as we reflect what Jesus called us to be through the gospel teaching.

GOSPEL
Luke 15:1–3

Jesus associates with sinners and tax collectors, for which he is criticized. But whereas his associates feel he should stick with those trying to live as he instructs, he recognizes that he is needed in the places where people live least like he wants for them.

Luke 11b–32

Story of the prodigal son, which is a parable not so much about the son (who represents us) but about the father (who represents God). The son messes up and makes bad choices, as do we, but reconciliation happens when we come back to God seeking forgiveness for our screw-ups. And the joy in such forgiveness and reconciliation is even greater than if we had never gone astray in the first place.

Bible, Decoded

Breaking down Scripture in plain language

Passover—This is a Jewish holiday that celebrates the "passing over" of the angel of death, thus saving their firstborns from being killed. They smeared lamb's blood on their doorposts while enslaved in Egypt, and then God sent death around to punish their Egyptian captors. Fun fact: Jesus was celebrating Passover with his disciples the first time he introduced him to the Lord's Supper (also called Communion).

Sin—A very loaded word. Basically, sin can be defined as anything we put ahead of God/love. So if it drives a wedge between us and God or you and our call to love unconditionally, it's probably sin.

Prodigal son—A churchy phrase for someone who takes off, screws up, and then comes back with a little more humility than before. We've all been the Prodigal son in one way or another. But we also have the opportunity, and responsibility, to be the father as well.

Reconciliation—Reconciliation is all about removing those "sin wedges" referred to above and closing the gaps between us, God, our call to love, true joy, or anything we long for but tend to fall short of achieving sometimes.

Points to Ponder

First Thoughts

It's not sin that keeps us from God but rather the unwillingness to confess that sin, to hand it over to

God. When we try to bear that burden on our own, our bones wear out, as the psalmist says.

Confession is vulnerable, revealing, humiliating. But it is through such confession that our load is lightened, and we help remove the barriers between us and God that we ourselves have built up.

The good news is that God goes out of God's way to meet us where we are. As long as we're honest, humble, and vulnerable in seeking forgiveness, there is no end to God's capacity for mercy and forgiveness. This, as Jesus notes, is gospel; it's really good news.

Digging Deeper

Mining for what really matters . . . and gold

What is our ministry of reconciliation? Are we called simply to forgive others as they seek forgiveness? Or are we called out into the midst of the surrounding brokenness to confess that if we are worthy of love, then certainly you are too?

Those we have yet to meet and reconcile with are worth going out of our way for, worth risking everything for. At one time or another, we've all been that lost sheep or that missing coin. We've been the son who blew it all and came crawling back on our knees. We've been the ones in exile, wandering aimlessly as we search for our way in the world.

And the whole time, love persists. It seduces us, waiting eagerly only for a "yes" from us to enter in. All it requires of us is to get real with ourselves, to look at ourselves in the mirror and name what we see. The beautiful and the bruised. The holy and the mundane. The lost and all that is worth hanging on to.

And then we are commissioned with going out into the world and helping others discover the same thing about themselves. How do we do that?

Too often, Christians fall back on pithy rhetorical catch phrases like "Jesus loves you" or "God has a plan for your life." But what if my life really sucks right now? What if my wife just left me, or my dog died? What if I'm an addict, mired in the bondage of my own making? What if I've been beaten down, ridiculed, ignored, marginalized?

Imagine how your pretty words sound to me if this is the state of my life.

Reconciliation doesn't happen simply by hearing an uplifting sermon, getting a sweet greeting card, or getting an affirming pat on the back. It is a long, hard process of healing that begins with intentional presence and radical vulnerability.

Take the story of the prodigal son, for example. We've heard the story before, most likely, and it's easy to see what the son is risking in coming back on his hands and knees to sleep among the pigs. He risks humiliation, rejection, and lifelong alienation from his loved ones.

But what about the father? What does he risk? Being taken advantage of again? What if his son comes back, only to fall back into his old habits and hurt him like he did before? What if he steals from him? And then there's the faithful brother, who now has to share his inheritance and his father's love with a brother who hasn't earned it. Understandably, he resists the invitation, but the father, who has so much to lose, begs for him to come to the party.

The last person in this story who should be begging for anything is the father. And yet here he is, risking all he has for one who might take it all away from him. He risks the loss of respect from the faithful son who could withdraw in response to the perceived injustice.

If the father was a pastor, his congregation might call him before the board for missing one too many potlucks because he was out walking the streets in search of the ones who need him most.

Heads Up
Connecting the text to our world

Excerpted from "MySpace to Sacred Space: God for a New Generation"

CHURCH OF THE PRODIGAL CHILD

In 2007, my wife, Amy, and I cowrote a book. In it, we surveyed more than 750 young adults about their perceptions of both God and religion. We included devout Christians, seekers, agnostics, and even atheists. One of the largest groups included those who felt some connection to God, and yet had little or no contact with organized religion.

With regard to influences on their faith, the "spiritual" group responded much like the overall averages with respect to people and their impact. However, the influence of both the Bible and church were significantly lower. Whereas 38 percent of all respondents said both the Bible and church strongly shaped their faith, only 6 percent of the spiritual group identified with these influences. Only 3 percent of the spiritual group attends church on a weekly basis, with most visiting church once or twice a year, or only for special events such as weddings and funerals. Less than 20 percent say their beliefs align with biblical teaching, less than 15 percent identify their beliefs with a certain church, and less than 10 percent feel any denomination echoes their views.

More than four in ten from the spiritual group had their initial church experience more than twenty years ago, with another 40 percent not claiming any church attendance history at all. Less than 10 percent began attending church fifteen years ago or less, which suggests most who have attended church did so as young children first. This idea is supported by the claim made by nearly 86 percent of the spiritual group that family took them or invited them to their first church encounter. The number of respondents from this group who had a positive experience their first time at church was only slightly lower than the average (74 percent versus 79 percent), but they took longer to decide whether or not they would return to church. Though just more than 20 percent of the overall respondents took a year or more to decide whether or not they would continue to attend church, the rate for the spiritual group was nearly double this (38 percent).

Though the spiritual group spends only slightly less time in weekly prayer or meditation than the average, they spend significantly less time with Scripture. However, one out of three reports spending at least half an hour each week reading the Bible. Not entirely surprising is that they have a relatively negative outlook on church. Less than 30 percent believe churches are necessary or healthy, and less than one in ten feels churches are responsible with money or important to their lives. Only 15 percent think the programs churches offer are relevant to them, yet an unexpected 49 percent say churches are still places of comfort.

The spiritual group is not dissimilar from the overall group in many respects about what they think the focus of church should be. Though worship and evangelism did not rank as highly important, issues such as social activism (85 percent), fellowship/community (77 percent), prayer, and moral issues (both 58 percent) were seen as "essential" or "very important." They tend to see church principally as judgmental (92 percent), intimidating (61 percent), and frightening (52 percent), though a significant number also view church in general as available (73 percent), strong (65 percent), energetic (47 percent), and engaged (45 percent).

Almost three fourths believe it's acceptable to question and doubt in church, but only one in five believes their opinions can be heard there. Ninety-five percent strongly feel everyone should be welcome in church, no matter what, yet few seem to think this reflects the climate of modern church. More than 80 percent say churches overstep their political limits.

Perhaps most important is that they are open to God's presence in their lives, and they are willing to engage in meaningful dialogue, prayer, and study about faith. Though traditional church worship settings may not immediately provide the greatest opportunity for bridging these gaps and reconciling some of the damage that may have been done, small group contacts outside of the church and one-on-one relationships provide the greatest opportunity for rebuilding the trust upon which a healthy corporate faith experience can be built.

If Jesus is the model for our ministry and evangelism, we can quickly realize that getting people through the doors of church is not the point. The central thrusts of Jesus's ministry were to bring healing to a hurting world, to sit and share time and stories with those otherwise rejected by society, and then to charge those who found hope and nourishment in his teaching to carry it with them to the corners of the earth. In many ways, he was his culture's poster boy for "spiritual but not religious." People believed he was who he claimed to be not because he held a respectable position within the church or because he demonstrated authority through acts of overwhelming power. His life and how he connected with the world set him apart, and he didn't stand behind a pulpit to do it.

Prayer for the Week

God, grant me the courage and clarity to name my own shortcomings, to confess them to you and to myself, and then to lay them down and accept that I, in all of my brokenness and imperfection, am still worthy of perfect love.

Popping Off
Art/music/video and other cool stuff that relate to the text

"Come Together," by The Beatles (song, 1969)

"Get Together," by The Youngbloods (song, 1967)

"Japanese Artist's Works Inspired by Faith on Display at Yale," from YaleNews (article, 2009): tinyurl.com/y884qjmc

O Brother, Where Art Thou? (movie, 2000)

Magnolia (movie, 1999)

The Straight Story (movie, 1999)

You'd Better Recognize

Lectionary Texts For
April 7, 2019 (Fifth Sunday in Lent)

Texts in Brief
My dog ate my Bible!

First Reading
Isaiah 43:16–21

A poetic passage that offers a testament to the intent of God (on whose behalf the author is speaking in first person) to invoke an entirely new order. This order is to be so profoundly different that even the animals and all of creation will bend to it. Finally, the reader or listener is challenged with a question about whether they recognize the change, which is already underway.

Psalm
Isaiah 43:16–21

A prayer offered to God, seeking to change our circumstances for the better. It is a prayer of lament, but also an appeal on the behalf of the people of Israel to return their tears of sorrow and regret with a reprise of joy.

Second Reading
Philippians 3:4b–14

Paul has lost a lot in his pursuit of following Jesus. He lost his culture, wealth, identity, and entire way of life. But looking back, he recognizes that none of it really mattered when compared with the value and importance of what he has gained in his new life pursuit.

It's also interesting that, whereas in other places in the gospel, we're implored to hate or despise the flesh (arguably hyperbole), here Paul actually expresses confidence that "the flesh," or human beings, can come around to right thinking and action.

Gospel
John 12:1–8

Mary anoints Jesus's feet with expensive oil, for which she is criticized. But actually Jesus is more harshly reprimanded, particularly by Judas, for letting her do it. The argument is that this oil is very valuable and could have been sold to feed a lot of people. But Jesus argues that she bought it expressly for the purpose of anointing his body at the time of his death. So this is a prophetic act, recognizing that he is beginning his preparation for death.

Bible, Decoded
Breaking down Scripture in plain language

Zion—This is the name of the mountain in Jerusalem where the Jews' holiest temples were located. It's considered the place at which humanity and God are most closely connected. Aside from being a holy site, it also represents hope in the future when God will send the Messiah and redeem humanity.

Righteousness—Paul drops this word so much he must have gotten a bulk discount on them at Costco. There are two kinds of righteousness Paul talks about a lot. One has to do with us, and in this case, our righteousness has to do with living a life that is pleasing to God. God's righteousness, on the other hand, is interpreted a lot of different ways, depending on who you ask. It seems to me that, for the most part, God's righteousness has to do with God's power to liberate humanity from our own sin and messed-up-ness.

Nard—A strange word for really expensive perfume. This is what Mary (Lazarus's sister) pours over Jesus's feet. Apparently she used so much that it was worth a year's salary back then.

Judas—Most notorious for his betrayal of Jesus before his death, Judas was also dipping into the coffers of Jesus's ministry. Yes, he complains about how the expensive perfume used on Jesus's feet could have been sold and the money given to the poor, but Jesus most likely knew the hypocrisy behind his criticisms.

Points to Ponder

First Thoughts

Isaiah notes that clinging to the past is a waste of time. We're invited instead to look ahead with hope and joyful anticipation. Even though we can't entirely know what awaits us, it is an act of faith in itself to look ahead with hope. If we hang on too tightly to what we have and think is important, or at least what has been important in the past, we might easily miss the best parts of life. As Paul notes, none of it has any real worth compared with what we're invited into as we follow a God-inspired way of living.

But for those of us who struggle in the present, or who are haunted by our past, this is more of a message of relief, rather than a mandate or challenge. Hope is bigger than present suffering; it can't be extinguished by our current struggles or even by a difficult past. Things can always change, and actually already are if we open our eyes to it.

Digging Deeper

Mining for what really matters . . . and gold

All of these texts have a common theme of hopeful anticipation of something better than the present situation. I particularly like Paul's attitude in Philippians, where he basically comes off like a rapper at a freestyle punk-fest. "If anyone has room to brag about their earthly achievements," he says, "it's me." And then he goes on to list all of his "cred." Then he follows that up by saying, "Of course, I'm not going to brag . . ."

Thanks Paul for that little dose of "humility!"

But the Gospel text in John is definitely the most intriguing of the four excerpts to me. There's so much going on there, it takes a little bit of teasing apart to get at all of the layers.

First, you have Jesus coming to Lazarus's house for dinner six days before Passover. There's a lot of symbolism here. For one, the Passover meal is when Jesus drops the bomb on the disciples about being on the verge of crucifixion. They don't know this at the time this dinner takes place, but the author of John is definitely pointing us in that direction.

It's also important that the dinner takes place at Lazarus's house. After all, this is one of only a handful of resurrection stories in the Gospels. So again the author of John is foretelling not just the bad news of the crucifixion, he's also offering a glimpse of the hope of resurrection.

And then there's Judas. He thinks he's pulling one over by acting self-righteous about wasting money on the nard-fest, but really he's just thinking about himself. And obviously he doesn't get it through his head this time around since he's also the one who sells Jesus out to the Roman authorities for a few pieces of silver.

Drawing a dotted line from John to Philippians, we see Judas doing exactly what Paul warns the church leaders in Philippi not to do. (Keep in mind most of Paul's work in the New Testament is from letters he wrote to new church starts spread out all over the place.) He's clinging to the things he sees as valuable in this world and this moment, meanwhile missing the big picture.

And ultimately, this approach leads Judas to commit suicide after serving up Jesus to Rome. So it's pretty obvious his strategy didn't pan out so well.

Finally, you have this intimate moment between Mary Magdalene (Lazarus's sister) and Jesus. Imagine how it would feel if someone poured a container of scented oil over your bare feet in front of all your friends, and then proceeded to bow down in front of you, using her hair to wash your feet with the oil. It's a vulnerable moment, really for both of them.

Keep in mind that this oil being used is usually committed for use in burial rituals. So clearly it's another piece of the prophecy puzzle, pointing to what is about to happen. But it's more than that. Jesus is participating in a moment that points to what all of these texts are telling us, which is to loosen our grasp on all the stuff we think is important in front of us and wake up to the fact that there are more important things going on.

Yes, you could argue that he's being self-indulgent and self-centered by "wasting" this perfume on himself. But it seems to me that he realizes this is the cost of the lesson he wants to convey to those present.

Oh, and let's not forget to mention that Mary, a "lowly" woman (and the one wrongly labeled by many as a prostitute), is the one who seems to actually get it. It's clear that, as the prophet asks us to, she sees the change that is already underway. Meanwhile, the disciples seem to be missing it. Judas, in particular, is looking for angles for self-enrichment even in this all-important moment. Regardless, God is creating a new thing. We just have to open our eyes to witness it.

Heads Up

Connecting the text to our world

Sometimes prophetic wisdom comes from the most unexpected places. We search Scripture, pray, sit in church, and wait for those mountaintop moments we hear other Christians talk about. We want to hear the voice of God, to feel the ecstasy of the scales falling away from our eyes, so that once and for all, we can see everything the way God sees it.

But what if God is speaking through a foulmouthed comedian instead of through winged angels playing harps on clouds? That's sooo Old Testament anyway . . .

I have been a fan of Louis C. K., who has made his living as a stand-up comedian for a long time. He drops about as many four-letter words as you can probably think of, and he pushes the envelope of propriety at every turn. Still, there's this sense in his work that he has a big heart and that his crusty exterior is basically an effective defense mechanism to keep people from getting too close. And since this was originally written, he has become entangled in the consequences of his own choices related to the #MeToo movement. Though I debated taking this illustration out because of his controversy, I determined that it's useful for us to recognize that truth sometimes comes through the most flawed of messengers.

After all, if we only shared stories from and about exemplary people, we would have a scarcity of content, including much of the Bible itself.

C. K. has a TV show called *Louie*, which is loosely based on his own life. Basically he takes his reality and fictionalizes the crap out of it at his convenience to make a good story out of it. Several times I've been watching the show and have been floored by the profound truth laid out in the middle of his barrage of toilet humor.

In one episode in particular, he's hanging out with another comedian friend of his who is really down on life. Everything he touches turns to shit. He's lost hope, and he's vocally contemplating suicide. Desperate to say the "right thing" to help turn things around for him, Louie finally slumps his shoulders and shakes his head in exasperation.

"I got my reasons to live," he says angrily to his friend. "I worked hard to figure out what they are. I'm not just handing them to you. Okay? You want a reason to live, have a drink of water, get some sleep, wake up in the morning, and try again like everybody else does.

"It's not your life. It's life. It's life as in 'bigger than you,' if you can imagine that. Life isn't something that you possess; it's something that you take part in. And you witness."

It's hard when we're struggling or suffering to remember that there is something bigger than us. Our tendency is to fold in on ourselves, draw back, and hide ourselves from the world. But Louis C. K. is right. We don't lay claim to this life. It's simply something we get to participate in for a while.

Yes, we're invited to fully love our lives. But as the old saying goes, if you love something, you have to set it free.

Prayer for the Week

God, it's easy for me to hang my hope and faith on present circumstances. Please help me recognize that hope is bigger than what happens today, this week, this year, or in my past. Hope is independent of outcomes, but that's easy to forget. Help me to loosen my grip on my own plans, things, and expectations so that I can see your plans for liberation more fully.

Popping Off
Art/music/video and other cool stuff that relate to the text

Life Is Beautiful (movie, 1997)

"40," by U2 (song, 1983)

The Pursuit of Happyness (movie, 2006)

I'm a Loser,
Baby

Lectionary Texts For

April 14, 2019 (Liturgy of the Passion)

Texts in Brief

My dog ate my Bible!

First Reading

There is no "first reading" this week, most likely because of how long the Gospel text is. The long version is 114 verses.

Psalm

Psalm 31:9–16

David is grieving the fact that he is beset by enemies on every side. He is scorned even by those who know him, and he feels almost like a "dead man walking." And yet, he seeks refuge with God, asking God to deliver him from a time of profound persecution.

Second Reading

Philippians 2:5–11

Paul writes to the early Christians in Philippi, reminding them of the example of humility and selflessness that Jesus modeled for them. If, he writes in verse form, Jesus can come in the likeness of God and still act in a such humble fashion, they have no basis to act in any other way but the example set by Christ.

Gospel

Luke 22:14–23:56 (long/full version)

Luke 23:1–49 (short version)

Both of these texts depict the trial and crucifixion of Jesus. First, Pontius Pilate—who is like a mayor—asks Jesus if he claims the be king of the Jews, to which he replies that Pilate seems to believe as much. Then he is taken before King Herod, who challenges him to demonstrate his divinity with some miraculous act, which Jesus refuses to do. So Herod and his attendants mock Jesus and send him back to Pilate, who sets him before a crowd and asks them whether he should convict Jesus or Barabbas. The crowd responds that he should crucify Jesus.

Pilate literally washes his hands of the conviction and sends Jesus to his death.

Bible, Decoded

Breaking down Scripture in plain language

Salvation—This is a big word in Christianity. For some it means protection from eternal condemnation and suffering apart from God. For others, salvation is more about healing in the present, divesting ourselves of the things in this life that cause suffering to live in greater peace with our circumstances.

Unleavened bread—This is bread made without yeast, which is the ingredient that causes bread to rise. Jewish people use this as part of their Passover celebration because it is a reminder of when the Jews fled captivity in Egypt. The story is that they had to leave so quickly that they didn't have time to let the bread that was being made finish rising.

Gentiles—This is a phrase that might closely translate in our reality to "those people." Back in the day, gentiles were considered everyone who wasn't Jewish. Today, sometimes Christians are considered to be gentiles. But it's still employed by some to refer to anyone outside "the circle," however they define it.

Points to Ponder

First Thoughts

The theme in Luke where Jesus exalts the servant over those with more esteemed status runs throughout this Gospel. The idea that "The first will be last and the last will be first" is sometimes called "The Great Reversal."

The psalmist is going through some pretty bad stuff. It almost seems like he's even making a joke of how bad his situation is when he says people look at him on the street and run away screaming. That's pretty bad! But the point is that the psalmist doesn't let hard times diminish his faith.

Jesus does not want to have to go through with the crucifixion. He even asks God not to have to endure it. But in the end, he remains faithful to what he feels called to do, despite the grief and fear that comes along with it.

In Philippians, Paul talks about the need for us to "empty ourselves out." Like last week's Pauline text, he points out that personal status, admiration, and titles trip us up when it comes to understanding who we are in God's eyes. When we get past such superficialities, the lowly among us become equal with the greatest among us: all beloved children of God. That sounds like a Great Reversal!

Digging Deeper

Mining for what really matters . . . and gold

One of the Bible verses with the greatest potential for misinterpretation is John 12:25, which says, "Anyone who loves their life will lose it, while anyone who hates their life in this world will keep it for eternal life." Yeah, I know. That's not one of the texts this week, right? But the sentiment is consistent with a lot of what we find in our verses here.

So are we supposed to actually hate ourselves or hate our lives? Does this mean that "emos" are, in fact, God's chosen people? I mean, they do have the whole "I hate my life" thing down, right?

We have to keep in mind that sometimes authors in Scripture use hyperbole or exaggeration to make their point. Take the author of Psalm 31, for example. Are we really supposed to believe that he is so hideously ugly that people run away screaming when they see the author coming? Or are they trying to say, in a way, that things really can't get any worse?

It seems that Jesus is in the same boat. Imagine being on death row for something you didn't do, and all you get from the authorities is more humiliation and torture. Hard to feel too good about life in that moment. In fact, Jesus's own followers fell way short of sticking with him once everything really went down. Addicts would call this moment for Jesus and the author of Psalms "rock bottom."

When we look at the Philippians letter from Paul, we can see him, once again, warning his folks not to get their identities hung up on their titles and accomplishments in the present life. After all, he knows that chances are good that many of the early church followers will end up facing a similar fate as Jesus did. A good many of them were executed, and he wanted to help make sure their faith was based on something real, rather than something that could easily be snatched away.

It's easier to be faithful when things are going right. The real challenge is if we can still look to God for our value, for guidance and hope, even when there seems to be no hope anywhere around us. It doesn't mean we can't gripe a little about hard times; the psalmist does this. It doesn't mean we can't stress out about adversity; heck, even Jesus sweated blood while praying for God to spare him the suffering of crucifixion.

But once we unload the burdens on our hearts (which God always welcomes us to do), we're encouraged to go back to the heart of who—and whose—we are. We're not as great as the world tells us sometimes, but we're not as crappy either. What we are is imperfect, flawed, beautiful, complex, vulnerable, God-inspired creatures capable of love, pain, joy, suffering, and everything in between.

So are we supposed to actually hate our lives in some sort of masochistic kind of way? Or are we called to keep life in perspective, understanding that there is always something bigger going on that simply life itself? It's humbling when things are going great, but in all the other times, it's nice to know that the world's fleeting and fickle evaluations of who I am and what I'm worth really don't compare to the love from which we emerged and to which we will one day return.

Heads Up
Connecting the text to our world

Mother Teresa is considered one of the most faithful, God-inspired, and inspiring people ever to have lived. She spent her time in the orphanages of Calcutta caring for children no one else wanted.

It's comforting to think that there are people in the world who can do such heartbreaking, backbreaking work and still love God in the process. But some letters discovered after Teresa's death suggest that even she wrestled with what some of us might call a "dark night of the soul."

"Jesus has a very special love for you," she wrote in 1979 to Rev. Michael Van Der Peet. "As for me, the silence and the emptiness is so great that I look and do not see, listen and do not hear."

How in the hell can I expect to keep my faith up if someone as incredible as Mother Teresa questioned the presence of God in some moments? At least for us, we have examples like Teresa and Jesus himself to look to. They don't like what is going on. In fact, their lives pretty much suck. And for Teresa, at least, it's enough to make her wonder whether or not God is even there.

So what is her response? To act as if God is, was, and will be there, even when she's not even sure that's the case. It's called "acting as if," or "cognitive dissonance" if you're into psychological parlance. When life offers us a big crap sandwich, it's easy to blame God. It's easy, too, for our suffering to blind us to the possibility of the existence of a greater grace or peace more enduring than our hurt.

But the hope embodied in the story of Jesus is that we can rest assured that it's true. Pain is temporary; love never dies. The world may tell us we're worthless, but God begs to differ. Teresa may have, from time to time, lost her faith in God, but Paul affirms for us that even in those moments, God doesn't lose faith in us.

God can handle our doubts, our pain, and our anger about it, just as God can endure our arrogance and self-reliance when we feel on top of the world. Thankfully, hope isn't harnessed to the present moment. It may be hard to believe sometimes, but it's part of the covenant—the holy promise between God and humanity—we have with our Creator.

Sometimes, though, we need a little reminder to keep on keeping on.

Prayer for the Week

God, I'm a screw-up, but that doesn't mean I'm unworthy of love. Today may be tough, but that's nothing compared to the peace I have in knowing I am wildly loved without condition, no matter what. Thanks for that gift, and please help remind me when I get too used to the judgments of the world around me and allow them to define who I am.

Popping Off

Art/music/video and other cool stuff that relate to the text

"Loser," by Beck (song, 1993)

"Creep," by Radiohead (song, 1992)

Yertle the Turtle and Other Stories, by Dr. Seuss (book, 1986)

Welcome to the Dollhouse (movie, 1995)

Little Miss Sunshine (movie, 2006)

Resurrection for Dummies

Lectionary Texts For
April 21, 2019 (Easter Sunday)

Texts in Brief
My dog ate my Bible!

First Reading
Acts 10:34–43

Peter speaks to Cornelius and a group of gentiles about the resurrection and about God showing no favor to a particular group of people. In addition to preaching that God's grace knows no boundaries, he is demonstrating this by the very fact that he is going out among those who are unlike him.

Psalm
Psalm 118:1–2, 14–24

A song of praise for the endurance of God's love through all time. It speaks of a stone rejected by builders now becoming the foundation stone for a new structure, which is a foretelling of the rejection, crucifixion, and resurrection of Jesus. The psalmist also rejoices in God's victory over death.

Second Reading
1 Corinthians 15:19–26

Since death came through a human being, Paul writes, the resurrection of the dead came through a human being too. This is his attempt to explain the role of the crucifixion to the early Christians in Corinth, and/or to give them tools for explaining it to others. Finally, Paul proclaims that death is the last enemy and that it has been defeated.

Gospel
Luke 24:1–12

The women (Mary Magdalene, Joanna, Mary, mother of James, and others) arrive at Jesus's tomb to anoint his body with spices, only to find the tomb empty. Two men in white explain to them that Jesus has risen, so they return to Peter to tell him. Peter joins them at the tomb and is amazed to find it empty.

Bible, Decoded
Breaking down Scripture in plain language

Galilee—Territory in what is today northern Israel, where Jesus lived most of his life. It was known in his time for being a region replete with political unrest, independent attitudes, and even the occasional politically motivated act of violence.

Cornelius—A "God-fearing man" known to be a pretty good guy among the Jews, even though he himself was a Roman soldier and a gentile (outsider). Although in this text in Acts he and Peter are only talking, this leads eventually to Cornelius being baptized as one of the first gentiles to become a Christian. This is considered a big deal in the birth of the early Christian church.

Points to Ponder

First Thoughts

Peter's name, given to him by Jesus, meant "rock." He was one of the disciples used as an object lesson in denying Jesus three times before his death. And yet he's also the first disciple to visit Jesus's empty tomb, and he is responsible in large part for Cornelius being baptized. The Psalm talks about the stone that is cast away by the builders becoming the foundation stone. Given Peter's name and importance in starting the church, it makes sense to think of this reference in the Psalm as a prophecy of Peter's role.

If you wrestle with the idea of resurrection, you're not alone. Jesus tells Peter that he'll build the church on his ministry, and yet he comes away from the tomb bewildered by its emptiness. The women, who seem to be the most faithful to Jesus before and after his death, seem to have developed amnesia about the resurrection prophecy. Good to know I'm not alone in scratching my head when it comes to resurrection.

I love the idea that Paul puts forward in the Corinthians text that Jesus has triumphed over death, our final enemy. It's beautiful, hopeful, and so liberating.

However, his language in the few verses just before this Scripture (1 Cor 15:12–19) sounds a whole lot like the "if-then" ultimatums that ran me out of the fundamentalist church. Basically he says if you don't believe Jesus was raised from the dead, everything is pointless. Let's put a pin in that and come back to it.

Digging Deeper

Mining for what really matters . . . and gold

Lots of ministers love preaching about the risen Christ on Easter Sunday without talking about what he went through to get there. It's a bad habit we Protestants have, but plenty of us skip right over Maundy Thursday and Good Friday to Easter. Part of this is because we don't like to have to deal with the darkness of Jesus's crucifixion, suffering, death, and burial, but it's also because we don't really understand the resurrection.

But in Corinthians, Paul is basically putting us all on notice, saying that if we don't believe in the resurrection, the whole of Jesus's life and our lives as his followers are meaningless. Hey Paul, let's back up the ultimatum truck, okay?

Growing up, I heard, "If you don't believe _____, then _____ terrible thing is going to happen." It used to scare the crap out of me because I wanted to believe, but it seemed like there was no room for questioning, doubt, or nuance in our understanding. Either you believed, or you didn't—period.

But I wasn't sure I did. Not in the way my church wanted me to, anyway.

We doubters seem to be in decent company. It's not as if all of the folks right around Jesus got it right away either. In Luke, the women show up and are surprised that Jesus isn't there. It takes a little reminder from the two guys in white (some say they're angels, but Luke's text just calls them men) that Jesus told them this would happen, back in Galilee. Kind of a big thing to forget, don't you think? They came with oils and spices, fully expecting him to still be in that tomb, and yet these are the women who stood by at the foot of the cross. Mary Magdalene was the one who washed Jesus's feet in precious oil not long before.

Then along comes Peter. Sure, he gets points for being the first disciple on the scene, but what is his reaction? The women have already told him that Jesus's body was gone, and I'm guessing they reminded him of the whole resurrection thing. Then he goes and sees for himself that, sure enough, the body isn't there. And yet he's bewildered.

Doesn't it seem like someone as faithful as Peter, the one on whom the church will be built, would get it? But resurrection is a mind-blower. It makes no sense. There's a part of us that, no matter how earnestly we want to believe, whispers in the back of our minds that resurrection is impossible.

For me, resurrection is a process rather than a one-time event. It's more like how Martin Luther King Jr. spoke of history's arc bending toward justice. God's arc for the whole of humanity is long, chaotic, and sometimes even violent. But it bends toward hope. It bends toward life and love. That love, though not yet fully realized, is a restoring love that is greater than the sum total of the destructive forces humanity can muster.

Resurrection literally means to make something right again. Though we are bent, bruised, and bloodied by life's darkness, God's love makes us upright once again. Maybe not today. Maybe not tomorrow. But faith in resurrection means that our entire existence bends toward God's fullness.

Heads Up

Connecting the text to our world

I'm an Olympics junkie. Not only that, but I'm also most ardently pro-American when watching them. My wife, Amy, and I were watching synchronized platform during the last summer Olympics (honestly, when else would we do that?), and she said she was kind of pulling for the team from Mexico to medal, even though it might mean pushing the Americans out of the running.

"What the hell are you talking about?" I asked, more than a little incredulous.

"We win so much already," she said. "This is a rare chance for Mexico."

"If you root for another country," I grumbled sarcastically, "the terrorists win."

I'm usually a fan of the underdog, and I'm not exactly a sports fanatic, but something about the national zeal combined with the athletic excellence brings it out in me.

Of course, there's a part of all of us that loves a winner. There's a reason why so many people wear the jerseys of their favorite teams or players (way more when that person or team is on top than not, by the way), why we revert to a sort of tribal level of passion—painting our faces, screaming rabidly—and why we practically make a religion out of our sports. At one level, it's inspiring to see someone achieve what appears to be unattainable. The idea of doing what most Olympians do—or all professional athletes, for that matter—is hard to comprehend. But when we get to witness it, it serves to embolden our faith in humanity a little bit.

Yes, we screw up a lot, we fight each other, and we're warming up the planet at an alarming rate. But once in a while, it's transcendent to watch someone do something amazing, beautiful, and a little bit closer to perfect.

Then there's a baser drive at play too. After all, if it was just about athletic ability, inspiration, and beauty, we'd have no need for medals and the whole "competition" thing. We love winners particularly because there are losers. In fact, the more losers there are, the sweeter the winners appear. I expect this taps into some very basic evolutionary stuff for us. Though we don't toss people into gladiator forums to fight to the death anymore (though we get pretty close), we love to pit two individuals or teams against each other to fight it out in an all-or-nothing decision.

We shower the victor with adoration, attention, and treasure while the loser, no matter how slim the margin, fades into obscurity.

Why? Because we crave a means of determining who is "the best" so that we can identify ourselves with them. Once we know Michael Phelps, the New England Patriots, or whoever is the best, we can buy their uniform, eat their cereal, and drink their sports drink, all the while feeling like we possess a little piece of them—without all that work, practice, and emotional tribulation stuff.

It's not unlike making an alliance with the pack leader, really. Once we know who the alpha is, we know who to cozy up to so we ensure our own safety and survival. It's funny that sports can be so inspiring and transcendent for the basic human condition while also appealing to our most primitive selves at the same time. No wonder they're popular.

Then there's Jesus, hanging out with the losers, the sick, the criminals; the kind of folks you would not likely see climbing to the top of the medal stand. And although I'd love to identify as often as possible with the big winners, more often than not my heart lands in the loser's camp too.

That's reason enough for me to love Peter. He tries really hard. He wants so desperately to believe and do the right thing. But he screws up . . . a lot. Jesus gives Peter his name (which means "rock") because he's a man of solid faith. Not perfect faith, but solid. He even names that Peter will be the cornerstone of the new church that will come next.

Despite that, it wasn't so long ago that Peter denied Jesus, and he was among the disciples who fell asleep while Jesus was praying in the garden of Gethsemane. These are only a few examples. Remember the whole "sinking in the lake" thing? That was him. Suffice it to say that in spite of his faithfulness, he's kind of a loser.

The good news is that God loves losers. In fact, the entirety of the Christian faith was built with them. The psalmist predicts this in our Psalm text, noting that the stone cast aside by the builders will become the cornerstone of the church. That's Peter.

We've all been Peter at one time or another. We've messed up, lost, fallen short, felt unworthy, doubted . . . you name it. And it would be easy enough in those moments to justify our own uselessness. *God can't use a loser like me. I'm supposed to have it all together, to have all the answers, to have Scripture memorized and to believe every word it says. I'm just not ready for all of that. I can't do it.*

If we waited until we all were fit to serve God, there would never have been a church to begin with. Yes, we'll screw it up. Yes, people will get hurt. But that's not a reason to sit on the sidelines, telling ourselves all the reasons why we're of no use.

Prayer for the Week

God, I know I'm not perfect. Sometimes I don't even know what I believe. There are times when I feel like Peter, the outcast, tossed to the side, discarded. But I'm still willing to try to do right, to understand, to discover all that I was made to be. I'm still not entirely sure what this whole resurrection thing means, but I do believe that your creation is imbued with love and goodness. Yes, there's evil in the world—and sometimes I'm a part of it—but I don't want that to keep me from taking part in the beautiful, amazing moments. Help give me the courage to do, to try, and to wonder, even when I don't feel like I can.

Popping Off

Art/music/video and other cool stuff that relate to the text

E. T. (movie, 1982)

Rocky (movie, 1976)

"Hallelujah," by Jeff Buckley (song, 2007)

"Easter Again," by Leo Kottke (song, 1986)

"Roll Away the Stone," by Kelly Joe Phelps (song, 1997)

Fact or Truth?

Lectionary Texts For
April 28, 2019 (Second Sunday of Easter)

Texts in Brief
My dog ate my Bible!

First Reading
Acts 5:27–32

Disciples are brought before the high priest and accused of teaching the gospel, which they had been banned from doing. They stand firm, emboldened by the Holy Spirit, claiming that they answer to God, a higher authority than any human authority, including the religious leaders accusing them at that time.

Psalm
Psalm 150

A psalm of effusive praise, urging us to praise God with all we have. In particular, it encourages praise of God through music.

Second Reading
Revelation 1:4–8

John of Patmos is writing to Christian churches in Asia from his island prison. He sends a letter of greeting to the early Asian Christian churches and proclaims the lordship and eternal reign of God through Jesus (the "firstborn from among the dead"). He claims that Jesus's death and "birth" (resurrection) is an act of liberation, specifically from the burden of sin.

Gospel
John 20:19–31

Jesus appears to his disciples and breathes the Holy Spirit into them. He endows them with powers of healing and forgiveness of sin. Thomas wasn't there and doesn't believe unless he sees Jesus for himself. Jesus reappears to the disciples, lets Thomas feels his wounds, and says, "Happy are those who haven't seen and still believe."

Bible, Decoded
Breaking down Scripture in plain language

Holy Spirit—For those who believe in a trinitarian expression of God (God the Father, the Son, and the Holy Spirit), this is the most mystical dimension of God. The Holy Spirit is often compared to the wind, and often appears in Scripture when people are being filled with God's inspiration. I understand the Holy Spirit as "God-given inspiration."

Jerusalem—One of the oldest cities in existence, which lies between the Dead Sea and the Mediterranean. It's been destroyed twice and attacked dozens of times. Scripture says that David established Jerusalem as the capital of the Jewish people, most likely because it was not part of the seven tribal lands occupied by the Jewish tribes. Today, it's at the center of the ongoing Israeli-Palestinian conflict.

Glory—This is a churchy word used all the time, but it is not often understood. Glory in a religious context is synonymous with praise or great honor.

John (Revelation)—There are lots of Johns in the Bible (no, not *that* kind of john, gah!), but they're not all the same guy. For example, the John to whom the fourth Gospel is attributed may or may not be the same John as the one who wrote 1–3 John later in the New Testament. It depends on which biblical expert you ask. And there is disagreement among biblical scholars about who the John writing Revelation is. While some believe it isn't either one of the Johns noted above, others suggest that it is the disciple John. Regardless, we often refer to him as "John of Patmos," named as such because he was believed to have written Revelation (note there is no "o" at the end) while imprisoned on the island of Patmos where he was in exile, most likely for publicly practicing Christianity.

Points to Ponder

First Thoughts

We've all heard the phrase "Doubting Thomas." Well, this Scripture in John is where it comes from. Thomas often gets a bad rap for questioning his fellow disciples' claims that they've seen Jesus, but they actually got to see him! Remember back when Mary and the other women told the disciples they had seen Jesus at the tomb? They didn't exactly believe either. So if you struggle with this whole "resurrection" thing too, you're in good company.

If you're like me, and you aren't a big fan of contemporary Christian praise music, this psalm just comes off as kind of annoying. What if we're still scratching our heads about what exactly God and Jesus are all about, never mind the Holy Spirit?

I used to think that you would understand the whole "praising God" thing once you really, truly believed it all. But now I'm getting more comfortable with the idea that I can offer gratitude, awe, and even a bit of humble praise while still swimming in the deep, troubling waters of doubt and mystery. Something happened, it seems. And that something changed the world, pretty clearly for the better. That's a pretty good place to start.

Let's just get this out in the open right up front—the book of Revelation is weird. In fact, it almost didn't get included in the Bible we use today because it's so strange. Some people think John had to write the book in code to get it past island guards. Others think maybe he was losing his mind while in isolated exile. But despite the fantastical imagery and all the weird, scary ways so many Christians have used Revelation, it still points to one important end I think we can all look forward to: God wins.

I've got to give props to the disciples for standing up to the high Jewish priest, knowing full well they could be facing death for it. It wasn't so long ago with Jesus still in their midst that they lost faith and courage, and now they're standing strong in the temple! The text says they were emboldened by the Holy Spirit. The way I interpret this is that they had some kind of "a-ha" moment when they really finally got what this whole "following Jesus" thing was about. They had a focus, a purpose. They were the ambassadors of Jesus on earth, the bearers of the new church. It's easier to stand up to forces of power when you believe, way down deep in your bones, in what you're doing.

Digging Deeper

Mining for what really matters . . . and gold

There have been so many efforts to attribute some artifact or another to Jesus that's it's kind of mind boggling. You're probably familiar with the Shroud of Turin, the supposed cloth used to cover Jesus while his body rested in the tomb. Most scholars today agree it's a fake, but still, millions of people have a longing to cling to something physical to connect them to Jesus.

If you ever visit the Holy Land, there are all kinds of holy landmarks for everything, from where Jesus was born to where he prayed in the Garden of Gethsemane before being handed over for crucifixion. But we don't *know* any of those kinds of specifics. These are nothing more than educated guesses. But it doesn't stop pilgrims traveling from around the world to connect with those holy sites.

Why do things like a piece of cloth and special landmarks matter to us? Because we're hard-wired to connect with the world through our senses. We want to see it for ourselves, touch it, smell it, and taste it to know it's really real. But Jesus knows, as he tells Thomas and the other disciples, that our own senses and even our brains can screw with us. We remember what we want to remember. We see what we want to see, hear what we want to hear. Jesus knew that even though we crave these kinds of physical connections, they'd end up leading us down paths of distraction and confusion.

Instead of focusing so much on the physical, historical facts about Jesus's life, why not spend more energy on wrapping our minds, hearts, and imaginations around what is true? In our Western mindset, we tend to see fact and truth as the same, but consider the parables (or stories) Jesus told so much. Were they factual? Did they really ever happen? Maybe the more important question is: does it even matter? The stories contain important truth whether they're based in fact or not.

So don't feel so bad if you struggle with the facts. The truth is, we don't have a lot about Jesus's life that we know for a fact. But there's so much truth in his life, wisdom, words, and in how he revealed his heart that any facts fall short of what was most important about his ministry.

Heads Up

Connecting the text to our world

I wanted to believe. I prayed to God to believe. But the older I got, the more questions I had. The more questions I had, the more strained my relationship with my youth pastor got. Finally, one day when I questioned his literal interpretation of the book of Revelation and also his rock-solid confidence that all of my non-Christian friends and family members would burn in hell, that was it. He'd had enough of me.

"If you can't believe every word in this Bible exactly how it's written," he fumed, his face turning a bright red, "then it doesn't mean shit!" And he threw the thing at me. Keep in mind this was a Baptist church, so he had one of those giant, floppy Bibles, and it barely missed my head. We agreed after the Bible-chucking incident that it was better if I took my doubts and questions elsewhere before I dragged other believers down with me.

I didn't come back to church for about a decade after that, and it wasn't because I'd finally figured it all out. I still have at least as many questions and doubts as I used to. The difference is that I found a community that gave me room to have those questions and actually celebrated it as a necessary part of the faith development process. Along the way, I came to terms with the idea that my questions were more important than the actual answers. Those places where I found doubt and struggle were the parts of me seeking most desperately to better understand God and the stories in Scripture.

Author, philosopher, and theologian John Caputo offered me a very simple key to the shackles of guilt I kept on myself for doubting and questioning so much. With one simple word, he made room for unspeakable joy on one day and utter disbelief the next. We created room for the highs and lows, and all points in between. I will forever be grateful to him for that word. It's helped me find more peace with God than anything else I've ever learned.

That word is, "Perhaps."

Prayer for the Week

God, I'm still not sure from day to day what I believe. But I'm working on it. I'm not sure what resurrection looks like, but I do believe that love is more powerful than anything, including death, corruption, or anything else humanity can heap on us.

Popping Off

Art/music/video and other cool stuff that relate to the text

"Doubting Thomas," by Nickel Creek (song, 2005)

Doubt (movie, 2008)

Oh, God! (movie, 1977)

Bruce Almighty (movie, 2003)

Feed Me, Seymour: A Search for Real Meaning

Lectionary Texts For
May 5, 2019 (Third Sunday of Easter)

Texts In Brief
My dog ate my Bible!

FIRST READING
Acts 9:1–6

Paul (called Saul until he converted to Christianity, then renamed Paul), the erstwhile professional Christian assassin, encounters Jesus on the road to Damascus. This is a pretty big deal for Paul, and the turning point after which he becomes one of Christianity's most influential leaders.

PSALM
Psalm 30

King David sings a psalm (song) of praise to God as part of the dedication of a new temple. God has given

David's life meaning, and he calls out to God for continued help and strength.

Second Reading
Revelation 5:11–14

A fantastical vision from John of Patmos, author of Revelation, wherein every creature on earth, as well as four angels, is praising Jesus. He hears them singing a song about Jesus being elevated to the right hand of God after enduring and overcoming death. Following their song of praise, they fall down in worship.

Gospel
John 21:1–19

Jesus's third appearance to the disciples after the resurrection. He appears to seven of them in this case, which often is considered to be a holy number in Scripture. Though they are trying to catch fish, they're having no success; Jesus tells them to try the other side of the boat, and they catch hundreds. While the other disciples pull in the nets, Peter puts on clothes (he was naked), and jumps into the water to go to Jesus.

Back on the shore, Jesus questions the disciples about their love for him and then charges them with going out into the world to care for others.

Bible, Decoded
Breaking down Scripture in plain language

Sea of Tiberius—Also called the Sea of Galilee. It's actually a freshwater lake, and it's the biggest one in Israel. Jesus spent much of his ministry at or near this lake. Various miracles took place here, including the miracle of the fishes and loaves, Jesus walking on water, and Jesus calming the storm.

Lamb—Lambs were really valuable back in Jesus's day. They were a source of food, wool, milk, and they even helped fertilize fields with their poop! They symbolized lots of things in the Bible. For example, they were used in sacrifices, thus the references to Jesus being the Lamb of God. They also represented innocence and vulnerability, like when Jesus tells Peter to feed his lambs. He didn't actually want Peter to feed sheep. Instead he wanted him to care for the most vulnerable of God's people.

Amen—There are lots of possible translations of this word, but generally, it's a word of affirmation or agreement. It can be understood to mean, "may it be so," or "this is true."

Points to Ponder

First Thoughts

There's so much in this Gospel account, it's hard to know where to start. First, there's the matter of numerology. It's explicitly noted that this is the third time Jesus has appeared to the disciples after being resurrected. The number three is important, as are lots of repeated numbers throughout Scripture. Oh, and PS: why the heck is Peter fishing naked with other guys?

Jesus has fish and bread for the disciples on the shore. The scene can cause us to think back to the story of the miracle of fishes and loaves. Also, Jesus hits on this number "three" again by asking Peter if he loves him. It's a kind of "un-doing" of the three times Peter denied Jesus before his death, but (spoiler alert!) it's also foreshadowing Peter's own death as a martyr.

David is king of the Jewish people, but he admits that all of his success has originated from God's provision. His relationship with God has given his life real meaning, and in singing a song of praise to God for all he has, he's also kind of reminding himself where all this good stuff actually came from.

Paul/Saul was kind of a jerk when it came to Christians. He worked for the Roman Empire, and the whole reason he was headed to Damascus was to hand out letters to the temple leaders to warn them that anyone caught teaching or practicing Christianity would be killed. But this encounter with Jesus along the way changes him completely. Like David, he is transformed, and his life finally takes on real meaning.

Digging Deeper

Mining for what really matters . . . and gold

In the sections both above and below, I kind of break down the whole thread of finding meaning in our lives that we can find in all of the texts. But for this part, I want to take a little bit of time to geek out on some really fascinating things we find in this Scripture from the Gospel of John.

If we read the Bible just like a straightforward book, a couple of things will likely happen. One, we'll probably never make it to the end, and two, we'll miss a lot of great stuff. But if we think of Scripture more like the TV show *Lost* or a Super Mario Brothers video game, we realize there are all kinds of "Easter eggs" hidden everywhere for us to discover.

First there's the matter of the numbers used. As I note above, this is the third time Jesus appears after his burial to the disciples. This number is used a lot to suggest completeness or some kind of resolution. We have the Trinity (God as Father, Son, and Holy Spirit) and also the literary concept that stories tend to have a beginning, middle, and end. In this case, an important chapter is closing, and a new one is beginning.

Also, Jesus asks Peter if he loves him three times in a row. Now, I know Peter comes off as kind of a dufus sometimes, but he's not an idiot. It's not that Jesus didn't hear him; this is meant to remind of us the three times Peter denied Jesus, just before his crucifixion. This is Jesus's way to sort of make that right. Kind of undoing the bad mojo between him and Peter and setting him on a new path as a core leader of the new Christian movement.

There's also the goofy bit about Peter getting caught in his birthday suit by Jesus. Let's set aside the obvious weirdness of him being naked and fishing with a bunch of others dude on a little fishing boat. But remember, instead of asking ourselves, "Did that really happen?," the more important question is, "What is this trying to get us to pay attention to?"

Consider the parallel that this has with one of the creation stories (yes, there are two) in Genesis. After Adam and Eve eat from the tree of knowledge of good and evil, they realize they're naked, and when God comes along, they're ashamed. Likewise, Peter has blown it big time by denying Jesus before his death, and now here's the very guy he screwed over, looking him in the face. He is aware of his nakedness when standing before Jesus/God, like Adam and Eve. However, the issue isn't literally his nakedness. The point is that he's beset by shame for what he's done, particularly for betraying Jesus at his most vulnerable moment, and Jesus wipes the slate clean, setting him on a new course.

Finally, there's the matter of the meal Jesus has prepared for the disciples once they drag their full-to-bursting nets onto the shore. He offers them fish and bread—sound familiar? Again, this is meant to remind us of the miracle where Jesus feeds five thousand people out of a kid's lunchbox—which, incidentally, happened pretty much in this same spot. Jesus also just multiplied the crap out of some fish, and this is the same spot where he was reported to walk on water and calm the storm. So this is bringing some closure to the evidence that this indeed is the Christ, the one his followers claim him to be.

Does that mean all these miracles happened literally the way they're depicted in Scripture? Maybe. But keep in mind the storytellers back then were less concerned about recording and relaying literal fact than they were about pointing us toward a greater truth.

After all, which is more of a miracle: feeding some hungry guys a magical breakfast, or offering them a new vision for life and giving them true meaning and something to live for—or even die for?

Heads Up

Connecting the text to our world

Scientists did this study with subjects in their experiment to see what really mattered to them in a job. When asked, most of the people in the study said that money ranked very high on the list of importance, if not at the very top of the list. But when the scientists did their tests, they found something very different.

They divided the subjects into two groups. One group came in to "work" each day and were given some fairly mindless task to do, like sorting widgets. They were paid a given amount for the day (let's say fifty dollars), but they weren't told why they were doing the job, or what—if any—point there was to it. But at the end of the day, they were told they'd get seventy dollars if they came back to do the same job tomorrow. Again, they weren't told why they were sorting widgets, but sure enough, they got paid at day's end. For day three, they were told they'd get ninety dollars if they came back and did the same job another day, but some of them didn't show up. By day five, nearly all of the workers in this group had quit.

In the second group, they started them out at the same basic rate, and they were doing the exact same widget-sorting job. But unlike the first group, they were told why they were doing it. They were part of a larger, very important project for which the widgets would be used. They were given goals, and they were reminded of the importance and purpose of their work on a regular basis.

Though the workers in the second group were never given a raise like those in the first group, they far outlasted the first group in how many of them stuck the job out.

The conclusion: finding meaning in what we do is more important to us than money, even if we think that money matters more. We want to know that we make a difference, that what we are doing matters. It's easy to get sidetracked by a safe career or a comfortable salary sometimes, but deep down inside, we all want our lives to have meaning.

David has found meaning, not in his power and wealth, but because he believes he is doing what he does on behalf of God. Paul is leading a joyless career as a pawn of the Roman Empire until his conversion on the road to Damascus. After that, he understands what he is meant to do. Jesus is forecasting a tough road for Peter as he spreads the teachings of Christ to all corners of the world—one that ultimately will lead him to be executed (by someone like Paul!). But he is emboldened in his mission because he understands its purpose. What he's doing matters, even more than life itself.

Turns out that meaning is more powerful than we might have thought! So, what gives you meaning? What is your purpose?

Prayer for the Week

God, it's so easy to get distracted why what's right in front of me or by what the rest of the world tells me is important. But what I long for more than anything is to have a life of meaning that matters to me and to others. Help me discover the meaning in my life, no matter what I'm doing.

Popping Off

Art/music/video and other cool stuff that relate to the text

Scrooge (movie, 1970)

Man's Search for Meaning, by Viktor Frankl (book, 1959)

"There's More to Life Than Being Happy," from *The Atlantic* (article, 2013): tinyurl.com/yclvyw2x

Amélie (movie, 2001)

Pay It Forward (movie, 2000)

Are You a Man or a Sheep?

Lectionary Texts For
May 12, 2019 (Fourth Sunday of Easter)

Texts in Brief
My dog ate my Bible!

First Reading
Acts 9:36–43

Peter is in Joppa and raises Tabitha (aka Dorcas) from the dead. Upon seeing her alive, her loved ones and mourners become believers in the God Peter was telling everyone about. This is further testament to the parallels between Jesus and Peter, which is not to suggest that Peter is divine; rather, Jesus has commissioned Peter with the special role of being the face and hands of Jesus's ministry in the world in Jesus's absence.

Psalm
Psalm 23

A psalm written by King David. By trade, he was a shepherd, and in this poem, God is humanity's shepherd. When tough times come, those who look for God, he says, will find what they're looking for.

Second Reading
Revelation 7:9–17

The Lamb of God (i.e., Jesus) is the shepherd of humanity. People from all nations have come through great trials and worship God and Jesus because Jesus has afforded them a way out of their earthly struggles and suffering. It is a hopeful prophetic vision of reconciliation and the end of suffering. In some ways, the boundary-breaking reach of God here is similar to the efforts of Peter to reach out to the gentiles in prior weeks.

Gospel
John 10:2–30

The Temple in Jerusalem has been dedicated. Jesus is in the temple, and some Jewish people there ask him to be straight with them about whether or not he is the Messiah. He says they won't believe him anyway, but that he is. He uses the sheep/shepherd image to symbolize the relationship between him and his believers.

Bible, Decoded
Breaking down Scripture in plain language

Lamb—Of course you already know what a lamb is. But the imagery of lambs is used all over the place in Scripture. Sometimes it's used to portray those who follow Jesus, who need protection and guidance. Other times it's meant to emphasize innocence. In the case of Jesus, especially in the Revelation text, it's meant to be seen as an object of sacrifice, since lambs were frequently slaughtered as part of Jewish temple sacrifices.

Throne—Not really an image we hold in high regard these days, but one that represented power and authority in a culture ruled by dictators. Basically, this was meant to show God as a new kind of Lord, unlike the human rulers, some of who claimed to be God.

Anoint—Placing some substance (oil, perfume, milk, etc.) on a person—often their head—to symbolize a welcoming of God's spirit. It was also used to represent the purging out of disease or bad spirits. Anointing is a ritual that far preceded Christianity, but it was one that Christianity incorporated and repurposed to mean something different for its followers.

Bible, Decoded

Breaking down Scripture in plain language

Sometimes I wrestle with all the symbolism of lambs and sheep in Scripture. To me, they're dumb, stinky, and fairly unhygienic creatures. So that's me? No thanks. But back then, sheep were very important. They represented sustenance (food, milk), wealth, and even protection (wool for clothing). And I suppose if Jesus can be compared to a sheep, I can get over my own sheepish hang-ups.

The kind of imagery presented in Revelation is troublesome for someone like me who isn't really on board with the idea that "Jesus died for your sins." It speaks of the worshipers' clothing being washed clean in the Lamb's blood, which is just gross, aside from being weird. But we have to keep in mind that Christianity is constantly borrowing and retooling pagan or Jewish symbols and rituals to mean something new. So whereas lambs used to be slaughtered to satisfy God's dissatisfaction with us, maybe it can mean something different for us as followers of Jesus today.

We've all probably heard Psalm 23 so many times that it's easy to stop paying attention when it comes along again. But there's a theme in this poem that connects with Revelation and John (and sort of even with Acts) about how God nurtures or shepherds us through the tough stuff in life. It's important to note, though, that this is not a shepherd who forces the sheep to follow. They have to decide to. So in this sense, those who choose to stay stuck in the valley of their own suffering do so by choice in not taking the way out that has been offered.

We've gotten kind of used to big healing stories, and even a resurrection here or there, when it comes to Jesus. But now Peter's doing it? The poor guy who got busted not long ago for failing Jesus now has the power to raise folks from the dead. That's a pretty big deal. Did this actually happen? Who knows. But there are two important points to take away. First, God's work wasn't stopped with Jesus's crucifixion. Second, God is a God of second, third, fourth . . . well, a whole lot of chances. We sometimes think we're beyond hope and repair. But God tends to think otherwise.

Digging Deeper

Mining for what really matters . . . and gold

In our culture, if someone calls you a sheep, that's not exactly a compliment. But it's different in biblical times. Sheep were prized possessions, worth guarding with our very lives. Given that context, it's not so bad being a sheep. Heck, even Jesus is a lamb in Scripture, while also being portrayed as a shepherd.

The shepherd part is easier to make sense of. Jesus offered wisdom, hope, compassion, and healing. Who wouldn't want to follow someone like that?

Well, maybe not so much when that becomes a sheep destined for the slaughterhouse.

This raises one of the toughest questions in the Christian faith: did Jesus die for our sins? The idea that the sacrifice of a living creature was required to appease God for one's sins has been around a lot longer than Christianity has. Mentions of animal sacrifice can be found throughout the Old Testament, and Abraham's faith is even tested when he's asked to sacrifice his own son.

This value of sacrifice as part of one's faith also was common in Roman culture, where the types of sacrifices usually were specific to the characteristics of the gods being worshiped. A god of the harvest would require an offering of produce, and so on. Some pre-Christian cultures, such as those from Carthage, even practiced human sacrifice, though the Romans generally condemned it.

Interestingly, a millennium prior to Anselm's understanding of blood atonement, there were very different understandings of Jesus's death germinating in the Christian collective consciousness.

In the fourth century CE, Gregory of Nyssa proposed that Jesus's death was an act of liberation, freeing humanity from enslavement to Satan. Seven hundred years later, around the same time that Anselm presented to concept of substitutionary atonement, a theologian named Abelard proposed that it actually was that Jesus's response of pure—some might emphasize nonviolent—love in the face of violence, hatred, and death was transformational in the human psyche, reorienting us toward a theology of sacrificial love over justice or atonement.

Contemporary theologian Walter Wink goes a step further than Abelard, claiming that atonement theology is a corruption of the gospel, focusing on an act of violence rather than the values of peaceful humility and compassion lived and taught by Christ.

Resolving the debate about the causes of and purpose behind Jesus's death is an impossible task. More important is to make clear that such a debate is going on. For too long, Christians and non-Christians have assumed that all who yearn to follow the way of Christ universally believe Christ died for our sins. For millions, this not only defines their faith but their understanding of the very nature of God as well. For others, it is the basis for rejecting Christianity, understanding it as an inherently violent religion, centered on a bloodthirsty God that requires death in exchange for mercy.

This is not the God in which I put my faith, and I am not alone.

Heads Up
Connecting the text to our world

An awful lot of Christianity has been focused on what happens to you after you die. We seem to be fairly obsessed with the afterlife. But the thing is, unless you have some special detour the rest of us don't know about, dying is still an inevitable part of the equation. The dying part, we're not so good with.

Instead of dealing with the reality of dying and all of the related loss, we try to gloss over it with some trite phrases that are supposed to make it all better.

"We can all rest assured that he's in a better place now."

"God needed another angel up in heaven, so she had to answer the call when it came."

Pretty words don't make death easier. Dying is hard, regardless of what's on the other side of it. Consider birth. Granted, the end result of being born is pretty amazing, but the process of going from a dependent fetus to an oxygen-breathing individual is traumatic. It's bloody, messy, and painful. Anyone who says otherwise is either fooling themselves, or they're test tube babies.

We'd love it if God would offer us a way around the hard stuff in life, or even in death. But that's not what we get. Instead, we're presented with a guide, a partner to help make the journey a little easier.

But why do we have to do this in the first place? If God really loved us, why let us experience suffering at all?

The idea of a life absent of all suffering sounds pretty good, but it's also a life absent of real humanity. We're as defined, like it or not, by our scars as we are by our accomplishments and triumphs. And it's not like God gets off the hook; Jesus suffers plenty. But he does it with us. He shows us a way out on the other side.

The only real way out is through.

Prayer for the Week

God, sometimes when I don't pray, it's because I don't feel like I deserve the hope and relief from my own struggles that I long for. I made a lot of these problems for myself, so it hardly seems fair to ask you for help. Please help remind me that love is an inexhaustible renewable resource, far more plentiful than the sum total of my screw-ups. Thanks for that.

Popping Off

Art/music/video and other cool stuff that relate to the text

The Mission (movie, 1986)

The Last Temptation of Christ, by Nikos Kazantzakis (book, 1960; movie, 1988)

Traveling Mercies, by Anne Lamott (book, 2000)

Lost (TV series, 2004–2010)

The Dark Knight (movie, 2008)

Batman: The Dark Knight (comic book series, 2011–2014)

The Unclean Crowd

Lectionary Texts For
May 19, 2019 (Fifth Sunday of Easter)

Texts in Brief
My dog ate my Bible!

First Reading
Acts 11:1–18

Peter is criticized for hanging out with uncircumcised gentiles (i.e., non-Jews). God's command, in a vision to Peter, is "What God has made clean, you must not call profane." The Holy Spirit tells peter to go with gentiles "and not to make a distinction between them and us."

Psalm
Psalm 148

A song of praise for all creatures of the earth and all people—old, young, meek, powerful, male, female, with no distinction. Interestingly, however, the next-to-last line mentions God raising a "horn" of strength: salvation (and by some accounts, even royalty) for the chosen people of Israel.

Second Reading
Revelation 21:1–6

A vision of a new heaven, a new earth, and a new Jerusalem. When this vision becomes reality, death and suffering will end; all things will be made new. The author hears a song about God coming and living among people to make them whole again. There is a reference to the human God proclaiming "It is done," much like when Jesus says "It is finished" at the moment of his death.

Gospel
John 13:31–35

Jesus knows his disciples want to go with him, but where he is going, they can't follow. Instead he commands them to love each other as he has loved them. He reminds them that the way people will recognize them as disciples of Jesus is by how generously they love.

Bible, Decoded
Breaking down Scripture in plain language

Horn—A symbol used a lot in the Bible, generally representing strength, salvation, and sometimes even royalty. Jesus is referred to as the "Horn of Salvation," and this psalm speaks of God raising such a horn for God's people.

Gentile—A term generally used by the Jewish people to refer to any non-Jew. It indicated someone was an outsider, an "other," and outside of God's special favor, reserved for the people of Israel.

Joppa—A city in Israel now called Yafo. This is the town where Peter resurrected Dorcas, Tabitha's sister. It is a port town, where the "cedars of Lebanon" reportedly came in for both the first and second temple of Solomon. It was a mishmash of Jewish and non-Jewish culture, having been occupied by the Phoenicians (Greeks), Romans, and even the Jewish Maccabean tribe.

Points to Ponder

First Thoughts

Tribal identity is a big deal in this part of the world back in biblical times. Different factions were constantly fighting over territory, and many ruling authorities had a nasty habit of enslaving the conquered people, or worse. So it wasn't just a matter of difference; there was real, time-tested historic hatred for each other among many different cultures. So when Peter talks about going among the gentiles, making no distinction between God's chosen people of Israel and the so-called pagan outsiders, this was a pretty radical (and probably unpopular) concept.

There's an interesting tension in Peter's vision about what is "clean" and "unclean." Of course, in the dream, he describes animals in particular, which would have referred to the types of animals Jews could not eat under traditional kosher law. But through this vision, Peter is told by God that those old lines of clean/dirty,

Jew/gentile, insider/outsider no longer apply. This is very similar to a better-known Scripture written later by Paul in Galatians 3:28, where he says, "There is no longer Jew nor Greek, slave nor free . . ."

It is interesting that although the psalmist regales the glory of God as being praised by all creatures of all walks of life, the psalm still ends with a special nod toward the people of Israel, believed by the Jewish people to be particularly favored or chosen by God. It's also worth noting the symbolism of God "raising the horn," since Jesus is called the "Horn of Salvation" in the New Testament. In the Gospel readings, Jesus appears to his disciples as resurrected.

I tend to think the fact that this scene with Peter is happening in Joppa is no coincidence. Consider that the timbers used to build Solomon's temple came through here. When that temple was destroyed, the cedar timbers from Lebanon used to rebuild a new temple came through here as well. Just like they say in real estate, when it comes to the Bible, it's all location, location, location.

In Revelation, many people get all hung up on the fantastical, somewhat terrifying images of Armageddon. But in this bit from the text, we see a very hopeful, affirming vision of the future. Something new is coming! Everything will be set right and made whole again, which is not unlike my interpretation of "resurrection" to mean "making things right again." It's also interesting how similarly this text reads to Isaiah 43:19, which says, "See, I am doing a new thing! Now it springs up; do you not perceive it? I am making a way in the wilderness and streams in the wasteland."

Digging Deeper

Mining for what really matters . . . and gold

We human beings love a fresh start. From new year's resolutions to the latest fad diet, we're always trying to find ways to start over. But somehow we end up falling back into the same old patterns again, no matter how hard we try to break free from them.

But maybe one of the problems is that we tend to start on the *outside,* with the hope that, by changing the exterior, the interior "us" will follow suit. But that's not really the way God works, it seems. God starts at the center of who we are, with the parts we'd just as well like to see stuck in the corner, shrouded in darkness. The things in us that make us feel unworthy, less-than, and undeserving of grace and love.

Then there are the constant reminders all around us of someone doing it better. Someone who is taller, smarter, prettier . . . *something.* But digging through all our old baggage to figure out what's worth saving is scary stuff. What if there's nothing left when we get to the bottom of the junk pile? Maybe it's better just to measure ourselves against other folks, to make sure that, even if I'm not so great, even if I'm less than happy with the way I'm handling my life, at least I'm better than *those people.*

We want to be special, favored, set apart. But according to Peter's vision, as well as the song from the psalmist and the beautifully hopeful vision from John in Revelation, those false constructs are being torn down in preparation for God's coming kingdom. That which divides, subjugates, marginalizes, and other-izes will be burned away. And what will emerge in its place is . . . well, something new. Something amazing.

But I want to know! Give me details! Where will I fit in the new order? Will I get more than those people? Will I finally stop feeling so desperate to change, and yet strangely incapable of living into the impossible image I create for myself?

The good news, although sometimes it's hard to accept, is that "those people," whoever your "those people" are, are God's beloved people. But there's more good news. We're all someone's "those people," which means that we're God's beloved too. We may not know exactly what that coming future looks like, but if it's built on a love that is all-encompassing and exceeds all human efforts to compare and compete, it sounds like something we can look forward to.

Heads Up
Connecting the text to our world

When Amy was in seminary in Texas, she and I led a youth group together in Fort Worth. It started out as a pretty small group, but once the word got out that we had free pizza and a gym, it grew quickly.

Soon, we had nearly one hundred kids a week of all ages, colors, and backgrounds. We called it Holy Chaos.

For our first youth Sunday, the kids planned the entire worship service. They did everything from the music to saying the prayers and serving communion.

The people in the church loved it, but when they found out later that during one of our practice sessions the communion trays had been hurled across the sanctuary like frisbees, Amy got called into the office.

"Amy, we have a problem."

"I know," she said. "I'm sorry about the trays. These are kids who've never been in church before, and they are still learning how to behave—especially in the sanctuary. I sat them down, and we had a little talk about what it means to show respect, what sacred space is all about, and how to take care of God's church."

"Well, it's not just that," said the pastor. "They bring their skateboards in. Our insurance doesn't cover skateboards."

"Okay—no skateboards. I'll tell them."

"And there are scuff marks on the wall. And one of the stalls in the men's restroom has some writing on it."

"I'll be sure they clean it up."

"And last week, a window got broken in one of the classrooms."

She knew what was coming, but she didn't want to hear it.

"Amy, this just isn't working out," sighed the pastor. "Those kids just need more help and supervision than we can handle. Maybe there is another church nearby that can host them."

But there wasn't. Most of the children lived across the street from that church, and they came because it was close enough to their home that they could walk.

We tried to carpool for a while, but many of the kids' parents weren't comfortable with us driving them around. Without weekly contact with them, we eventually lost touch, and the group—though much smaller—moved over to another church in a neighborhood on the other side of town.

A few months passed, and one day we got a call from the associate pastor of the church where we'd had the holy chaos youth group.

"Amy, you have got to come see our new ministry," he said. "I am so excited about this. Can you make it over this afternoon?"

We were optimistic. "Maybe they figured out a way to bring the kids back!" we thought.

We walked into the office and the whole church staff was huddled around a little model building encased in glass that was sitting on the table. As we got closer we saw what looked like a miniature castle. It had sort of a brick fortress with big wrought-iron fencing all the way around the outside.

A new playground? We wondered . . .

"Is that fence to keep people out or in?" Amy joked.

"Isn't it wonderful?" they said.

"What is it?"

"Well, this isn't the main attraction. This is just the space that we'll build to hold it."

"Hold what?"

They pointed to a picture hanging on the wall above the castle. It was familiar, but strangely different. It was the Last Supper, but not da Vinci's painting. It looked bigger, more modern.

"This," said the pastor, "is the largest wax rendering of the Last Supper in the world!" They were excited.

It was hideous.

To me, the statues looked like nothing more than oversized candle—something you'd see in the bargain bin at the drug store.

"Now, all we have to do is raise one million dollars for the building, and we'll be able to bring in the exhibit. And then we'll have to consider the cost of cooling a building that size."

That would be important—especially in Texas.

If the building wasn't properly cooled, the wax statues would melt. And nobody wants to be responsible for melting Jesus and his disciples. Nobody would want to do anything to hurt Jesus.

Right?

Prayer for the Week

God, help me always see myself in whoever "those people" are to me, whether they're non-Christians, Christians, Republicans, Democrats, the poor, gays, women, older people, or the jerk in the car ahead of me. Make something new in me, something that yearns to find reasons to love other people rather than picking them apart.

Popping Off

Art/music/video and other cool stuff that relate to the text

X-Men (comic series, 1963–; movie series, 2000–)

Freaks and Geeks (TV series, 1999–2000)

Revenge of the Nerds (movie, 1984)

Lost (TV series, 2004–2010)

It's Not Fair!

Lectionary Texts For
May 26, 2019 (Sixth Sunday of Easter)

Texts in Brief
My dog ate my Bible!

FIRST READING
Acts 16:9–15

Paul has a vision, and the disciples go to Macedonia, a Roman colony. They meet Lydia on the Sabbath, and her family converts to Christianity. She invited them to stay in her home, "if you have judged me to be faithful."

PSALM
Psalm 67

Another psalm of praise for how God has blessed humanity, and for judging them with "equity."

Second Reading
Revelation 21:10, 22–22:5

John, the author, has a vision of the "new Jerusalem." He sees what he calls a River of Life and a tree that bears twelve different kinds of fruit, one each month. The fruit from the tree heals the nations of the world (representing the twelve tribes of Israel). Everything in the holy city will be blessed and also holy.

Gospel
John 14:23–29

Jesus speaking about his ascension to heaven to be with God. He makes clear that the gospel is not from him, but rather he is conveying the good news from God. Those who adhere to the invitations in the gospel message express their love for God, and they will be loved by God in kind. He tries to offer comfort, reminding them not to be upset that he has to leave them since he will be going to join God. And if they love him, they should want this for him.

or

John 5:1–9

Jesus heals a man who has been waiting by the healing pool in Jerusalem for thirty-eight years. He also does this on the Sabbath. Before healing him, Jesus asks him if he wants to be made well, to which the man offers a complaint about being passed up at the healing pool for so long. So Jesus orders him to get up and be on his way, which he does.

Bible, Decoded

Breaking down Scripture in plain language

Selah—A holy pause, noted in Scripture, meant to instruct the reader to stop and allow space into which God's spirit can enter.

Sabbath—A holy day of rest, which varies from culture to culture. Jews observe the Sabbath from sundown Friday to sundown Saturday. Most Christians consider Sunday to be our Sabbath day. It's based in the story of the seven days of creation, when God rested on the seventh day, after all things in the universe were made.

Light—God and Jesus are both referred to as light a lot in the Bible, but there are more light comparisons in John than most other books. This is, in large part, because the author of John was writing to the Gnostics, a non-Christian mystical sect, who believed that God was manifest in certain people through a "divine spark."

Twelve—This number appears a lot in the Bible, often in reference to the "twelve nations." These are the twelve tribes of Israel, led by the sons of Jacob, who had twelve sons. In the Old Testament, God tells Abraham (Jacob's grandfather) that his descendants will give birth to the nations of the Jewish people.

Israel—Though this is the name of the Jewish nation in the Middle East, it is historically used to represent the whole of the Jewish people. Jacob also became known as "Israel," which means "persevere with God."

Points to Ponder

First Thoughts

What do we imagine when we hear the word *judgment?* What kind of image of God does it render for us when we think about God's judgment? Some people say that God can't be both all-loving and still condemn people to hell. Others says that God's love can't truly be genuine unless it's also tempered with judgment. Is this true? Can there be more than one kind of judgment?

The text in Revelation paints a beautiful picture of this heaven-on-earth that is the New Jerusalem envisioned by the author. But there's this whole "But nothing unclean will enter it, nor anyone who practices abomination or falsehood" part. How do I know if I'm on the inside or the outside? Is there an outside? What about this tree that feeds and heals all the nations? Is God's salvation particular and conditional, or is it universal?

Does anyone other than me read the psalmist's praise of God for judging humanity with equity as more of a plea or a wish than a praise? Kind of like those "Thanks in advance for not smoking" signs. What if God's judgment is unequal or unfair by our human standards? Does that change our faith? Does that make God any less . . . God?

Digging Deeper

Mining for what really matters . . . and gold

We have to consider what we mean when we are talking about the judgment of God. There are many expressions of judgment throughout Scripture, but generally, they can be divided into two distinct categories: retributive judgment and restorative judgment. At the risk of sounding terribly modernist in drawing such distinct lines, retributive judgment is principally concerned with making things fair. Restorative judgment, on the other hand, is focused on making things right or whole.

Retributive judgment believes there is a price to be paid for every wrong, and that balance must be pursued until those who were wronged are satisfied. Let the punishment fit the crime, says retributive judgment. Meanwhile, restorative judgment goes deeper and broader, seeking to better understand the context in which the offense took place to being with, and then to address the fundamental root causes that led to the problem.

Restorative judgment doesn't seek to repay wrong with appropriate punishment; it seeks to undermine the entire system of retributive judgment to incline the course of humanity toward an ultimate resolution. Retributive judgment is punitive in nature; it requires satisfaction. Restorative judgment, however, is discerning, surgical, and strategic in helping free people from self-perpetuating systems of brokenness and our seemingly hopeless enslavement to our own desire.

We crave justice, fairness, and for things to be made right according to our standards. But if even a nine-year-old can see the futility of retributive judgment, why can't we? Do we need God to be "fair" in order to understand God to be just?

We try to fill one void by creating another. We want our loss to be made whole by someone else paying an equal price. It's only fair.

But what if God's judgment really does raise up the so-called valleys and lower the mountains, creating a level playing field for everyone? What if the only true way to make it all right is to stop trying so hard to be fair?

Most of us are all for judgment of some kind, so long as the line is drawn somewhere south of us. But the God of my understanding erases the line, and God's judgment is about making all things whole, upright, and like new again.

That's the kind of judgment that I'm able to reconcile with a God that is also all-loving.

Heads Up

Connecting the text to our world

"I heard someone dropped a bomb on Boston," said Mattias, my nine-year-old son, over breakfast while I scrolled through the breaking news reports.

"Not exactly," I said. "It was two guys. Two brothers who came from Russia to go to school. They put homemade bombs in and around trashcans by the finish line of the marathon."

"Why?" he asked.

"I really don't know."

"Maybe they were angry about something, and they didn't know how to talk about their feelings."

"Maybe so," I nodded.

"Did they hurt people?"

"A lot of people," I said. "More than a hundred."

"And they didn't do anything to deserve that."

"No," I said. "They didn't."

"Did they kill anyone?"

"Three people," I said, hoping his questions would stop, while also knowing well enough they wouldn't.

"Who died, dad?"

"Well," I sighed, "a young woman who also was a student, and a boy . . ." I watched his face fall and his mouth go slack. We sat in silence for at least a minute, though it felt like hours.

"That's really terrible," he whispered. I nodded in silence. "That kid didn't do anything."

"It's pretty messed up," I said. Then his face began to harden.

"If I saw those guys," he raised his voice, "I would take a cinder block and . . ." his voice trailed off as he realized the hopelessness of trying to make anything right out of such chaos, such senseless violence.

"I know, buddy. It's hard to understand. And it's okay to have feelings about it."

"I hope they feel really bad about what they did," he scowled. Amy helped slip his backpack over his shoulders as we scooted him toward the front door. He was late for school. "Oh, and don't forget to bring cupcakes by the school today for the carnival," he said. "Store-bought only."

"All right buddy. Try to hustle so you won't get a tardy slip."

Store-bought cupcakes. Because God knows what someone might do to homemade treats for elementary school kids.

God knows what someone might do.

Prayer for the Week

God, I admit to a longing for judgment against others, for fairness to be doled out on my own terms. Help me focus on restoration rather than retribution.

Popping Off

Art/music/video and other cool stuff that relate to the text

"The Rewards of Revenge," from *Wired* (article, 2011): tinyurl.com/ycl4d278

Stanford Prison Experiment: www.prisonexp.org

Les Misérables (musical, 1980–; movie, 2012)

Charlotte's Web, by E. B. White (book, 1952; movie, 1973, 2006)

The Interpreter (movie, 2005)

Going Up!
(aka Jesus in Space)

Lectionary Texts For
June 2, 2019 (Ascension Sunday)

Texts in Brief
My dog ate my Bible!

First Reading
Acts 1:1–11

The author of Luke/Acts is writing to someone called Theophilus. The disciples are to be empowered by the Holy Spirit soon. Following Jesus's death, it says that Jesus appeared to them many times to give evidence of his resurrection to them. They want to know when; Jesus tells them that timing isn't any of their business. Then Jesus ascends into heaven, and as they are looking up, two men appear (like the two who appeared to the women at Jesus's tomb) and ask them why they're staring off into the sky for someone who is gone.

Psalm

Psalm 47 or Psalm 93

Both psalms of praise, depicting God as ruler on high, and as a God that uplifts creation.

Second Reading

Ephesians 1:15–23

Paul's letter to the Christians in Ephesus proclaims the authority and lordship of Jesus over all of creation, as endowed by God. He also prays that they will receive the power of wisdom from God. He wants them to be fully aware of the scope of generosity behind all that has been given to him.

Gospel

Luke 24:44–53

Jesus gives the disciples the power to understand the Scriptures clearly. He reinforces, once again, that he is the fulfillment of Scripture foretelling of a coming messiah. He claims he is given the ability to impart this power to them from God. He leads them out to Bethany, and then ascends to heaven, and they wait for further instruction in Jerusalem, praising both God and Jesus in the meantime.

Bible, Decoded

Breaking down Scripture in plain language

Theophilus—The name of the author credited with writing both the Gospel of Luke and the book of Acts. It means "lover of God" in Greek.

Baptized—A ritual Christians use to indicate dying to the "old ways" of the world and being born again into a new life with Jesus.

Apostles—Another word for disciples. The longer name for the book of Acts is "Acts of the Apostles," or basically what they did to start the Christian church after Jesus's resurrection.

Christ—Some folks mistakenly think Jesus's last name was "Christ." Actually, he was known as Jesus of Nazareth, or Jesus the Nazarene. "Christ" comes from the Greek word *christos,* which means "anointed." Anointed means to be particularly marked, chosen, or empowered.

Points to Ponder

First Thoughts

It's all about the *power* this week. Makes me think of Jesus more like He-Man with his giant sword on top of Grayskull: "I have the powerrrrr!" Levitating Jesus is hard enough to comprehend, then we have the God presented in the psalms, who is all about being lord and sitting on a big throne floating in the sky. Between you and me, I could relate a lot better to the pre-crucifixion Jesus.

From these texts, we can definitely see where people would have gotten the sense that heaven is "up there" somewhere in the clouds. But it wasn't that long ago in the garden of Gethsemane that Jesus was calling on God to bring God's kingdom to the earth. Are they separate? Is God closing the gap? Why did Jesus have to go away anyway? Why couldn't he have hung out for, say, a couple thousand more years to help us sort this whole faith thing out?

It's hard to know what kind of relationship we're supposed to have with God and Jesus. In Genesis, God hangs out with Adam and Eve in the garden, but then as the books of the Bible go on, God becomes booming voices from the sky and magic burning bushes and stuff. Then Jesus comes along and is literally so down-to-earth that we can relate to him. He's one of us. But then he's, well, not. Can we believe in a God that is both close and abstractly big and overarching? Can we cling to a Jesus that is both human and divine? What if we can't make sense of one or the other?

Digging Deeper

Mining for what really matters . . . and gold

There are lots of big, supernatural images in these texts. We have Jesus floating up into outer space, for one. And then there's God on a big cloud-throne thing, looking down on us human folk. If you come from the kind of background I did, where you're expected to believe these kinds of texts literally and without question *or else,* they probably make you kind of nervous. I know they make me squirm a little.

Oh crap, I said to myself when I first saw the lectionary texts for this week. *Please, not the ascension.*

But sometimes we get so hung up on the big, fantastical stuff that we miss what some might call the "minor miracles." Yes, there's the power conveyed in this mighty, lord-like God, and in the superhuman Jesus floating skyward as the disciples look on, slack-jawed.

But there are other expressions of God's power here: ones that we can hang on to, even as Jesus drifts up into the ether.

In Luke, Jesus gives the disciples the power to discern Scripture more fully. Up to this point, we've seen them get baffled by pretty much everything Jesus does, even though much—if not all—of it is predicted in the holy texts. But now they're going to be the ones doing the heavy lifting of telling his story to those in all corners of their world. So it stands to reason they could use a healthy dose of clarity to embolden them in their auspicious task.

There's also the blessing from Paul in Ephesians, wishing for them the kind of divinely inspired wisdom they'll need to keep going with their job, even as they hit challenges and setbacks out in the field.

Sky thrones, space Jesus, and the like continue to be a bit of a head-scratcher for a small-brained creature like me. But longing for (and on a rare and blessed occasion, receiving) wisdom, clarity, and discernment is something I can relate to. Maybe if we start with those, the rest will begin to make more sense in time.

Heads Up

Connecting the text to our world

I shared the story earlier in this book that Tony Campolo offers about throwing a party for a prostitute in a café in Hawaii in the middle of the night. But like when the Gospels share a story more than once, I think it's worth considering this anecdote in the context of ascension.

It's fair to say that Agnes is no angel. She has made decisions about her life that have limited both her professional and personal choices in a lot of ways. And of course, most people who choose to sell their bodies for a living don't set out with this as an aspiration from their elementary-school days. Life intervenes, and things happen. Sometimes we find ourselves in circumstances where we may feel we have no choice, and we do what we have to in order to survive.

Agnes likely wasn't proud of selling her body for a living, but the world is all too ready to judge her for it. And yet God sees something pure in Agnes, something untouched by all of life's darkness. There's a light that still shines, however dimly, even if most choose not to see it.

Like the disciples, though, we're called to open our eyes wide and to see with the vision that Jesus had for all of creation. And not to say that Tony Campolo is Jesus (though some may argue he's close), but that day, in that dingy diner in Hawaii in the middle of the night, his eyes were opened. As a result, so was his heart. And this started a chain reaction of revelation for others around him.

When Agnes came in the diner the first night, she was more or less nobody. She was good for one thing in the world, and one thing only. Her friends made fun of her for even mentioning her birthday. Imagine being so small, so invisible.

And then imagine some stranger coming along, going out of their way to make sure you feel special, to assure you that you're noticed, that you matter.

Sounds like ascension to me.

Prayer for the Week

God, I try to understand, to believe; help me in my unbelief. Though I struggle sometimes to understand the supernatural dimensions of the divine portrayed in Scripture, I embrace those "aha!" moments when the clouds seem to part, and things become clearer. Help me trust that you're in these moments just as much as you're in the bigger ones.

Popping Off

Art/music/video and other cool stuff that relate to the text

Kung Fu Panda (movie, 2008)

"The Ascension," from *Divine Comedy Symphony*, by Robert W. Smith (song, 1995)

The Ascension of Christ, by Salvador Dali (painting, 1958)

"Birthday Party," by Tony Campolo (sermon from Christian Community Development Association Conference, 2006): tinyurl.com/ybb5tezb

Holy Rollers and Drunk Disciples

Lectionary Texts For
June 9, 2019 (Pentecost Sunday)

Texts in Brief
My dog ate my Bible!

FIRST READING
Acts 2:1–21

The beginning of Pentecost, or the birth of the church. The disciples are filled with the Holy Spirit, though observers think they're drunk. They begin speaking in the native languages of all those present. Peter explains that this is fulfillment of prophesy. He describes fantastical visions from the prophet Joel about "end times" and concludes with Joel's claim that "everyone who calls upon the Lord shall be saved."

or

Genesis 11:1–9

The story of the tower of Babel. People decided to build a tower all the way to heaven to memorialize themselves, which pisses off God. He punishes them by making them all speak different languages and spreading them out to all corners of the earth.

PSALM

Psalm 104:24–34, 35b

A song of awe and worship for God the Creator of all things of the earth, a God that has power over life and death.

SECOND READING

Romans 8:14–17

A very beautiful text from Paul, in which he claims we are born into a spirit of adoption by God, meaning we are inheritors of God's kingdom just as Jesus is. There is no slavery in this spirit and nothing to fear because we are not servants or slaves to God, but rather we are brought in like adopted children into a family. The pretense of the relationship, then, is based on love, not power and authority.

or

Acts 2:1–21

See description above under "First Reading."

Gospel
John 14:8–17, 25–27

Phillip still doesn't get that Jesus and God "the Father" are one. But Jesus gets over being annoyed pretty quickly and assures him that he (and we) can and will do even greater things than Jesus when we do them in God's name. We're endowed with the Holy Spirit, or the "spirit of truth," to keep us on the path that Jesus laid out for us.

Bible, Decoded
Breaking down Scripture in plain language

Holy Spirit—There are lots of different understandings of what the Holy Spirit is, from a feminine expression of the divine to a supernatural kind of ghost. For me, the "spirit of truth" that Paul refers to resonates a lot. It is this compass, given to us, that helps guide us along the path Jesus illuminates for us.

Prophecy—This is another word with disputed meaning. Some think of it more like fortune-telling, where a prophet reads the future. For me, I understand it more as a spirit of clarity or discernment, which might also include having a clearer understanding of what's coming up ahead. And in the truest sense of the word, a prophet is a "truth teller."

Pentecost—The word literally means "fiftieth day." Back in ancient Israel, it marked a Jewish festival in observance of when the Jewish laws were handed down from God to Moses on Mount Sinai. Interestingly, this was not the Ten Commandments, and these laws weren't actually written down in the Jewish Talmud, or sacred text. After the event described in the text from Acts, it's better known in Christianity for being (roughly) fifty days after Easter, and it is considered the "birthday" of the Christian church.

Abba—No, this is not some Biblical reference to a Swedish pop band from the '80s. It's actually Hebrew for "daddy," or "papa." What's worth noting about this is how intimate the expression is, especially when compared with how God is referred to in other places, like this week's psalm.

Points to Ponder

First Thoughts

The whole idea of the Trinity (three different manifestations of God as God the Father, Son and Holy Spirit) can be pretty confusing when you start thinking about it. For one, we talk about these separate entities, but then Jesus says he and God are one. So are they separate or not? Some people like my wife, Rev. Amy Piatt, call themselves "infinitarians" instead of Trinitarians because they see God expressed in infinitely different ways throughout creation. But the number three is big symbolically in the Bible, generally representing wholeness, perfection, or completeness. For me, when I think of the Trinity, it helps to imagine God the Father as "God beyond," Jesus or "God the Son" as "God within," and the Holy Spirit as this sort of connective tissue that holds us together, or "God among."

I love the idea that onlookers think the disciples are drunk when they're overwhelmed by the Holy Spirit. It just goes to show that people have always thought Christians were a little bit weird! For some, this is where the ideas of what we often call the "Pentecostal" church come from, where, during worship, people often will speak in tongues, have prophetic visions, or some other dramatic spiritual experience. We "frozen chosen" mainline Protestant types are sometimes uncomfortable with this expression of faith, or else we assume we're doing something wrong if we don't worship this way. But just like the disciples were sent out speaking all the different languages of the people around them, there are as many ways to engage God as there are people in the world. Don't worry about trying to do it right; stay focused on what is meaningful for you.

It's interesting to consider the parallels between the Pentecost story and the tower of Babel story. In the latter, the diversity of languages bestowed upon the people is a punishment for them trying to be too much like God. But in the story in Acts, it's a gift of the Spirit, empowering them with the cultural toolkit they'll need to spread the gospel all over the world.

I don't know about you, but when Jesus makes a claim like saying, "I'm going to do greater things than him," it kind of freaks me out! Paul, too, seems to put us on the same level with Jesus, when he talks about us being adopted in the Spirit, and that we are joint inheritors of God's kingdom with Jesus. It's all a little bit overwhelming to consider, but in a good way. It's beautiful, terrifying, heavy, and liberating.

Welcome to the call of the gospel.

Digging Deeper

Mining for what really matters . . . and gold

I love the story of Pentecost, in all its weirdness. On the one hand, we have the disciples with their heads on fire (no Michael Jackson or Richard Pryor jokes, please) and speaking weird foreign languages. Then we have Peter, laying this creepy, end-times prophecy from Joel on us.

And yet, in the middle of all of that strangeness, there's something really incredible happening. I think of it as divine inspiration taking hold, with God "breathing" the gospel into them to the point that they're overwhelmed by it. They know what they have to do, and they have the tools they need to go do it. Did they really turn into big, drunk disciple candles? Did they really magically speak in a dozen languages all at once?

But *something happened,* and whatever it was set things in motion in a way that helped bring us together here and now. We're still trying to make sense of it all. Sure, we may not speak in tongues or dance beneath a blood-red moon, but we know what it's like to be really inspired when we're open to it. And when we feel God leading us toward something new, that combination of unbridled excitement and abject terror might feel a lot like this Pentecost scene, even if it's only on the inside.

So, is this speaking in tongues thing a blessing or a curse? In Genesis, it's a bad thing, and then in Acts, it's a gift from the Holy Spirit. Consider that the folks who created the stories found in Genesis were primarily interested in addressing one big question: *Where did we come from?* And how better to talk about the existence of this vast, sprawling diaspora of cultures, colors, and languages than with a story? God made us this way, the story goes, because we messed up. We tried to be too much like God, and so there were consequences. Sounds a whole lot like the garden of Eden story, right?

But it's also worth noting that whether something is a blessing or a curse may all be a matter of context, or what the person in question makes of the situation. It's natural for us to try to evaluate our circumstances as good or bad, especially in comparison to others. But what if we approached each new situation with a more childlike curiosity? Rather than a "Wow, this is awesome!" or "Hey, this stinks!" attitude, what if we cling to a mindset closer to "Hey, wow. Look at this! I wonder what'll happen next?" Imagine how much broader and more exciting the possibilities for the future might be.

Heads Up

Connecting the text to our world

I'm a fan of stories from Zen Buddhism called Koans. They're a lot like Jesus's parables, especially in the sense that they don't drive home the point or moral of each story. Instead, they're meant to give us a moment of pause, letting us reflect on the wisdom we find in them.

One of my favorites is about a farmer who had worked most of his life in his fields. He was doing fine until one day his horse ran away. His neighbors shook their heads and sympathized about what bad luck it was for him to lose his only horse.

"Maybe," he said

Later the horse came back and brought with it a small herd of wild horses. His neighbors cheered his unexpected good fortune.

"Maybe," he said again,

The next day, when his son was trying to ride one of the wild horses to tame it, the horse threw him, and the son broke his leg. The neighbors now were sure that this was a sign of bad luck.

"Maybe," said the farmer.

Soon after that, when the army instituted a military draft, his neighbors congratulated him on his good luck that his son didn't have to go to war.

"Maybe," he said again.

Prayer for the Week

God, help me focus less on placing a value judgment on my current situation. Instead, lend me the gift of prophetic, inspired vision for what could be. I may not understand everything in my life, but I do believe that I am born from a Spirit of love and that I can do even greater things than my limited human imagination can dream of.

Popping Off

Art/music/video and other cool stuff that relate to the text

"Tree Branch Commercial" by Allstate Insurance (commercial): tinyurl.com/n5x2ybz

"The Waiting," by Tom Petty and the Heartbreakers (song, 1981)

"With Great Power Comes Great Responsibility" scene from *Spider-Man* (movie, 2002): tinyurl.com/y8hy4s63

Hey, Wise Guy!

Lectionary Texts For
June 16, 2019 (Trinity Sunday)

Texts in Brief
My dog ate my Bible!

First Reading
Proverbs 8:1–4, 22–31

Wisdom (a feminine figure) longs to reach out and share her message with all people. The Bible claims that she (wisdom) has been around since the forming of the universe. We were fashioned, or cocreated, by this wisdom, which is a "master worker" beside God.

Psalm
Psalm 8

The psalmist says that although humanity is a "little lower than God," we have dominion over all the creatures of the earth.

Second Reading
Romans 5:1–5

Paul claims we are justified by grace through our faith in Jesus. He also contextualizes suffering by noting that suffering leads to endurance, endurance to character, and character to hope. Hope, he says, doesn't let us down, because we are filled with divine love.

Gospel
John 16:12–15

Jesus is heir to all that is of God. He vows, in turn, to entrust it to us. He notes that we can't yet handle all he has to tell us, but that the spirit of truth (a masculine figure) will guide us in time toward what we require.

Bible, Decoded
Breaking down Scripture in plain language

Grace—This is one of the slipperiest words in Scripture. Basically, grace is favor or unearned mercy. Grace is revealed most often when we do something to need it. One thing to note is that grace comes without strings or conditions and is available for all to accept. Otherwise it wouldn't be grace; it would be favoritism.

Sovereign—One who has independent authority over a territory. This goes along with the images of God as Lord, which make plenty of sense within a largely feudal or imperial system. Sometimes such images of God are comforting; other times, they can be a real turnoff. In order to better understand this, we have to break down what we mean by "authority." To be continued . . .

Dominion—This is similar to sovereignty, in that it means one who has dominion has more or less unchecked control over something else.

Wisdom—Sometimes we confuse wisdom, intelligence, and knowledge. Wisdom is distinct in that it is understanding and judgment specifically based on experience.

Bible, Decoded

Breaking down Scripture in plain language

It's strange to think of wisdom as something that's existed since before humanity's creation, since it seems like it requires our experience to manifest itself. But here, this is meant to suggest that wisdom is freely given by God and is a gift that undergirds all of creation.

Some people take this passage in Psalms about God giving us dominion over the earth to mean that we have the responsibility of stewardship, or care, over all the earth. Others see this as permission to exploit nature for our pleasure and convenience. Still others, often called "dominionists," believe that this means God means for our nation—if not the world—to be governed by a Christian-based power of government. So yeah, I'd say we're coming away from different perspectives here that warrant some teasing out.

In this context, grace is generally understood as God's gift of not giving us what we deserve for screwing up. Many Christians suggest that grace is conditional, based on acceptance of Jesus as our personal lord and savior. But can grace be conditional? Is it still grace?

It is interesting that wisdom is portrayed as female (*Alethia*) and the spirit of truth is portrayed as male (*Pneuma tis Alitheías*). It's worth considering if we feel there is something inherent in the characteristics of both that are masculine or feminine, and how this might help inform our approach to things like our dominion over the earth and our understanding of God's mercy.

Digging Deeper

Mining for what really matters . . . and gold

There are a few potentially contrasting things at play in these texts. And actually, the contrast comes more from how we choose to interpret the texts more than from the texts themselves. As theologian and preacher Fred Craddock says, there's no such thing as uninterpreted Scripture, so it's incumbent on us each to be honest about what filters and agendas we bring with us to the Bible.

For some, this idea of having dominion over the earth is more of a call to stewardship: an honorable but daunting responsibility. It means we're responsible for the future well-being of our planet and for our brothers and sisters who inhabit it. Even some evangelical Christians are refocusing on what they call "creation care" based on their understanding of this and other Bible passages.

And then we have others who seem to take a diametrically opposite meaning from the very same words. Some, like Christian millennialists (not to be confused with the generation known as the millennials, mind you), believe that the apocalyptic images depicted in Revelation don't depict a world on the verge of destruction but rather the coming of a golden age, during which faithful Christians will rule the earth for a thousand years (thus the term *millennialist*).

We hear predictions pretty often about when this will happen, and some claim it is just around the corner. And the sooner, the better for those waiting to be at the top of the new human food chain. So anything that helps invoke the rapture is seen as hastening this golden age. So if ecological and/or socio-political instability help speed the process along, then bring it on!

It's interesting to me that while there are both feminine and masculine attributes afforded to wisdom and truth, respectively (see above), in these passages, it could be argued that these two takes on our role as the dominant species on earth fall into similarly masculine and feminine camps. One approach is more of a nurturing, caretaking perspective, while the other is more of a conquering, forceful (or we might even argue, exploitive) approach.

If we as Christians are supposed to look to Jesus for the best example of how to live and how to engage Scripture, it seems reasonable to consider Jesus's nature on similar situations. Yes, he knocked over the moneychangers' tables in the temple, and sometimes he had strong words for people who were wrong-headed about what was most important to them. But in the end, when he was being urged to ride into Jerusalem and take it back in the name of Israel from the Roman occupiers, he entered instead as a servant, a martyr.

Jesus's brand of lordship was not one of a conquering hero as much as it was one of a humble caregiver. When people were fixated on end times, he told them to stop worrying about it and to focus on the work at hand, right in front of them.

One of the hardest things about sovereignty and dominion over all the earth is that no one tells us what to do. Rather, we're inborn, the Scriptures suggest, with a kind of wisdom that precedes creation itself. And just like Paul's call to use our experiences—even the bad ones—to further forge our character and cast a future of hope ahead of us, we're called to learn from history, from our former mistakes, and to discern what is true and what is right from a place of wisdom.

And not just any kind of wisdom, but from *sophia,* the feminine wisdom into which we are born and from which Jesus himself formed his ministry and identity. And if that's not enough to help us discover what it means to be a true Christian, maybe we're spending too much time sitting around and waiting for further instructions.

Heads Up

Connecting the text to our world

Following was a fascinating excerpt from a recent article by Russ Pierson that appeared on Sojourners' website, Sojo.net:

Alas, while it was sunny in Seattle, it was theologically cloudy in Dallas, where one of Seattle's famous residents—young, hip pastor, Mark Driscoll—was speaking at a major evangelical conference: Catalyst. By many accounts on Twitter and in the blogosphere (see Nate Pyle's blog), Driscoll said: "I know who made the environment. He's coming back and he's going to burn it all up. So yes, I drive an SUV."

And after presenting his driving credentials, Rev. Driscoll reportedly added: "If you drive a mini-van, you're a mini-man."

Now it seems these comments came early in his session and were not intended to be his primary point. But it's no wonder they have attracted attention. They suggest a throwaway theology that sees the created world as disposable and "burned up" as rubbish while Christians are snatched away. His comments also, oddly, link masculine identity with an attitude of destructiveness to the natural world.

It suggests not only that the world is both our playground and toilet to enjoy as we see fit but also that those who aren't Christians (and this assumes we agree with Driscoll's take that we'll be raised up to heaven, and the "others" will be left here to deal with our mess) will have to live out a life absent of God's grace, beyond our concern.

And as if this isn't breathtaking enough, he ties masculinity in both with the kind of car we drive and the sort of attitude we take toward the environment.

I can only imagine what he'd say about my Prius-driving, recycling, organic-food-buying, biodegradable-soap-using hippie Christian self. By all estimations, I'm among the "others" in Driscoll's equation, so maybe it makes a lot of sense for me to keep caring about the planet. I'll be left here on it long after he and the other chosen are airlifted to paradise.

Prayer for the Week

God of truth and wisdom greater than all creation, help me see your authority less like that of a fierce dictator and more like an author, creating an ongoing story of which I am a small part. I am grateful for the chance to contribute to that story, and to help preserve it and pass it on to those who will know a similar kind of wisdom, even if they never know my name.

Popping Off
Art/music/video and other cool stuff that relate to the text

The Fifth Element (movie, 1997)

Dogma (movie, 1999)

Wall-e (movie, 2008)

The World Without Us, by Alan Weisman (book, 2007)

"Mark Driscoll: Gas Guzzlers a Mark of Masculinity," from Sojo.net (article, 2013): https://tinyurl.com/yc6pld6g

Which Way Did He Go, George?

Lectionary Texts For
June 23, 2019 (Second Sunday after Pentecost)

Texts in Brief
My dog ate my Bible!

First Reading
1 Kings 19:1–4 (5–7), 8–15a

Elijah gets in trouble with King Ahab and Jezebel for killing their prophets. He hides in the woods and waits to die, but an angel gives him food. He retreats to mount Horeb for forty days. God appears to Elijah and tells him to retreat to the wilderness in Damascus.

and

Isaiah 65:1–9

The prophet Isaiah is condemning those who do not observe Jewish law and do not worship the God of Abraham. He says they will pay for these sins and for turning their back on Isaiah. He prophesies destruction for them but not for the land. Rather, he predicts that the descendants of Judah will inherit the land of the unrighteous.

PSALM
Psalm 42–43

A song of mourning about being forgotten by God and being ridiculed by those who do not follow the same God. He longs to be reconciled with God in God's dwelling place on the mountain. Despite being of poor spirit, he still offers praise and expresses hope.

and

Psalm 22:19–28

A song of the persecuted asking God for protection and providence.

SECOND READING
Galatians 3:23–29

In Paul's letter to the Galatians, he proclaims that they are no longer beholden to a series of laws but rather are justified and guided now by their faith in Christ as revealed in the gospel. Distinctions between people and groups such as male/female, Jew/Greek, and slave/free no longer apply, as we are all one in Jesus.

GOSPEL
Luke 8:26–39

Jesus heals a man of demon possession. He sends the evil spirits occupying his body into a herd of swine that jump off a cliff and drown. Observers tell people in the nearby town about this healing, and they are afraid of Jesus and ask him to leave. The healed man asks to stay with Jesus, but Jesus sends him back to tell people about what God has done for him.

Bible, Decoded

Breaking down Scripture in plain language

Gergesenes—this is the location where the man possessed by demons was reported to be healed. Although the location itself doesn't seem to be particularly important, it is interesting that different accounts of this story call the town where this took place several different things, including "Gerasenes," "Gadarenes," and "Gergesenes." And in one account, there are even two men possessed rather than just one.

Judah—The fourth son of Jacob and the man from which the Israelite tribe of Judah is said to have come from. This is particularly important in considering the Jews' identity as God's chosen people. Also interestingly, one of Judah's sons is Onan, who David Ackerman wrote about in his most recent "Year D" study.

Mountain—The symbolism of hilltops and mountains appears throughout these lectionary texts. And since we are interested in the symbolic significance of patterns that recur in Scripture, it should be noted that this is where Elijah encounters God. Mountaintops are considered holy dwelling places or places of retreat.

Points to Ponder

First Thoughts

Elijah is afraid for his life because Jezebel is threatening to have him killed. But what exactly does he expect? He has put the hit out on all of the king's prophets. He is grieved to the point of welcoming death, and yet God calls him to continue on his mission. I think we can all relate to these times when we feel compelled or called to do something that is right even though we are terrified or exhausted, or both.

It is interesting that the possessed man is the one who recognizes Jesus for who he is. It causes one to ask whether it is the man himself or the evil spirits within him who recognize him as the Christ. Also, after he performs this miracle, this is one of the few times I can recall in Scripture where people are scared by his power and try to run him off. And yet, the man who benefited from the healing wants to follow him but is required to stay among those who reject Jesus to profess God's great works. Kind of a mixed blessing I guess!

The stories about Elijah are generally filled with tales of justified violence, magical providence, and a sort of cage-match battle of the gods, none of which I find easy to relate to. But finally, in this passage, Elijah exhibits a little bit of humanity. He is afraid and discouraged, and one might even argue he's depressed. In fact, he's suicidal. And although God doesn't make it all okay, he does provide what you need to take the next step, and then the next one. What comes after that? Who knows, but Elijah seems to summon the faith that God will be with him wherever that ends up taking him.

I am fascinated by the idea that while Elijah is on the mountaintop, there is a violent wind, but God is not in the wind. God is not in any of the great natural wonders he is witnessing, but rather in the piercing silence that comes after the awesome displays. How often do we ever make room for such silence in our lives? When we sense that God is distant, is it possible that we have just become so used to all the distractions and static of our daily life that we cannot any longer hear the still, small voice of God that still lingers there in the silence?

Digging Deeper

Mining for what really matters . . . and gold

This week we are hit with the double whammy of being sent into the proverbial lion's den, surrounded by those who are hell-bent on hating us and what we stand for, while also feeling hopelessly distant from God. What a setup! Why in the world would God do something like this to the people who demonstrate such deep faith?

Shouldn't they be the ones sitting up on the thrones, making all the decisions, having servants feed them grapes, and waving palm branches behind them to keep them cool? Where's my reward? Where is the justification for all the hard work that I do in the name of my faith?

This week in particular, we would find kindred spirits in King David, the prophets Elijah and Isaiah, and probably in the man who was healed by Jesus, only to be sent back into hostile territory to talk about the miracles of the God of Jesus. He was the very man who was just run out of town by those who were afraid of him. Jesus himself, as we know, doesn't fare much better when it comes to his own ministry. So why does the work of our faith so often have to be so damn hard?

It would be much nicer to retreat to a mountaintop, build a nice shelter, kick back by a stream, and do some fishing. Now that sounds like a place I could find God! But meanwhile, the world's suffering and brokenness persists, and I hide myself away because of my own fear of the consequences. Consider Paul's vision of the erasure of all divisions between people. It is a beautiful thing, considering the idea of there no longer being a distinction between us and the "other," but I think if we sit around and watch from the sidelines, waiting for God take care of it all and make it better, we're missing the point.

Maybe we are missing out on our mission, our role in the coming kingdom and in the elimination of those barriers between us. What if the only way those divisions that cause such violence will ever be overcome is if we find the strength and courage to face them head on and overcome them ourselves? Granted, it may not be the answer we were looking for, but if what we ultimately want is a life filled with meaning and purpose, it seems we may have to choose between what we want, what feels comfortable, and what really matters.

Heads Up

Connecting the text to our world

I came down to the basement of our house just after Amy and I got married to find her sitting on the washing machine, crying. I asked her what was wrong, assuming I had done something (which was usually a safe guess), and she looked up with tears in her eyes.

"I have to go to seminary, dammit!," she said.

A few months later, we had packed up everything we owned in a truck and drove through an ice storm in Colorado down to Fort Worth, Texas, where she began her three-and-a-half-year stint at divinity school. There were times when she came home assuring me that there was no way she was going to be able to finish. Of course, I had quit my job in Colorado and moved a thousand miles away, so I was less than excited to hear about her loss of confidence.

She made it through, obviously. But there have been other times in our ministry together over the past fifteen years—many times, in fact—when we both wanted to just pack it up and walk away. We would yearn for God to remove the longing from our hearts to continue to do ministry, to give us a passion for something else that didn't take so much out of us and didn't make us so . . . weird.

What we got instead was renewed endurance and a persistent conviction that, no matter how difficult it was from day to day, we were doing what we were supposed to be doing. Not exactly an answer to prayer by some accounts, but certainly a way through the struggles, doubt, and darkness rather than a simple shortcut out of it.

Just another one of those examples of God not giving us what we want but rather us finding what we needed—sometimes in spite of ourselves.

Prayer for the Week

God, sometimes it doesn't feel like you're there. I feel isolated and alone, and I feel like giving up. Help me find the courage, hope, and strength to keep looking.

Popping Off

Art/music/video and other cool stuff that relate to the text

Beyond the Lectionary: A Year of Alternatives to the Revised Common Lectionary, by David Ackerman (book, 2013)

"Up to the Mountain (MLK Song)," by Patty Griffin (song, 2007)

"Did You Feel the Mountains Tremble?" by Delirious? (song, 1995)

"I Still Haven't Found What I'm Looking For," by U2 (song, 1987)

From Rock God to God Nerd

~~~~

Lectionary Texts For

June 30, 2019 (Third Sunday after Pentecost)

Texts in Brief

My dog ate my Bible!

FIRST READING

2 Kings 2:1–2, 6–14

Elijah keeps trying to leave Elisha behind, but Elisha keeps following him everywhere. Elijah is getting ready to be swept up to heaven by God, and Elisha asks for a double dose of his spirit. Elijah gets swept from the banks of the Jordan River by a chariot of fire, and Elisha freaks out. But based on his superpowers to separate the waters of the Jordan, it appears that his wish was granted.

and

1 Kings 19:15–16, 19–21

Elijah anoints Elisha as the prophet to take over his place when Elijah is gone. Elisha accepts the new calling, says goodbye to his family, and slaughters the oxen he has been raising, giving away the meat to the people.

Psalm

Psalm 77:1–2, 11–20

This Psalm refers to the story of Moses leading the Jewish slaves out of Egypt. It says that God's ways are through the waters but that there are no footprints left behind as evidence. This helps draw a deeper connection between the stories of Moses and Elijah.

and

Psalm 16

A psalm comparing the way of life of the God of Abraham to the way of death of all other gods. The God of Abraham offers followers a path to life, joy, and abundance.

Second Reading

Galatians 5:1, 13–25

The call of Christ is to one of freedom, both from the authority of legalism and government and also from sin itself. Paul warns the early Christians in Galatia, however, not to use this newfound freedom as a way to be lazy and self-indulgent. Rather, he calls them into a relationship of mutual obedience to one another and humble servitude. He reminds them of the greatest commandment to love your neighbor as yourself and contrasts the so-called fruits of the spirit with the destructive and toxic fruits of the flesh.

Gospel

Luke 9:51–62

Jesus is near the time of his ascension to heaven and on his way to Jerusalem. Samaritan villagers along the way do not treat them with hospitality, which pisses off the disciples. They offered to burn the village down, and Jesus condemns their inclinations toward violence. Along the journey someone offers to follow Jesus wherever he goes. He warns them that there is no rest or home in such a path. Another person offers to follow him after completing burial rights for the dead. Jesus tells them to let the dead bury the dead and to concern themselves only with the kingdom of God.

Bible, Decoded

Breaking down Scripture in plain language

Elisha—Chosen by God and anointed by Elijah to be the next leader of the sons of the prophets after Elijah was taken to heaven. Supposedly he has a double dose of the Holy Ghost and was a powerful prophet and leader for Israel for several decades.

Oxen—Considered beasts of labor and burden, they were controlled by farmers with a yoke. Often times, as is the case in the letter to the Galatians from Paul, a similar yoke is evoked to describe the enslavement of the people of Israel, both literally and figuratively. Oxen also were beasts of sacrifice, as they were very valuable, and their slaughter would be considered a demonstration of faithfulness.

Jordan River—The Jordan is an important "character" throughout Scripture. It delineates the eastern border of Israel, and it is the site both of John the Baptist's ministry and of his activism for Jesus, which started Christ's anointed ministry in earnest. Part of the reason this river is considered so important to John the Baptist is because it is the site where Elijah was swept up to heaven. It is also important to note the parallels between Elijah and Moses in the stories of parting the waters.

Points to Ponder

First Thoughts

There are a lot of interesting parallels to consider in these texts this week. There is the coming ascension of Jesus, which has an important parallel to Elijah's ascension. There are references to the parting of the waters, which draws a connection between Elijah and Moses. And then there is the symbolic significance of the Jordan River. All of these, in a broad sense, are meant to reinforce the notion that Moses, Elijah, and Jesus are all anointed by the God of Abraham, and that those who follow them are on the path of righteousness and life.

While Jesus tends to be more inductive about his guidance in matters of how to live and behave, Paul—even in quoting the greatest commandment held up by Jesus—gets very specific about the kind of behaviors that are okay and those that are examples of a life gone astray. This could partly be because Paul is a bit of a control freak, but it is also likely it's because he is seeing the evidence of destructive behaviors manifesting themselves in these early Christian communities.

It's a pretty bold move for Elisha to ask Elijah for a double dose of the prophetic spirit and power that this great prophet has held. Even Elijah notes that this is a big order to fill. But keep in mind this would have been written looking back in history on to the prophetic ministries of both Elijah and Elisha. Although Elijah came first, it is meant in a way to suggest that those who succeed their predecessors will do even greater things than those who came before them. This sounds an awful lot like something Jesus said in our texts a couple of weeks ago.

We see a few examples here of the friction between the idea of following a great prophet or even the Christ himself versus the reality of what it actually means. As we have seen just last week, Elijah was so grieved by his own ministry at times that he prayed for death. It's not the glamorous, rock-star life that some groupies might be hoping for. But one reason it seems clear that Elisha is the right man for his particular job is because he is so willing to lay everything down and just walk away. Similarly, we will see Jesus challenge many people who claim to want to follow him throughout the Gospels.

Digging Deeper

Mining for what really matters . . . and gold

It's funny how much emphasis many Christians seem to put on the day when a "new Christian" becomes baptized, joins the church, or make some other public statement of faith. It's an exciting time and a cause for celebration for many, but it turns out that there is a hell of a lot of fine print that is left out during these warm, fuzzy experiences.

Sometimes, following God and trying to live out a Christlike path really, really sucks. And honestly, why should we expect anything different? If, after all, the path of Christ leads to some sort of common destination, consider where it led Jesus! If we used today's measures, by all accounts, Jesus was a complete failure. He died poor. He died alone. He was reviled and ridiculed. Not exactly the path to prosperity that some of our TV evangelist brothers and sisters would like to paint for us, is it?

This isn't to say that God calls us to a life of misery. Far from it; suffering is inevitable, no matter which path we choose. Can we have a choice either to run from it or to accept the suffering as a natural byproduct of life itself? If so, we can learn to keep it in perspective when compared with the joy, peace, and encouragement that comes from a life lived with real meaning and purpose.

It's not God's fault that such a path leads to hardship along the way. The fault there lies with the culture around us that doesn't want to be called on its obsession with superficial interests and trinkets of distraction. After all, if we live in a way that suggests such things aren't really that important, what does it say about those around us who treat such things like gods?

Some people talk about the path of Christ being narrow, as if it is a tiny gateway to a private club where very few are welcome. But what if it is a narrow path because it isn't a particularly popular one? The path trodden by the majority of the world is well-worn and fairly easy to navigate. But like Sarah Palin's famous bridge, ultimately it leads nowhere.

Heads Up

Connecting the text to our world

When I got to college, I was what I would call "A-B-C: anything but Christian." At my large, progressive, and fiercely independent campus, a guy could have gotten more dates admitting he had herpes then telling a girl he was a Christian. Though I had grown up Southern Baptist, I had been thrown out of the church only a year or so before, so steering clear of the religious weirdos was no hard feat. In fact, my stories of apostasy actually added to my reputation as a good, solid non-Christian.

But I was a seeker. I was insatiably curious. I wanted to understand everything from the meaning of life the origins of creation itself. I looked to all of the great philosophers and even a good number of theologians, ever mindful to steer clear of the religion of my childhood. I found intellectual and even some spiritual nourishment through other avenues. I found an identity as a musician. I found comfort in the occasional romantic relationship. I found escape with copious amounts of drugs and alcohol.

Not all of this was necessarily bad (well, maybe the excessive drugs and alcohol), but they still left me wanting . . . something. Surely, it couldn't be the very thing that I had walked away from, could it? Certain that there was nothing in that past for me but heartbreak and disappointment, I forged ahead for many years in search of the past that would lead me where I wanted to go—so long as it didn't require me to look to Jesus or the Bible to do it.

It turns out, there are a whole lot of ways to do Christianity. Yes, some of them can be incredibly hurtful, and it can be debated whether this group or that denomination are even legitimately Christian by someone else's definition. But the good news is that Jesus didn't tell people to go to church in order to get their heads and hearts right. He told them to set everything down that was getting in their way, to stop being their own greatest enemy and biggest stumbling block, and to walk unburdened, without the yoke of fruitless pursuits, toward the fruits yielded by a life led by the spirit.

If you found some of my old college buddies and told them I was leading a Bible study online and had married a minister and founded a church, they would probably be pretty certain you're nuts. Just goes to show that I, in all my shortcomings, missteps, and tragic flaws, am in very good company when it comes to trying to understand this Jesus guy.

Prayer for the Week

God, it is so very easy for me to get distracted from a path you set ahead of me that leads me to the things in life I really longed for in my heart of hearts: peace, contentment, and joy, all unbound by present circumstances. Help me let go of those things that don't satisfy and to trust that although the path may be narrow, we don't have to travel it alone.

Popping Off

Art/music/video and other cool stuff that relate to the text

"Wade in the Water" (gospel spiritual)

Rock Star (movie, 2001)

Can't Buy Me Love (movie, 1987)

Life and Death Decisions

Lectionary Texts For

July 7, 2019 (Fourth Sunday after Pentecost)

Texts in Brief

My dog ate my Bible!

FIRST READING

2 Kings 5:1–14

Naaman is a great warrior for King Aram, but he suffers from leprosy. Elisha invites Naaman to his house in order to be healed. When Naaman gets there, Elisha sends a servant who tells him to bathe himself seven times in the Jordan River. Naaman is offended that Elisha doesn't come out in person and almost goes home. But his servant convinces him to follow through on what Elisha has told him to do, and he is healed.

and

Isaiah 66:10–14

Israel is described as offering the nourishment and comfort of a nursing mother. Isaiah assures the people of Israel that they will be protected and cared for as the chosen people of God.

Psalm

Psalm 30

This is a song of praise in four parts that was offered at the dedication of the temple of David. He offers praise to God for being delivered from death, and although there are dark times, they do not compare to the joyful ones.

Psalm 66:1–9

This is another song of praise that seems to be referencing the deliverance of the Jewish people from Egypt. It mentions the parting of the Dead Sea, which also harkens back to the parting of the Jordan River in our recent study.

Second Reading

Galatians 6:(1–6), 7–16

Paul warns the Christians in Galatia to be gentle in dealing with people who sin. He reminds them that each person must ultimately be responsible for themselves and that, although we support one another, we can't fix one another. He goes on to remind them to stay focused on matters of the spirit rather than those of the flesh. Placing value in matters of the flesh leads only to death, he says. And the only path to real life is to stay focused on matters of the spirit.

GOSPEL
Luke 10:1–11, 16–20

Seventy evangelists are sent to all corners of the region to share the news of the gospel. They are encouraged to take nothing with them but rather to depend on the hospitality of those they encounter. They are urged to stay as long as they are welcome, but to shake the dust off of their sandals and move on if they are not welcome. The evangelists report back in amazement that even demons submit to them, but they are warned not to rejoice in their own power but rather in the assurance that they will be with God in paradise.

Bible, Decoded
Breaking down Scripture in plain language

Circumcision—We all know what circumcision is but often do not understand the religious basis for it. In Genesis 17, Abraham uses circumcision as a demonstration of his covenant with God. From then on, Jewish males have been circumcised on the eighth day after birth. Although it is not required to be circumcised in order to be Jewish, it is believed by some that there can be spiritual consequences without it. Paul continued to hold up this practice for new Christians in the early church, as he also was a Jew.

Demons—Any number of physical and psychological maladies were attributed in these days to demon possession. There are stories, like the one we recently studied when Jesus casts a man's demons into the group of pigs, about the God of Israel's power over evil in the world. This reference to the demons submitting to these new evangelists is an affirmation of their authority to speak on behalf of God.

Transgression—More or less synonymous with *sin*. Sometimes the words *sin* and *transgression* are used interchangeably, even in the Lord's Prayer. Both words have a slightly different etymology, however. Whereas a transgression is the crossing of some kind of line or boundary, the word *sin* means literally to "fall short" or "miss the mark."

Points to Ponder

First Thoughts

The comment from Paul about the largeness of his letters seem strange at first. But it is likely that many of his letters are either transcribed, or even partly composed, by secretaries. Here, he is making a point to let the church in Galatia know that he is adding a personal note himself.

We can definitely see the references back to the deliverance of the Jewish people from Egypt as a metaphor for God's deliverance of his faithful people from death into life. Elisha demonstrates a similar power with Naaman, which is meant to further validate the sovereignty of the God of Israel. And this theme continues with the seventy Christians sent out to spread the gospel.

It is interesting that he almost allows his own ego to get in the way of his healing. It is also worth noting that, once again, it is a servant (one of the outsiders or marginalized people) who recognizes the potential in the situation and holds out hope for healing. This seems to echo the servant mentality that both Paul and the author of Luke call their followers to as they engage other non-Christians.

It is debatable whether the discussions about life and death are focusing more on the afterlife or the presence of life that we are living today. Of course, some place great emphasis on the endgame of Christianity being about salvation in eternity after death. But by most accounts in these texts, we are dealing with people struggling with physical and spiritual matters of life and death here and now.

Digging Deeper
Mining for what really matters . . . and gold

Is Jesus more concerned with what happens to us after we die or how we're living here and now? This is one of the fundamental questions that seems to divide Christians more than any other. Whereas Christianity historically has focused on the salvation of souls, there is a growing movement that emphasizes salvation of lives and the world in real time.

This is not necessarily a new concept. At the very beginning of the twentieth century, Walter Rauschenbusch gave rise to movement that is now called the Social Gospel. He felt that Christians up to that point had focused far too much on individual sin and had largely neglected inherently broken—or sinful—social systems. He took a new approach to the Lord's Prayer offered by Jesus, suggesting that the words, "Thy kingdom come, thy will be done, on earth as it is in heaven," is a call for us to strive to realize a Christlike vision for our world rather than waiting for some idyllic afterlife as a reward for individual faithfulness.

His notion of evangelism was not one of rhetorical argument to coerce someone into a confession of faith, but rather to take on a servant's heart and to invest ourselves in righting the wrongs within our communities. The Social Gospel movement has been picked up more recently by those advocates of what is called a "missional church" model. It even seems more conservative evangelical Christians have begun to take on more and more social causes like ecological conservation, poverty, gender issues, and in some cases, even equality of rights for the LGBT community.

Do we all agree on the significance of the death of Jesus and what it means for our faith? Definitely not. Will we ever? Not likely. But all who read the Gospels can certainly find common ground in the call to serve those who are suffering, marginalized, or otherwise cast outside of various social circles and denied equal access or opportunity. This may look different for each Christian, and it should. We are all called to different respective ministries. God places on our hearts a longing to rectify those particular things we see as the world's deepest needs.

And it will take such a diversity of efforts to help realize the kingdom vision that Jesus cast for the world.

And the best part is that we have the opportunity to help ensure that this vision becomes a reality.

Heads Up
Connecting the text to our world

We all love feeling like VIPs sometimes. It's fun to get some special treatment to help us feel like we are set apart, as if we are really special, at least for a moment. In fact, there are entire industries built on the assumption that we will go to great lengths to feel important.

My brother-in-law used to work in Las Vegas. He worked for limousine company that specialized in making people feel like rock stars for one night. And believe me, they paid for it! One night, he took me by one of the nightclubs that his customers frequented, and he introduced me to many of the service personnel he depended on to help these tourists feel like VIPs. Although there were hundreds of people milling around in the main area of the club, I noticed that there was a red velvet rope separating off one corner of the room.

"What's that about?" I asked him.

"That's the Platinum Club section," he said.

"Sounds fancy," I said. "What's the difference between over there and over here?"

"About five hundred bucks a night," he winked.

Naaman was a VIP in Israel. He was close to the king, and what he did and said mattered. He was used to deference from those around him and was shocked when Elisha didn't offer him the same respect. In fact, he was so put off by Elisha's reclusive behavior that he almost became his own worst enemy, denying himself the gift of healing that was right in front of him.

Most of us don't walk through life expecting people to bow down and lay palm branches before us as we walk down the street. But when a group of young Americans was asked what they wanted to be when they grew up, the number one answer, far and away more popular than any other response, was "to be famous."

Meanwhile, I observe people wrestling to accept even the simplest kindnesses when they visit a church. We used to offer something we called giveaways every month at our church in Colorado. We would offer something simple, like a meal, a car wash, or a garage sale, and when people offered a donation, we would refuse it. Most people were baffled but pleased, but some people simply refused to accept the gift. One man actually shoved a few dollars out of his window as he drove away to ease his own conscience!

"This is really nice and all," a woman once said to Amy, "but why? Why do you do all of this?"

She would just smile and say, "Jesus says that grace is supposed to be free, but we thought we might start with a carwash."

If people wrestle with the very idea that they are worthy of something for nothing while, on the other hand, clamor for validation from something as superficial as a stupid red velvet rope, there is certainly plenty of spiritual and emotional triage work left to be done. Seems like a big task, but we can start small and simple with . . . oh, I don't know . . . a car wash?

Prayer for the Week

God, help me remember to take on a servant's heart while also accepting kindness and hospitality from others, even when I don't feel that I deserve it. Help me worry less about what awaits beyond this life; help me focus instead on using what I have today to make tomorrow a little bit better for my brothers and sisters.

Popping Off

Art/music/video and other cool stuff that relate to the text

Leaving Las Vegas (movie, 1995)

Joe versus the Volcano (movie, 1990)

Myth of the Self-Made Man

Lectionary Texts For
July 14, 2019 (Fifth Sunday after Pentecost)

Texts in Brief
My dog ate my Bible!

First Reading
Amos 7:7–17

God tells Amos that he will hold a "plumb line" up against the people of Israel in an act of judgment. Amos, who is in the northern territory of Israel, begins to tell people to get ready for God's fierce judgment. Amaziah, a key priest in the court of King Jeroboam II, tells the king what Amos is saying, and the king pressures Amos to head south toward the territory of Judah. Amos resists, and instead offers dire predictions for the king and all in his family.

and

Deuteronomy 30:9–14

A promise is offered by God to the Jewish people who hold God's commandments sacred. They will be prosperous in everything as long as they turn to God with all of their heart and all of their soul in everything they do. The author notes that this commandment is not too hard, out of reach, or complicated for anyone; rather, it is on our hearts and lips already.

Psalm

Psalm 82

A psalm of unknown origin and authorship. At first, it seems to suggest a polytheistic reality. But more likely, the "gods" referred to, over which the one true God rules, are the leaders of countries or kingdoms on earth. The psalm says that they were blessed with godlike authority and status but have fallen short of their duties. As such, they will suffer the fate of all human beings and will be judged by God for their transgressions.

and

Psalm 25:1–10

King David is pleading with God to teach him the ways of a righteous ruler. Basically, he is doing exactly what the commandment in our Deuteronomy text says he should do.

Second Reading

Colossians 1:1–14

A letter of praise to the early Christians in Colossae for their faithfulness. It is evident by the fruits of their faith that they are following the teachings of the gospel. As such, Paul, Timothy, and the other leaders in the Christian movement pray for them and their ministry every day.

GOSPEL

Luke 10:25–37

A lawyer is either trying to trap Jesus with rhetorical logic or find a loophole in the greatest commandment for himself. He asks Jesus how to inherit eternal life, and Jesus responds with the commandment. The loophole comes when he asks Jesus who his neighbors are. Jesus responds by telling the story of the good Samaritan. The priests and politicians from the territory of the man who was beaten and robbed don't help him at all, but it is only when a Samaritan man came by that he receives help. Jesus says this is what the man—and implicitly, the rest of us—should also go and do.

Bible, Decoded

Breaking down Scripture in plain language

Plumb line—In construction, a plumb line is used to tell when something is straight. In this case, the root word often translated as "plumb line" is *anak*. This is literally translated as "metal" or "tin," but it is generally believed to be referencing this building and design tool. So God is going to hold a similar yardstick up to the people of Israel and judge them on where they have strayed from the "straight and narrow" path established for them by God.

Judah—This is the southern territory of the Jewish people. It is generally considered more faithful to God's law and orthodox in their religious practice than the more "liberal" or secularized north, known as Israel. Basically, the king is pressuring Amos to go south where people actually care about his prophetic teaching.

Amaziah—The chief priest of Bethel, one of the major territories within Israel at the time. There was a great deal of church-state collusion going on, which led to an awful lot of lapdog leadership in religious life. Granted, this convenient marriage was how much of the stability was maintained in the region, but it was believed the religious leaders often kissed up to the political process rather than holding them accountable to their people or to God's law.

Points to Ponder

First Thoughts

Interestingly, the root words for "tin" and "moaning" are very similar in Hebrew. So there may be a bit of wordplay going on, in that God is holding up the plumb line to determine the righteousness of the Jewish people. But it is also a sort of foreshadowing of the moaning that will result from their judgment.

One of King Jeroboam's sons was killed in a recent political uprising, which helps explain why the king would be particularly sensitive to Amos's prophecies about him and his sons dying by the sword. It also helps to explain why the political powers would be so eager to hold religious leadership close, both to help keep people in line and also to help inform them of potential insurrection, such as what might have been fomented by Amos's prophecies.

Psalm 82 is especially curious on first reading. It sounds much more like old Greek or Roman theology, with the council of gods and one leader trying to manage them all. Some scholars have argued that it is actually a celestial context in which God is managing dissident angels. As such some suggest this is a reference to the legion of rebel angels that Lucifer rallied to overthrow God before being cast out. However, the more generally accepted understanding is that this is an indictment of the kings and lords on earth—all of whom generally would have been treated like Gods in their own right—for falling short of their divine mandate to submit first to God and care for their people, as the commandment in Deuteronomy dictates.

Digging Deeper

Mining for what really matters . . . and gold

It interesting to consider the parallels between the leaders and nations being called to account here and our present-day world. For centuries, the spread of Christianity has been dependent upon a complicit relationship with the powers of authority that embrace them. Basically, the priests bless the rulers in their conquests so they may go and take territory. In return, Christianity is recognized as the religion of the kingdom, giving the church a central the role the new territories and colonies.

At its heart, this is the essence of "theocracy," a system of governance in which the lines between church and state are blurry at best, and at worst are ignored for expediency and the acquisition of power and wealth. It is no surprise, when someone goes back to the history books and reads about Emperor Constantine's work or myriad leaders since then that they cast a skeptical eye toward the Christian faith.

If Amos were here today, what would he have to say to our political and religious leaders? If the author of Psalm 82 saw how we deify celebrities, athletes, and even our leaders, how quick would they be to remind us and them of our utter mortality, and of falling so woefully short of that simple commandment—simple but far from easy to live out every single day of our lives—first laid out in the fifth book of the Old Testament, thousands of years before Jesus was even born?

Privilege, power, and all that come with them should always be met with a sense of humble gratitude as well as heartfelt responsibility. They are the mantles we bear, not simply the inevitable fruits of a true meritocracy.

We hear the story of the good Samaritan so often that it is easy for it to lose its meaning. But to me, sometimes all a parable needs is a more modern context. What if the man in the ditch was a Christian, maybe even an American executive, and the Samaritan actually a Muslim woman in a full burka? Imagine the man being passed by those whose eyes were glued to their smartphones, with far more pressing matters than to notice the suffering right in front of their faces. Take a closer look at the face of the passersby. Does it look familiar? Maybe like looking into a mirror? And now look again to the ditch. Who do you see? The child who was forced to mine the minerals to make that phone in your hand? The woman whose village was burned down to make way for the new oil pipeline to feed our hunger for oil? Or maybe just a friend, distraught and broken down by hopelessness, loneliness, despair?

Just keep going. Don't look up. Someone else will come along soon enough who can really help.

But they see us. They may not know our names, but they know we are here. *Who is my neighbor?* they wonder. *Will they notice me?*

Heads Up

Connecting the text to our world

All of these texts this week remind me of the parable of the faithful servants, which comes up in Luke 12. Basically, the moral of the parable is "to whom much is given, much is also expected."

One of the biggest illusions of so many of us have, at least in the United States, is that of the "self-made man." We love the idea of someone who comes up from nothing, and through hard work and determination, finds themselves "blessed" by the fruits of their rigorous labor. Granted, this happens sometimes, and it's an inspiring story when it does, but it's only really part of the story.

Yes, I work hard for the grades I got in school. I withstood rejection after rejection in more than one career for finding some measure success in my chosen vocation of writing. But if I were to credit myself primarily for being here, it would be a tremendous act of hubris and self-deception.

We are far more interdependent than we realize, or at least than we care to admit. I think back to when I worked in a small public school in Pueblo, Colorado, which was at risk of losing its federal funding because of its poor standardized test scores. I was given the task of working intensively with a small group of teachers to turn around the hardest academic cases with the hopes of saving the school.

There was one little girl who was particularly bright but hardly said a word when more than one person was present. To call her a wallflower would be an understatement. It was obvious that she was dealing with some sort of trauma back home. And while she did perfectly well with any task I put before her, she often struggled to stay awake, even through the shortest lessons.

Finally, I asked her what was wrong. Was she not getting enough sleep? Was she bored? Had she not had a good breakfast? It was then that she told me about her mother, who was trying to raise her three children alone, but had a revolving door of sorts for boyfriends and other hangers-on who frequented the house. They would party into the late hours, and more often than not, once alcohol was involved, things got violent. She was afraid to go to sleep because she felt responsible for her brothers and for her mom. The last thing on her mind was getting a good education and thinking about her future.

Tell me that girl has the same opportunities that any other girl her age has in this land of the free and home of the brave. Tell me that a child doesn't have to worry about where their next meal comes from or whether they can sleep through the night without harm doesn't have an advantage.

And to those who have such advantages—particularly, those in positions of power and authority to do something about the systemic poverty, hopelessness, violence, and oppression that help manifest these issues—woe unto us who stand by, congratulating ourselves for our good fortune while doing nothing for our neighbor.

Prayer for the Week

God, help wake us from our slumber. Help the cloudiness clear from our eyes so that we may see with the eyes of Jesus. Help still my hands from the busywork that distracts me so often so that we may reach out with the hands of Jesus. Slow my stride and guide me along the path of compassion so that I may walk in the path of Jesus.

Popping Off

Art/music/video and other cool stuff that relate to the text

"The Three Rules of Epidemics," from *The Tipping Point*, by Malcolm Gladwell (book, 2006)

"The Good Samaritan," from *Seinfeld*, season 3, episode 20 (TV series, 1989–1998)

The Secret Life of Walter Mitty, by James Thurbur (book, 1945; movie 1947, 2013)

Get Outta My Tent!

———————⟋⋀⋁⋀⟍———————

Lectionary Texts For
July 21, 2019 (Sixth Sunday after Pentecost)

Texts in Brief
My dog ate my Bible!

First Reading
Amos 8:1–12

God shows the prophet Amos a basket of summer fruit and then proceeds to drop the cataclysmic prediction for the people of Israel on him. Aside from the general wailing, gnashing of teeth, and skies turned to darkness, the vision is one of a spiritual famine: one in which God's people search for God but will not find him. This, like our passage from Amos last week, has to do with the northern territory of Israel and its people straying from God's ways.

and

Genesis 18:1–10a

God appears to Abraham, and Abraham asks God not to pass him by. He invites him—actually, Abraham sees three men—to stay for a meal, and they accept. He has his wife, Sarah, prepare bread for them while he serves them milk and meat from a choice calf. While the men are dining under the tree, God tells Abraham that he will revisit soon and that Sarah will bear him a son.

PSALM

Psalm 52

David's song of reproach for those who persecute the people of God and turn their backs on God to pursue earthly riches. He warns that they will be "snatched from their tents" while the righteous watch and laugh at them.

and

Psalm 15

A poem about who God welcomes into God's presence. It includes those who resist evil, have compassion for the poor, and who stand by their commitment to God, even when it poses a risk to them.

SECOND READING

Colossians 1:15–28

Paul describes Jesus in his letter as the firstborn of all creation, one created in the image of God, the source of life in the midst of death and the reconciliation of all humanity to God. He recognizes that the Colossians have sinned but that Jesus has made it right between them and God. Despite this gift of grace, he warns them to stay on the path of righteousness and to follow the commands laid out by Jesus in the Gospels.

GOSPEL
Luke 10:38–42

Martha invites Jesus into her house. Her sister, Mary, sits at the feet of Jesus and listens to his words of wisdom. Martha, however, is preoccupied with housework. Finally, she gets frustrated that she is the only one doing work and complains to Jesus that Mary should be helping her. But Jesus says that Mary is doing the right in taking the time to learn something more important than busying herself with daily chores.

Bible, Decoded

Breaking down Scripture in plain language

Ephah—An ancient unit of dry goods measurement, roughly equal to today's bushel.

Shekel—An Israeli coin, currently worth about one United States quarter.

Tent—A symbol used throughout Scripture to represent holy ground. Often synonymous with a temple in an earthly context, and with heavenly paradise in a metaphysical sense.

Mamre—The site where Abraham is camping, historically known as the location for a famous Canaanite cult shrine.

Points to Ponder

First Thoughts

The prophecy in Amos gets the heart of what people in Israel are placing before God, which are material riches. So the prophetic threat is that the entire economic system will be turned on its end, with valuable things becoming worthless and scraps of the poor becoming great treasures.

It is significant that Abraham has set up camp near Mamre. His tent is, in a sense, holy ground in the midst of ungodly cult territory. Keep in mind that Abraham is considered the forefather of all of the people of Israel and that the land of Israel is considered by the Jewish people to be, much like Abraham's campsite, holy ground in the midst of a spiritual desert. So this is a sort of foreshadowing the birth of Israel.

The basket of summer fruit in Amos seems like a total non sequitur without some cultural context to help explain why it is there. Amos is a simple herdsman when he is called to be a prophet of God. He is a man of the land. He is also called a "gatherer of sycamore fruit." This fruit is like a fig but with a very bitter skin. Those who harvested the sycamore fruit actually had to scrape or bruise the skin of the fruit in order to help it ripen and become edible. This, then, is a sort of metaphor for what Amos's job is among the Jewish people. He has been sent to rough them up a little bit, to bruise them, but with the purpose of preparing them for living more fully what God has created them to be.

We have to keep in mind that David is both a warrior and a king, but in his psalm the righteous stand by and laugh at the suffering of others, which is terribly un-Christlike. This sounds much more like the God of Elijah; it places greater emphasis on sovereignty and superiority than on compassion and grace. Perhaps this is the unrecognized mystery that Paul is referring to; maybe it's clear to him that those who came before him simply didn't have the entire picture without Jesus.

Digging Deeper

Mining for what really matters . . . and gold

Growing up with the Baptist church, I always thought it would be awesome to be a prophet. They get to know people, never got in trouble, and everyone was afraid of them! There was the whole martyrdom thing, but in general it seems like a pretty good gig back in the day

But whoever got excited about seeing a prophet come their way? The locals would probably cringe, because you know he probably isn't bringing good news. And everyone else probably thought you were a whack job. The powers that be were always gunning for you, and if you were lucky, your reward is a fancy dinner of locusts and honey.

But this is Amos's job. He is to help scrape away the bitterness on the surface of God's people to help them get at the real meat of who they are.

But no one welcomes being scraped or bruised. We would rather be told how great we are and what a good job we're doing. I'm sure the churches under Paul's oversight paused for a moment or two at the mailbox when they saw a new letter from him. Sure, it might have a kind word or two, but it was sure to have new challenges or criticisms aplenty.

Jesus didn't exactly tell people what they wanted to hear either. They were expecting a Messiah, but not this kind of Messiah. They longed for salvation, but not this kind of salvation. They called out for the kind of peace found in victory, what they got was the peace found in a humble servant's heart.

Come to think of it, maybe pass on the whole prophet gig. After all, the pay sucks, you always work alone, and the severance package is almost always the same. And man, it ain't pretty.

Heads Up

Connecting the text to our world

Summer is a relatively slow time in church life, and it is usually the time when we have a chance to get away with family for some much-needed rest and relaxation. This past week, we went to visit Amy's mom, who lives on a twelve-acre ranch on the Rio Grande in New Mexico. It is a beautiful spot: our own heaven on earth, especially to the kids.

Mattias brought one of his best friends from Colorado with him, and the first night, they decided they were going to sleep outside in the apple orchard in grandma's tent. So like a good and dutiful dad, I spent the next hour and a half wrestling with tent stakes and canvas in order to create something vaguely tent-like. All the while, the boys were so eager to get into the thing that they could hardly stand it.

The moment I gave them the go-ahead, they dashed inside as if paradise itself awaited them. Not surprising, little sister Zoe decided that she wanted to join them. And although she is five years younger and very mild mannered, she is still a little sister. As such, she was banished hardly before she had her head through the tent opening.

As they zipped up the tent behind her, her eyes filled with crocodile tears. She had been cast out. She was in social exile. Never mind that the only thing inside the tent was a dusty tarp, a handful of eager mosquitoes, and some wiggly boys. The only thing she wanted in that moment was to be inside the tent with them. It meant everything to her.

What kind of tentmakers are we? Are we more like Martha, so preoccupied with busywork that we neglect our neighbors, the guests of honor? Do we stand by and rejoice in the misfortune of others as they suffer the consequences of their own doing, rather than inviting them in and making room for them at the table, under the protection of our shade? When we see a stranger come by, do we drop everything, bring out the best of what we have, and sit at their feet in humble service?

Granted, plans might have to change, we might have to share, and God forbid, something might get broken. But our tents only become holy ground when they are open to the stranger. Otherwise, they're just four more walls in a world of walls, keeping us all farther apart and further away from the realization of God's kingdom.

Prayer for the Week

God, help me fling the door of my tent open wide, and help me do likewise with my heart.

Popping Off

Art/music/video and other cool stuff that relate to the text

Chicken Little (movie, 2005)

Evan Almighty (movie, 2007)

Jesus Found
My Wallet!

_____⌇⌁⌇_____

Lectionary Texts For
July 28, 2019 (Seventh Sunday after Pentecost)

Texts in Brief
My dog ate my Bible!

First Reading
Hosea 1:2–10

Hosea is ordered by God to Mary Gomer, and they have three children. The names of the three children—Jezreel, Lo-ruhamah and Lo-ammi—represent forthcoming consequences of Israel's abandonment of their covenant with God. The harshness is softened in verse 10 when God promises that the future of Israel and its people can still be great.

and

Genesis 18:20–32

God intends to destroy Sodom for its wickedness, but Abraham is concerned that some good people will suffer for the deeds of others. Abraham goes into used-car salesman mode and starts bargaining with God about how many faithful he would have to find in the city in order for God to spare it. Ultimately, God says that if Abraham can even find ten good people in Sodom, he will spare the city.

Psalm

Psalm 85

A song of thanks to God for being merciful and generous. The fortunes of the house of Jacob are stored in the future of the people of Israel, and it is hopeful and prosperous.

and

Psalm 138

Another song about the mercy, protection, and provision of God. The psalmist notes that God is always faithful to us whether or not we are faithful to God. God is concerned with the welfare of the meek and the oppressed, and endeavors to deliver God's people from their oppressors.

Second Reading

Colossians 2:6–15, (16–19)

Paul reminds the early church in Colossae that in being baptized in Christ, they died to all of the previous values, practices, and ways of thinking of the world and were reborn into the fullness of God's grace. Paul is almost giddy about the disarming power found in the crucifixion, and he urges fellow followers of Christ to lean on such power rather than earthly powers.

GOSPEL
Luke 11:1–13

Jesus teaches the Lord's Prayer to his disciples. He also explains that God provides what is asked for by God's faithful people. God is not interested in sleight-of-hand or bait-and-switch tricks, but rather God looks upon us as children. Jesus assures us that God's love is far greater than even that which we possess for our own children.

Bible, Decoded
Breaking down Scripture in plain language

Jezreel—Hosea and Gomer's first child, whose name means "he sows." This sounds benign enough, but actually it is a reference to the consequences that will be reaped by the Israelites for their unfaithfulness. The name has several violent connotations, pointing to "Jehu's Purge," in which the kings of Israel and Judah are killed. It is also a reference to the location where Naboth was killed by his king, who was greedy and wanted to acquire Naboth's vineyards for his own.

Lo-ruhamah—Hosea and Gomer's second child, a daughter, whose name is more explicitly dark. Though it is sometimes translated as "not pitied," it can actually be more accurately interpreted to mean "not loved by one's parent," or even one who is neglected or abused.

Lo-ammi—the couple's third child, a second son, has a name that is a direct reference to the covenant between God and the Jewish people. The word *ammi* is used in Exodus when the covenant is established to note that the people of Israel are God's people. This is effectively a negation of that and can be translated as "not my people."

Points to Ponder

First Thoughts

The God presented in both Hosea and Genesis is particularly harsh on first examination. We are presented with a God figure who is intent on exacting brutal violence on those who transgress. But there also is a pervading thread of mercy, love, and hope throughout all of these passages. It is worth more than a moment to pause and consider whether these consequences are self-made by the people in the stories, or if indeed we believe in a vengeful God who requires satisfaction through the shedding of blood of his own creation.

Paul's writings are often used to support the idea of sacrificial substitutionary atonement: the idea that Jesus had to die in order for God to forgive our sins. But in this beautiful verse from Colossians, Paul notes that in being willing to be crucified as an innocent and not repaying blood with blood, Jesus "disarmed the rulers and authorities and made a public example of them, triumphing over them in it" (Col 2:15). It is a glimpse of a nonviolent conquering hero, and the power found in it is incredibly good news.

The assurances from Jesus in Luke are certainly comforting. We like the idea that God provides what we ask for, but at the same time, this text has been distorted and abused in profound ways. From this, we have prosperity gospel ministries that teach Jesus wants us to be rich and presents us with a vending-machine God that fills our orders. But if we note the prayer taught by Jesus, there is simplicity and humility in the requests made of God: sustenance, forgiveness, and deliverance. No Rolexes. No McMansions. No prosperity gospel.

Digging Deeper

Mining for what really matters . . . and gold

We find ourselves at a theological crossroads this week, juggling both a God of infinite love and mercy with a violent, punishing, and vengeful God. René Girard suggests that every ancient religion has this sort of friction of apparently opposing God images within it. We find it with Dionysus, Zeus, and throughout our own Scriptures.

But if we consider these early stories, particularly ones from the Old Testament, to be metaphors for the state of the Jewish people, we have to consider the likelihood that they were written in retrospect, looking back after the fallout from horrible tragedies was already evident. It is in our nature, then, to ask, "Why me? Why us? What did we do? Why did this happen to us?"

As such, the authors of the Scriptures draw connecting lines between such tragedies after the fact and points at which the people of God have broken their covenant with the creator. This is not necessarily to say that God did these things to the world, but perhaps it is more of a cautionary tale that God's covenant is one of restoration, deliverance, and prosperity, though not always in the forms the world tells us we should want or expect.

The residents of Sodom often are accused of any manner of sexual deviancy. But the sexual acts referenced actually tend to point to something bigger. The acts described were generally used in two ways within that culture: military rape or religious ritual. As such, the real "sin" here is worshiping a false God or oppressing God's people with force and humiliation. The story in Hosea points to economic greed and collusion among the powers of authority to maintain an affluent standard of living at the expense of the poor.

When we strip away the fantastic imagery and sexual connotations, we get back to an ever-present theme; God calls us to humble service, fulfillment of an eternal promise of faithfulness, and to seek out justice for those being crushed by the systems under which they live. In turn, we will find the life we seek and the meaning we long for, and we will not want for anything. It may not mean that God fulfills our every whim but rather that God fashions our priorities and longings around those things that truly give life.

Heads Up

Connecting the text to our world

When I was eight years old, I lost my first wallet. Aside from it being a proud status symbol of my pending membership in the "grown-up club," it also had ten dollars inside it. That represented nearly a month of allowance for me at that time, and to say I was prudent would be putting it lightly. I was a saver. I loved having that money in my back pocket and knowing that when I saw something I liked, I could buy it, even if I didn't. There was something in the assurance of knowing I could that actually was better in some ways than actually owning the thing itself. It was power!

When I lost my wallet, I lost that sense of identity and power at the same time. I panicked. After looking everywhere I could think of, I did what every good, young, Southern Baptist boy would do: I prayed for Jesus to help me find my wallet.

A few minutes later, I came across it, tucked underneath some dirty clothes near the head of my bed. I was elated. I ran to show my mom, beaming. "Look," I said. "Jesus found my wallet for me!"

Looking back on this today, I encounter a chilling but all-too-familiar God. One who helps me find my Naugahyde wallet but neglects the empty bellies of millions in sub-Saharan Africa. A God who affords me the comfort of carrying money I don't actually need in my back pocket while turning a blind eye to young girls who sell their bodies for a meal and a place to sleep.

This is not my God. God had no more to do with me finding my wallet than God had to do with me losing it in the first place. God created humanity, and in affording us the latitude to live by our own will, the seeds of brokenness were planted.

I believe in a God of love and of infinite grace. I also believe in reality beset with consequences. But the two don't have to coexist in some seemingly contradictory Godhead in order for me to feel loved. I found my own wallet that day, and rather than waiting for God to fix the ills of the world, perhaps it's better that we reflect on the abundance of resources and gifts already before us and get to work on making it right with what we've got.

Prayer for the Week

God, I know I tend to break my promises. I tend to want more than I need. I fantasize about a life without consequence. Help me realize my own fullness and then to release it so that others might feel the same way.

Popping Off

Art/music/video and other cool stuff that relate to the text

Groundhog Day (movie, 1993)

Get Lazy
for Jesus

Lectionary Texts For
August 4, 2019 (Eighth Sunday after Pentecost)

Texts in Brief
My dog ate my Bible!

First Reading
Hosea 11:1–11

A poem of lament of sorts, spoken on God's behalf. God is mourning the fact that the people of Israel continue to turn their backs on God, despite being delivered from Egyptian bondage and being sustained and nourished during the exodus. Instead they worship pagan gods and are inclined toward violence. Despite God's disappointment, there is a vow not to strike out in anger but to keep calling out to God's children. Regardless, the consequence of their actions will likely be that they will be delivered again into bondage in Egypt.

and

Ecclesiastes 1:2, 12–14; 2:18–23

The author laments the apparent vanity of life. Why work, simply to pass on the spoils of one's labor to another generation, which could very well be made up of screw-ups? In the end, all of the hard work—mental and physical—adds up to little or nothing, which causes the author no small amount of despair.

Psalm

Psalm 107:1–9, 43

A hymn of thanksgiving to God for providing for the deepest needs of God's faithful. When they seek it, God offers them peace and a sense of contentment that is unmatched to any earthly fulfillment.

and

Psalm 49:1–12

This psalm speaks in a strangely roundabout way of the preciousness of life. One can't work enough or amass enough wealth to justify the gift of life we're given by God; it's priceless. Brilliant minds and idiots all die in the end, so clearly, wisdom isn't the key to eternal life. Our bodies all become worm food.

Second Reading

Colossians 3:1–11

Paul calls on the church members in Colossae to set aside longings that are bound to earthly things that tend to occupy our lives—like greed, sexual appetite, anger, vengeance, and the like—and to enshroud oneself in a new skin, one stitched for us by Christ. It is a sort of living death-and-resurrection experience to which Paul calls the early Christians.

Gospel

Luke 12:13–21

Jesus is approached by brothers to settle a dispute over an inheritance. He warns that material wealth doesn't make for a rich life. He tells the parable of the farmer who stores up grains in great barns. Just as he gets to a place of wealth and comfort, God calls him out, saying he's about to die, so what was the point? The warning is that a life spent storing material treasures but not dwelling in the richness of the spirit is a life of vanity.

Bible, Decoded

Breaking down Scripture in plain language

Ecclesiastes—The Hebrew word for this book is *Qoheleth,* which means "one who speaks to an assembly." In other words, the author—or at least the speaker portrayed by the author—is generally considered to be a religious leader, like a priest or rabbi.

Baal—as noted in previous studies, we can easily mistake the name "Baal" for one particular pagan god. But the passage in Hosea reminds us that we're dealing with "Baals," or hundreds of possible false gods in which the people of Israel are placing their faith.

Points to Ponder

First Thoughts

Qoheleth is undergoing a pretty serious crisis of faith. For those of us who struggle with—or who have even come to accept—doubt as part of our faith experience, there can be some real solace in a figure of religious authority going through something similar. Much of the faith crisis he is going through (we can assume it's a male, given the time period and social standing) revolves around the idea that living life seems like an act of vanity. Believe it or not, this actually reveals some remarkably *good news,* which I'll explore in more detail below.

Most—if not all—of us know that circumcision has to do with removing part of the penis foreskin of a male. Sometimes this is done still today because it is thought by some to help prevent some diseases. It can be seen to be somewhat consistent with other preceding Jewish laws of cleanliness. However, rather than this being done to infants, Paul calls on adult males seeking to covenant with Christ to get circumcised as adults to demonstrate their faithfulness and a sort of death to the flesh. Let me just go on record now as saying how incredibly glad I am that this is no longer a common adult male Christian ritual!

These texts remind me of a statement made recently by Walter Bruggemann at our denomination's general assembly (I'm paraphrasing): God is not impressed with your ability to amass wealth within the context of a kingdom of abundance. I guess it's kind of like spending your life collecting as much salt or sugar as you can, only to load it all onto a sinking ship. Talk about pointless.

Digging Deeper

Mining for what really matters . . . and gold

Some take the verse found in Colossians 3:11 as some kind of politically correct mandate to become color blind or otherwise indifferent to the differences among us. We're all just people, right? Why distinguish one from another based on things like gender, economic status, intelligence, nationality, or anything else?

But that's not what Paul is saying. His point is that these other labels—these means by which we find our identity and value—fall far second to the identity of one who is reborn in the spirit of Christ. And far from a call to some nice, politically correct living, he's suggesting we should expect more of one another. We should look deeper, gazing upon one another's souls, to see the vulnerable, childlike faith that lies beneath.

Such depth of knowing is quite literally disarming, and though it doesn't make us cease to notice other distinctions and differences, it does forge a love that is a stronger bond than the dividing force those differences might otherwise have within our communities.

The kingdom of God is not about making everyone basically the same. That would be boring anyway. It's about connecting us all with a more precious common thread, and holding us together through our struggles, doubts, and mistakes. Put another way, it's not about getting rid of the different parts so that we're one monolithic, homogenous whole. Rather it's about making the whole stronger and greater than the respective parts so that together, we can endure all things and make each other that much greater in our unity.

Heads Up

Connecting the text to our world

The pastors I know are some of the most burned-out folks you'll ever meet. They're overworked and tired, and it's really no surprise to me that a significant number of them end up walking away from their calling to ministry in time, if not their faith all together.

One pastor I know lasted only three years in his final ministerial position. In that time, he lost about forty pounds, along with his faith. When he resigned as pastor, he decided to move to Hawaii and start practicing *reiki*. Not that there's anything wrong with this particular style of quasi-mystical massage, but it ain't exactly downtown Christian church ministry.

Why is this? Aren't our religious leaders supposed to be the ones who are faithful in spite of, well ... everything? Aren't they the ones who are supposed to help us through our hard times by leaning on their own faith and wisdom? This is pretty much what is happening to the religious leader portrayed in Ecclesiastes. It wouldn't surprise me to find out that just past the end of this book, he took off for Hawaii to do *reiki*.

But ministers, like most everyone else, fall victim to the same kind of earthly traps as anyone else. They get preoccupied with making the budget, building an endowment, expanding the membership rolls, and putting on the perfect worship service. But in the end, people come and go, they are born and die, they find faith and lose it. Does it all really make a difference?

When Amy and I finally decided it was time to leave Pueblo, Colorado, where we started and nurtured a new church to life for eight years, she was terrified by the prospect that it might wither and die in our absence.

"And what if it does?" I asked. Does that mean that the experience we had, the moments in which we felt so close to God we could nearly taste it, were all for nothing? After all, if we measured Jesus's ministry the way we measure most of ours, he was a total failure. There has to be more to life, it seems. And yet we're so easily tempted back into the same old ways of thinking and acting, even in the church.

Prayer for the Week

God, I occupy myself with plenty of vain activities every day. And yet, I look around, seeking real meaning in my life. Help make clear to me what in my world is truly of value so that I can aside those things and activities that yield nothing but a life of vanity.

Popping Off

Art/music/video and other cool stuff that relate to the text

The Great Gatsby, by F. Scott Fitzgerald (book, 1925; movie, 1974, 2013)

All In

Lectionary Texts For
August 11, 2019 (Ninth Sunday after Pentecost)

Texts in Brief
My dog ate my Bible!

First Reading
Isaiah 1:1, 10–20
God finds all of the offerings given by the people of Sodom to be repugnant. He tells them to stop making offerings and instead to focus on personal conversion and care for the outcast. The admonition concludes with a promise that if they are contrite, their transgressions will be forgiven.

and

Genesis 15:1–6
God promises great rewards to Abram for his faithfulness, but Abram is distraught because he has no

children to leave his estate to. God promises that he will have an heir of his own blood and that his descendants will outnumber the stars.

Psalm
Psalm 50:1–8, 22–23

God is described as a devouring fire that judges all. God warns people that their offerings do not grant them an indulgence from God; the sacrifices were merely a sign of covenant between God and humanity. Rather, what God requires for forgiveness is a grateful heart and a willingness to change.

and

Psalm 33:12–22

No army or personal strength is sufficient to overcome death. God's love is the only thing standing between us and destruction.

Second Reading
Hebrews 11:1–3, 8–16

Paul explains that faith is manifest in assurance that those promises not yet fulfilled or entirely understood by humanity will indeed come to be. It is this kind of "assurance of things hoped for" that binds us to God rather than good acts or sufficient sacrifices. He points to the blessings bestowed on Abram/Abraham as an example of how God keeps God's promises.

GOSPEL

Luke 12:32–40

Jesus reminds us that wherever we invest our hearts, whatever we deem important by giving it our time and effort, that is what we will yield for ourselves. He also reminds us that only heavenly things are not destroyed in time. He invites us to be like the hopeful servant who waits by the door for his or her master to come home. He may not see the master but has faith in his imminent return.

Bible, Decoded

Breaking down Scripture in plain language

Slave—It's easy to get hung up on the word *slave* in Scripture, and for good reason. First, this is an example of how cultural norms dictate what is considered humane and what is wrong, rather than there being some absolute guide that is eternal and permanent. But it would also be a mistake to draw too many parallels between biblical-era slaves and American slaves earlier in our history. Throughout the Old Testament, there are specific rules about the human treatment of slaves, and generally it is believed they were more like live-in servants in most cases than the way slaves were treated in colonial America.

Abram/Abraham—Considered to be the genealogical ancestor for all of Christianity, Islam, and Judaism, it is from Abram's lineage that all of the tribes of Israel emerged. God renames Abram as Abraham to indicate

292 | SURVIVING THE BIBLE

the covenant they have together. His name means "father of many."

Zion—The city high on a hill on which David's city was built. It suggests God's divine favor and protection as well as the fulfillment of a promise.

Points to Ponder
First Thoughts

Folks tend to get hung up on the idea of sexual sin as the reason the city of Sodom was cursed by God. But in this passage from Isaiah, we see that God's consternation stems from the peoples' habit of making sacrifices as a sort of "salvation Band-Aid" so they could justify continuing to do whatever they really wanted to. But God doesn't accept sacrifices as payment for sin; rather, God requires a change of the human heart for true salvation. God doesn't need anything from us. The act of sacrifice is merely supposed to be an outward expression of an inward promise.

Despite the content given above about the nature of slavery during these times, I struggle to get past the parallel Jesus draws between us and God as being like the relationship of master/slave. Why not parent/child, or husband/wife? Chances are that Jesus was speaking—as he tended to do—to those on the margins of society. Those form the wrong side of the tracks, without a stellar pedigree. Probably the kind of people who would have served as house servants or slaves back then. So rather than seeing this as Jesus condoning slavery, it makes more sense to consider he was speaking to his audience in a context that would make the most real-world sense to them.

The early Christians who received this letter from Paul, found in Hebrews, were probably struggling. As we know, most of the early churchgoers were harshly persecuted for practicing this new, subversive religion. So if they got too hung up on present circumstances, it could be easy to understand why they might lose heart. Paul is encouraging them to keep their eyes set on a broader timeline, a greater goal. In other words: present struggles do not change the fact that God keeps the promises God makes.

Digging Deeper

Mining for what really matters . . . and gold

There are several rich elements to pick from in this week's texts. From God's promises to humanity, to the kind of faith to which we're called, and even to the treatment of slaves, the verbal soil is broad and rich. But personally, the theme of the role of sacrifices speaks volumes to how we should reframe our understanding of Jesus's crucifixion.

Historically—or at least in the past few hundred years—it has been the consensus among most Christians that "Jesus died for our sins." Basically, it's been practically universal doctrine to assert that at the core of our Christian faith is the belief that humanity's sins are intolerable in God's presence, and that without a perfect, innocent sacrifice found in Jesus, we would have been lost forever.

But here's the thing: Jesus forgave sins before he died. And generally, we tend to agree that Christians understand Jesus and God to be one and the same. So which is it? Can God tolerate sin or not? Perhaps it's a matter of volume; after a certain critical mass, the sin just becomes too much to handle without blood atonement. Or perhaps it's one of those things where God just got tired of forgiving sin one at a time, opting instead for a panacea that would fix the problem once and for all.

But as we can see as early as the prophet Isaiah, or even back in Genesis regarding the city of Sodom, sacrifice in and of itself is basically worthless to God. If we're using any sacrifice—be it a check in the offering plate, a burnt offering on an ancient altar, or even Jesus's death on the cross—as an excuse to carry on as we always have before, there's no value to it. We get so hung up on the act of Jesus's death as the big thing that we miss the covenant—the holy promise—to which it is meant to point.

And what is that promise? That no matter what we do, where we run, or how badly we fail, God will welcome us back. God would give up everything for us, but will we be equally committed to the relationship? God puts it all on the line, and just offering a token of faithfulness isn't good enough. There's no balance in such a relationship. We have to be all in.

Heads Up

Connecting the text to our world

When I was a little kid, probably in the first or second grade, my dad worked late. He was an insurance salesman, working in one of those little makeshift booths in a shopping mall. Because he was the low man on the totem pole, he was given the late shift and had to close down every night. As such, he usually came home well after I was already in bed.

What my mom didn't know was that I rarely, if ever, actually fell asleep until I knew he was home. I would listen as the cars drifted by in the dark, listening intently for his car, which I could distinguish from at least a block away. I would smile and pull the sheets up tight near my neck as I saw his headlights sweep across the wall in my room as he pulled into the driveway. I would only close my eyes after I heard the back door close and the muffled sound of his voice greeting my mom.

He almost never came in to kiss me good night. As far as he knew, I had been asleep for an hour or so. And it wasn't so much that I needed him to come in as I wanted to know he was home and that we were, once again, a whole family. For some reason I slept better knowing he was there, even if I hadn't actually seen him.

This is the kind of faithful anticipation Jesus implores us to have in our anticipation of our complete reconciliation with the divine. In another text, Paul suggests we should meet God's call daily with the childlike anticipation equivalent to, "What's Next, Papa?" The child's question in this sense is absent of all pretense and expectation, filled instead with eager trust that, no matter what happens, everything ultimately will be all right.

Can we muster such faith? The kind that holds no conditions over God? The kind that trusts without seeing, that asks, "What next?" even as the idea of an uncertain future terrifies us? I think I can, or at least I could once. What a wonderful gift my younger self could offer, if only I had held on to such innocent trust and anticipation.

Prayer for the Week

God, I know I tend to only wade into your deep waters of grace only halfway. Help me go all in, to follow your example, and to trust your promise that, even if things seem tough right now, there's a peace that passes all understanding and a grace that holds the world together in the end.

Popping Off

Art/music/video and other cool stuff that relate to the text

Hoosiers (movie, 1986)

Moneyball (movie, 2011)

Burn It Down

Lectionary Texts For
August 18, 2019 (Tenth Sunday after Pentecost)

Texts in Brief
My dog ate my Bible!

FIRST READING
Isaiah 5:1–7

The prophet compares the people of Israel to a vineyard planted by God. The vineyard was supposed to yield nourishing, healthy grapes but instead yielded wild fruit. Although God established Israelites to seek peace and righteousness, they have turned to bloodshed and suffering. So Isaiah prophesies that God will turn God's back on them, and they will suffer the inevitable consequences of their own actions.

and

Jeremiah 23:23–29

The prophet Jeremiah delivers a word from God, reminding the Jewish people that God is ever-close and not far removed from our lives. God warns the turning of the people of Israel toward the prophets of false gods (Baal) and reminds the reader that the true word of God will cut through all falsehood and burn it away.

PSALM

Psalm 80:1–2, 8–19

A song of praise to God for delivering the Jewish people from the land of Egypt and preparing a place for them called Israel. The psalmist uses the same vineyard metaphor as Isaiah, thanking God for provision and protection, and vowing that God's people will no longer stray from the path laid out for them.

and

Psalm 82

A song of mourning from God's perspective about having given particular stature to the Jewish people, effectively placing them on level ground with their creator. However, they did not live up to their honored status by behaving in a godlike manner. They acted selfishly and without regard for the poor and vulnerable. They did not show compassion to their neighbor in the same way that God showed compassion to them. God, with a heavy heart, welcomes judgment upon them for their shortcomings.

Second Reading
Hebrews 11:29–12:2

Paul lists many stories throughout the Bible in which people of faith persevered and emerged victorious because of the faith in God that they demonstrated. He also notes the many martyrs who have suffered or even died on behalf of their faith. He reminds them that they are part of a greater body, which he calls the great cloud of witnesses, who are there to help us endure the struggles and stay on the righteous path. Run the good race, he says. Stay focused on the final goal rather than being distracted by the hills and valleys along the way.

Gospel
Luke 12:49–56

Jesus harshly criticizes the crowd for not recognizing the state of the world right in front of them. He labels them as hypocrites for speaking of one set of values while living out another. Although people believe he has come to bring peace, he turns that notion on its head, noting that he is instead here to bring division, even to families.

Bible, Decoded
Breaking down Scripture in plain language

Crowds—We never know how many people the Gospel authors are talking about when they refer to Jesus speaking to "crowds." But the number doesn't matter; what's important is what it's supposed to tell us, the reader. Just like when Jesus—or other prophets, for that matter—speaks from a hillside or mountain, speaking before a crowd indicates that he is saying something important. Is this account in Luke one that someone who was there wrote down? Maybe, but not likely. Rather, it's an essential truth of Jesus's teaching that the author is trying to get us to really pay attention to.

Vineyard—Back in Jesus's day, vineyards were pretty important, especially in the valley. They were a way of life for many, aside from the enjoyment of drinking wine or nourishment of eating the grapes. Grapes and their byproducts were major staples of the region and held big cultural significance in the surrounding culture. One reason biblical authors and Jesus all reference wine, grapes, and vineyards so much is because it was an important part of life to which everyone could relate.

Cherubim—the plural form of "cherub," these are angelic beings who tend to indicate the nearness of God in Scripture. They first appear in Genesis as guardians of the path to the tree of life.

Points to Ponder

First Thoughts

How we interpret the bad stuff that is to descend upon the people of Israel tells us a lot about our image of God. If God is actively punishing them, is God a sadist? If God allows bad things to happen, is God indifferent? If God can't stop the consequences of human free will, is God weak? Rather than settling too quickly on an answer, it might be more helpful to wrestle with each of these questions, along with the feelings they raise in us.

One could interpret Paul's text in Hebrews as a departure from the Old Testament Scriptures that seem to draw direct lines between the faithlessness of the people of Israel and the crises that befall them. Instead, Paul notes that, time and again, promises are fulfilled for God's faithful. Nonetheless, some seem to be called to an existence beset with struggle and even great suffering. But Paul says if we focus too much on the present difficulties, we miss the big picture . . . we fail to engage with the imagination of God. Consider this: if you're exhausted from running, would it be easier to keep going if you knew the end was close rather than if all you could think about was how bad your legs and lungs were killing you? Keeping our eyes on the horizon helps place the present in a healthier context. Good advice, Dr. Paul!

Some people really struggle with this text in Luke and how it portrays Jesus. Most of my friends who are members of the NRA love it! In some translations, Jesus says he comes with a sword rather than just coming to bring division. So while there's room to interpret this as one of the only times Jesus may be advocating violence, that's not what I take away. Rather, he is welcoming the "refiner's fire," which will help separate those things that are life-giving from what is life-taking. And sometimes those life-taking forces can be found even within our own families. So maybe the division that Jesus speaks of here is more about liberation by separating us from what binds us rather than creating a violent, fractured culture for fun. Yes, ultimately he comes as the Prince of Peace. But can there really be peace while so many are still in chains, both literally and figuratively?

Digging Deeper
Mining for what really matters . . . and gold

The fifty-cent word for the question raised in the first paragraph above is *theodicy*. Namely, how do we reconcile our understanding of a loving, gracious, forgiving God with all of the suffering we witness and experience in the world? Is God doing this to us? Or is God at least letting this happen to us? And what does this tell us about the nature of God?

These seemingly contradictory images of God have existed long before the Judeo-Christian tradition came along. I think part of the problem emerges when we try too hard to humanize God, to create God in our own image, so to speak. I find that when I liberate my understanding of God from the trappings of human will, consciousness, and emotion, the whole issue becomes a lot clearer.

Take the phrase "God is love." Semantically, we would call this a synonym, meaning that we could use the words "God" and "love" interchangeably. Who among us, having experienced love, has not been hurt along the way? There is even the old classic rock song that warned us decades ago that love hurts. We know this, and for the most part, we don't try to blame love for the pain. We understand it is part of the risk, an inevitable part of life.

We don't love because of the promise of the absence of suffering; we love in spite of the inevitability of suffering. It's hurt before, and it will hurt again, but we resolve to keep going, to avail ourselves of the risk. It is in the midst of that risk that we find the stuff of real life. We find God. We find love.

Heads Up

Connecting the text to our world

It's easy to attribute prosperous times to God's blessings and, especially for those who believe in an actively punishing God, to presume that the lean times are some sort of penance meant to teach us a lesson. In my own life, I know I don't sit around and ask "Why?" when things are going well. Those kinds of reflections only arise when I'm in the midst of struggle, mostly because I want the struggle to stop.

Yes, I would love to say that in the midst of my suffering, I am able to center myself and focus on the potential wisdom to be gleaned from the moment. But in most cases, I would be lying. Generally, I'm just as desperate as anyone else to find the solution, to get back to the way it was, to make the hurting stop.

There is no question that the church is in the midst of one of those difficult times. There is no shortage of people looking around, arms in the air, asking "Why?" But like in our own personal lives, most of those questions emerge from a place of seeking a quick solution, a way to avoid any more discomfort and to get back to the good old days when everything seemed to be going well.

And then we have this text from Luke 12:49–56, where Jesus says that rather than coming to bring peace, he comes to bring division. Wait a minute . . . isn't this supposed to be the Prince of Peace guy? What about all the beatific scenes with Jesus holding cute little lambs and patting children on the head? Those kids and those sheep come with no encumbrances. No baggage. They don't come to Jesus with some set agenda about how they want their life to turn out, or how they plan to see their congregation get turned around, back to some magical 1950s–era ideal. They just come with their whole selves. That's it.

Seems to me they don't need to be divided from anything. There's nothing weighing them down, keeping them from traveling down that narrow path. But like the rich man who asks how to enter the kingdom of heaven, we come with so many demands, expectations, wishes, caveats, and conditions to God's table that it's hard to tell who's really under all that crap.

Maybe we need some help sorting through the baggage in our lives and our churches. Maybe some of it—more likely a hell of a lot of it—needs to be tossed in the fire. We're the emotional and institutional equivalents of a subject on the show *Hoarders* who sits around in the piles of shit, wondering why, in spite of all the stuff, we feel so isolated, alone, and desperate.

Ok Jesus, help cut and burn away all the crap I can't seem to set down on my own. Give it away, throw it on the garbage pile . . . whatever you want. Maybe then, with a clearer head and unburdened arms, I'll have a little bit more time and energy to invest in this whole peace thing.

Prayer for the Week

God, I can't seem to lay all of my crap down on my own. Help burn it away for me. Show me what really matters, and let the rest slip through my fingers like sand.

Popping Off

Art/music/video and other cool stuff that relate to the text

Brewster's Millions (movie, 1985)

Ruthless People (movie, 1986)

Chill Out

Lectionary Texts For
August 25, 2019 (Eleventh Sunday after Pentecost)

Texts in Brief
My dog ate my Bible!

First Reading
Jeremiah 1:4–10

The prophet Jeremiah explains the experience of being anointed by God to speak on God's behalf and to have power over the nations. He explains that God knew him since before he was born, and God will not hear his complaints of inadequacy. God assures Jeremiah that he will have what he needs for the job.

and

Isaiah 58:9b–14

The prophet Isaiah offers a promise of renewal and rejuvenation from God to the people of Israel. But in order for this blessing to come, they must choose themselves to remove the un-godlike attitudes and actions from their midst. The promise of blessing is certain, and they are the only things keeping themselves from it.

PSALM

Psalm 71:1–6

A prayer offered to God, seeking rescue and refuge from the world. The psalmist acknowledges that God has been with him since the moment of his creation.

and

Psalm 103:1–8

A song of praise to God for offering rejuvenation and renewal; a return to use, as it were. God is just, compassionate, slow to anger, and abundant in love.

SECOND READING

Hebrews 12:18–29

The apostle Paul offers words of wisdom to the early church. He reminds them of their history, of the covenants between God and Moses, and of God and Abel. He reminds them of the importance of heeding the words of the prophets, and how this was essential to the delivery of the people of Israel from destruction. He notes that this new covenant offered by Jesus is even more important and binding, as are his words of warning not to cling too tightly to the material world. Jesus notes that these things ultimately will fade away, and that the unimportant things of the world will be consumed by divine fire. What is left will be the incorruptible, unshakable kingdom of God, of which they are invited to be a part.

GOSPEL
Luke 13:10–17

Jesus gets in trouble with the leaders of the synagogue for healing a crippled woman on the Sabbath. He calls them out as hypocrites since each of them would care for their animals on the Sabbath. Shouldn't, then, this woman who is seeking out God's healing be afforded at least the same compassion that a vulnerable animal would be? His critics are silenced, and the crowd praised him.

Bible, Decoded
Breaking down Scripture in plain language

Sabbath—A divinely sanctioned day of rest once a week, intended to be given over to God and to the body's need for rest and renewal. It is based on the story in Genesis following the creation of the heavens and the earth, when God was said to have rested on the seventh day. However, some religious leaders were trying to use this and other Jewish laws to get Jesus in trouble, as he did not conform to the social order that they managed.

Fire—Usually when we think of fire, we think of something destructive. But when this symbol is applied to God in Scripture, it tends to be something that helps remove the things that get in the way of our relationship with God. Rather than something to be feared, like the images of hell portrayed in Dante's *Inferno*, it is something to be welcomed as a source of liberation.

The pit—This phrase is used fairly interchangeably in the Old Testament with the Jewish understanding of *sheol*. We sometimes mistake this for a modern understanding of hell, a place of eternal conscious torment. There was no such belief in ancient Jewish culture. Rather, the pit—or *sheol*—was a place of rest for all of the dead, both good and evil. When someone is rescued from "the pit," it is more about being delivered from a death-dealing, fruitless life than it is about protection from existential suffering in the afterlife.

Points to Ponder

First Thoughts

This passage in Luke is yet another example of Jesus leaning on the rule of love rather than the rule of law. He recognizes that the laws given to the people of Israel have become a tool by which those in power control and even oppress others. And as he always does, he is careful not to simply toss the law aside. Rather, he reveals the weaknesses and flaws in their application of the law, rendering it fairly impotent, especially compared with the rules of love found in the greatest commandment.

Sometimes we need to be reminded where we came from. One of the most important things that Paul did in guiding and encouraging the early church was to constantly remind them that they were part of something bigger, a continuing narrative that is part of a much longer, richer story. This is not unlike what we have to do with our children, who inevitably believe at one time or another that the things they are going through are utterly unique to them, never having been experienced by anyone in history before. And it's not that we have to minimize those feelings. In offering a broader, more mature perspective, we can hopefully help avoid making some of the same childish mistakes, over and over again, be they personal or institutional.

Digging Deeper
Mining for what really matters . . . and gold

There are a couple of recurring themes in these texts for the week. First, there is the idea of Sabbath, or renewal. It is interesting to point out that simply taking a nap or stopping work for a while does not connect people in these texts to the source of what rejuvenates them. It does, however, require them to set aside the rest of their busyness and distraction to make room for the waters of renewal to well up from within them.

Sometimes people talk about the Sabbath as if God is lonely or jealous and requires some sort of joint custody agreement with the rest of our demands. But actually, that Sabbath time is for us; it is the source from which we draw not just to get through the other six days of the week, but that from which we find the necessary perspective to work with purpose and the inspired sense of conviction that helps us keep going when the going gets tough.

There is also this theme of being known since the beginning of our creation. It feels, in a sense, like the stories about guardian angels that some people tell, about having that presence guiding them when they could not do it themselves, illuminating the path when they felt like they were blindly stumbling in the darkness. It is a reassuring image, but it also helps me gain some healthy perspective on what God-like patience must be. When we pray, we want results, not soon, not later—right now!

But to think that we were crafted with such love and care, and then allowed over the years and decades to find our own way, screwing it up over and over again—it points to a grace and patience that I could not conceive of summoning in myself.

Heads Up

Connecting the text to our world

There's rich irony in me writing about Sabbath. I'm one of the most notorious violators of days of rest that I know. Technically, I have one "day off" a week. But of course, I am writing this lectionary study on a Monday! So yes, I am as much of a hypocrite as the rabbis trying to corner Jesus for doing good work on the Jewish day of rest.

Of course, God never intended for an invitation to Sabbath to be a means by which people would be controlled, manipulated, or even punished by those in power. God knew—and God knows—that we can always find more to do. And sometimes we find it much easier to occupy ourselves with work (in parentheses or any host of other activities, for that matter) rather than slowing down and spending intentional time with the still, small voice within us.

That's the thing about God, at least these days. I don't know about you, but I have seen no pillars of fire, no burning bushes, no fat little naked kids with wings telling me things that are magically going to happen in my life. That's not how God works with me. In fact, God never insists God's self on me. I consider it more of a standing invitation, an open call back to the wellspring, as it were. But God is not in the business of pinning me down and force-feeding me the waters of renewal.

I often employ the phrase, only half-jokingly, "There is no rest for the wicked." But honestly, when I think about the message and the values of the culture around me, and when I think of the insistent voices in my head, always telling me to do more and be more, it is a corrupted, distorted notion of what it means to live well. And if in fact a life of balance, hard work, and occasional renewal is ordained by God, then I am (and I will go out on a limb and guess that most of you are) living counter to God's intentions for me.

Why should you listen to a hypocrite like me, writing about Sabbath on his day off? You probably shouldn't. But like the prophet Jeremiah, sometimes God places words of wisdom in the mouths of fools. Busy, distracted, overworked fools.

Prayer for the Week

God, help me shake the mistaken belief that rest is the same as laziness. Remind me that I am so much more than the sum total of what I can do. Even when I turn my back on your invitation to Sabbath, please keep the invitation open.

Popping Off

Art/music/video and other cool stuff that relate to the text

"KidGuilt: Are Parents Working Too Much?" from News.com.au (article, 2012): tinyurl.com/ya4sym3v

God Grew Tired of Us (movie, 2006)

I'm Awesomely Humble

Lectionary Texts For

September 1, 2019 (Twelfth Sunday after Pentecost)

Texts in Brief

My dog ate my Bible!

First Reading

Jeremiah 2:4–13

The prophet shares God's mournful disappointment that the people of Israel have turned from God, even after being delivered from the desert into a land of plenty. Their transgressions are twofold: forsaking God and trying to create new false gods for themselves.

and

Proverbs 25:6–7

A wise call to humility, the author of the proverb warns that it's better to place yourself in a lower social standing and be elevated by those around you than to assume you belong in an elevated position, only to be knocked down a few notches by someone else.

PSALM
Psalm 81:1, 10–16

The psalmist echoes the mournful observations of Jeremiah, noting that although God promises protection and bountiful nourishment for God's people, God also does not force human hearts to turn away from self-serving ways. Much good awaits those who turn to God, and much woe falls on the heads of the self-righteous. But it is by their own choosing that they stray.

and

Psalm 112

This psalm presents the other side of the coin, so to speak. It celebrates the lives of the faithful, noting that their faithfulness not only is rewarded by God but that it also is obvious in all that they do. They share generously with those who have less, and they have nothing to for in the face of their enemies. Meanwhile, the unjust long for fulfillment from things that will never yield what they truly desire.

SECOND READING
Hebrews 13:1–8, 15–16

Paul offers a sort of quick guide to a faithful life. As is the case with Jesus, he places love first; from this, everything falls into place. Remember the imprisoned, honor marriage vows, care for the poor, and offer hospitality to the stranger. Just in case people aren't sure what to do, they should look to their spiritual leaders for example.

GOSPEL

Luke 14:1, 7–14

This is the scene of one of several "great reversal" stories in Luke. As is the case quite often, in this Gospel, those who think they're awesome are knocked down a few notches, and those who act out of humility are elevated. He also warns those in attendance not to use what they have to leverage favor with others; rather, he urges them to offer freely what they have to those who have nothing to give in return.

Bible, Decoded

Breaking down Scripture in plain language

Banquet—Jesus's parable focuses on a dinner banquet, which is a common theme throughout the Gospels, and some might suggest it's a metaphor for the kingdom of God. It represents community, ritual, nourishment, and inclusion . . . many attributes found in Jesus's description of the kingdom. And although we have all-you-can-eat buffets on every corner, the idea back then of a plentiful layout of all the best food and drink was a pretty special thing.

Sacrifice—Paul outlines the new kind of sacrifices required by God's faithful: constant praise, generosity, and acts of mercy rather than burnt offerings. Such is the way of the new covenant. We can see glimmers of this turn away from the kind of sacrifices offered by Jewish people and pagans as early on as Abraham and Isaac. When God stops Abraham from sacrificing his son, it is effectively a call for the end of so-called burnt offerings, which usually were animals that were slaughtered and then burned in honor of God.

Righteous—Often times, the righteous in the Jewish culture were considered those who knew the Jewish laws well and followed them closely. But God apparently isn't impressed with simply following written laws, and especially those who elevate themselves above others because of their adherence to the law or because of social status. Rather, Paul, Jesus, and the psalmist all point to acts of love, mercy, compassion, generosity, and hospitality as the means by which we demonstrate righteousness—and through doing so humbly, with no expectation of anything in return.

Points to Ponder

First Thoughts

The texts urge us to offer what we have generously to others with no expectation of anything in return. But this is really hard for us humans. Whether we truly ever do anything from a place of pure selflessness is debatable. Though some might suggest altruism is something we can really achieve, others could reasonable contend that is it more of an ideal we can look toward but never reach. Perhaps Jesus knows this, as he hangs the promise of a reward in the coming kingdom for those who can really pull it off. So maybe it's more about delayed gratification—really, really delayed—rather than trying to be entirely selfless. Still not easy, but maybe a little bit more manageable.

Though it's not in this week's lectionary texts, all the talk of humility makes me think of the Scriptures from Galatians and Corinthians to boast only in Christ. I'm not sure what this means, but given the fact that one of the words most commonly associated with Christians when folks are surveyed is "arrogant," I'd wager we aren't exactly getting this one right. I think what Paul means is that when folks try to celebrate or elevate us, we should use it as an opportunity to tell them about the source of our inspiration and purpose in Jesus. I find it hard to imagine that Paul would approve of jingoist hyper-nationalism or using Christianity as a bludgeon to subjugate others. Rather, we're meant to divert attention off of ourselves and toward God by way of the teachings and life of Jesus.

Digging Deeper
Mining for what really matters . . . and gold

The Christian ethic of humility is so counter-cultural, especially in our increasingly cluttered, noisy, and competitive world. If we're not going to actively promote ourselves, telling folks how incredibly awesome we are, who will?

Interestingly—sadly, really—when young, school-age children were asked recently what they wanted to be when they grew up, the number one answer offered was "famous." And in fact, we have a media culture that enervates mediocrity as its own curious virtue. If you don't agree, watch an episode of *Jersey Shore*. We're so desperate for attention, for validation, that we'll go to insane lengths to get it.

Leaders are admired in our culture—those who can rise to the top and achieve greatness—especially if they can seem to do it on their own. Self-reliance is practically its own American religion, and pulling oneself up from the bootstraps is a quasi-spiritual practice. But this is not what God requires. In fact, Jeremiah goes as far as calling this sort of thinking and behaving as akin to worshipping false Gods. Ouch!

As someone who makes his living in the public eye, traveling the world talking about myself and my work, this cuts to the quick. Can such work really be done in the name of service to God, or am I (along with so many of my peers) fooling myself to accommodate a way of life I really want selfishly at the expense of what the gospel calls me to?

Suffice it to say that this will be the mantra of my prayer this week.

Heads Up

Connecting the text to our world

Amy once offered a sermon on humility at our former church in Colorado. One guy, whom I'll call Hector, always had something interesting to say in response to the sermon, but this week was a chart-topper. And although it was one of the funnier moments I can remember in my time in ministry (I still have bite marks on my lip from the experience; self-control isn't easy for me), it was pretty obvious from his comments that he didn't get it.

"That was a really good message today," Hector nodded, shaking Amy's hand. "I always like hearing about how humble we're supposed to be in our Christian walk." Then he took a deep, thoughtful breath. "Personally," he said, "I'm a pretty humble guy. I'm actually much more humble than I tend to give myself credit for."

Oh, how many times I have longed to have that phrase printed on a T-shirt! But for some reason, Amy won't let me.

But the reason Hector's comments were so funny wasn't just because he kind of missed the whole point, or because his celebration of his own humility was so richly ironic. It was funny, at least to me, because he was actually the most honest person in the room that morning. After all, most of us would like to think of ourselves as humble, and if we're telling the truth, we'd love to be recognized for that humble disposition. Part of the appeal of someone like Mother Theresa isn't that she lived in squalor with the untouchables of Calcutta for decades but rather that she's been elevated to sainthood for it.

Who doesn't want to be a saint? Who wouldn't love to have statues of themselves in front of the great cathedrals of the world or in the parks of every big city? Maybe if we present our humility in just the right place and time, we'll finally get the credit we deserve. We'll get elevated to the spot where we know we actually belong.

Hang on, says Jesus. If there's any ulterior motive behind our acts of humble faithfulness, then it's not actually humility or faithfulness. It's self-serving, which is counter to the fundamental message of the gospel: *It's not all about you; get over yourself.*

Prayer for the Week

God, help me better understand how I can pursue serving you while also finding real joy and meaning in my life. Help me not find worth in the praise of others, or in book sales, blog metrics, job titles, or socioeconomic status. Rather, help me use any opportunity I can to point people more toward you.

Popping Off

Art/music/video and other cool stuff that relate to the text

Mean Girls (movie, 2004)

What Women Want (movie, 2000)

Stay Green,
Christians

—–∿–—

Lectionary Texts For

September 8, 2019 (Thirteenth Sunday after Pentecost)

Texts in Brief

My dog ate my Bible!

First Reading

Jeremiah 18:1–11

Jeremiah witnesses a potter turning a worthless pot into something usable and beautiful. God tells Jeremiah that he can do this and much more with the people of Israel. Basically, no person or nation is beyond the redemption of God.

and

Deuteronomy 30:15–20

The author of Deuteronomy is warning the people of Israel what will happen if they stray from God's commandments, which is, of course, precisely what does happen when they do just that. Basically, there are two paths laid out: one of life and prosperity, and one of death and destruction. Those who obey God will find life, and those who look elsewhere for meaning will watch all that is of true value slip between their fingers.

Psalm

Psalm 139:1–6, 13–18

A beautiful piece of poetry about how intimately and thoroughly known by our Creator we truly are. God knew us before we were born, helped get us together in our mother's womb, and knows us so completely that every hair on our head is counted. No one else on earth knows us for what we truly are like God does.

and

Psalm 1

Another word of warning that resonates with the cautions laid out in the Deuteronomy text. Those who cling to God and God's Word will prosper; those who stray will perish.

Second Reading

Philemon 1:1–1:21

Paul and Timothy write a letter to Philemon on behalf of Onesimus. Paul has become somewhat of a father figure and mentor to him, and he asks that Philemon put him to work for the cause of the new Christian community. Formerly, Onesimus was considered less than human, fairly worthless. But now Paul says he is of great value, and so Paul is pleading on his behalf. He wants to see that all of his former debts are settled and that he is treated as an equal, a brother, rather than a lesser person or as property.

GOSPEL
Luke 14:25–33

Jesus is speaking in measured hyperbole to those who are following him about the cost of being one of his disciples. Basically, when met with the question, "What does it take to truly be a disciple of Christ?," his response is, "Everything you've got." Not only do you have to be willing to give up all of your possessions, but even your emotional bonds to friends and family. It is an investment that cannot be made through half measures.

Bible, Decoded
Breaking down Scripture in plain language

Potter—The metaphor of God being the potter and of us being God's clay is common throughout Scripture. Basically, it speaks to our need to submit to whatever it is that God will make us into. Today's modern-day equivalent might be that God is the programmer, and we are the code.

Disciple—Lots of people followed Jesus around, but there were few that actually became disciples. They were kind of like the samurai of the early Christian movement, and like the samurai, there were probably plenty of people who thought it would be cool to be like them. But Jesus was pretty sure that most of them had no idea how much it would cost them to really be a disciple. The ones who gave their lives over to discipleship of Jesus left everything and everyone behind. Most of them ended up being killed for following him, and yet they did it anyway. The pay sucked, the hours were long, and there really wasn't much respect or glamour in the gig. For most, the calling to discipleship would require a price far too high. Jesus wanted no one to be caught by surprise by this.

Points to Ponder

First Thoughts

Christians tend to get into a lot of trouble when it comes to hate. There are plenty of us who are quick to show disdain, judgment, or intolerance toward anything different than us, and when we come across Scriptures like this one in Luke, it seems we can even find justification in the example of Jesus to lean on human hatred. But as was often the case, Jesus spoke in extremes to get people's attention, to really get them thinking about how serious his mission and ministry were. Does he really mean we have to hate our loved ones? No, but if we place them before our obedience to what is right, they can become more of a hindrance than a blessing.

Sometimes we mistake rigidity for faithfulness. We believe that keeping things the way they are is what our calling is in fulfilling the mandates of the gospel. But really, very little ever stayed the same during the life and ministry of Jesus, from what we can tell. He didn't stay in one place for very long, he hung out with all kinds of different people, and his message changed depending on who he was talking to. Paul, too, talks about flexibility as part of our cultural competency in connecting with other people as Christians. But so often, we value our traditions and rituals above the people we are meant to serve, and in doing so we become like brittle branches, splintered and broken by the slightest change.

Digging Deeper

Mining for what really matters . . . and gold

Is anyone ever beyond God's redemption? Is it ever too late, or can we ever go so far that God can no longer make use of us? Certainly we have all felt this way at one time or another. We know people who have said as much to us, either about themselves or others. But if the one who created us has truly known our inner workings—our motivations, our flaws, and our true potential all along—then how could we possibly be beyond repair?

There is a flipside to this. We have seen the tendency of some Christians to feel as if they could get away with nearly anything, so long as they have their fire insurance in place and have a decent sense of timing when things go down. But this is not when any of the texts this week are talking about. None of it is about any of us getting what we do or don't deserve. Rather, it is more about what keeps us from living into our full God-given potential. And the only thing that seems to be that stumbling block is us.

There are temptations and distractions everywhere we look, but the only power that they really have over us is what power we give them. If we keep all of these other things in their proper context, and if we keep our hearts and minds firmly fixed on the commandment that the only thing that really matters is love, those things that hem us in, constrain us, heap false value upon us, or incline us to play it safe lose their effectiveness on us.

Jesus didn't hate the world or anything in it. Time and again, throughout the Bible, we hear about how God so loved—and loves—the world. The difference is that Jesus knows not to cling too tightly to those things that are not firmly anchored, that ultimately will crumble away. The only truly sustainable, enduring resource is that of divinely inspired love. But the cost of submitting to that love is cutting ties with everything else that has any power in our lives.

Heads Up

Connecting the text to our world

My son, Mattias, wanted to do something special for the last day of summer before he went back to school. His mom and sister were going to the nail salon for pedicures, and that didn't quite fit with what he had in mind. So the boys headed to the skate park.

He's always been an adventurous boy, and certainly more fearless than I ever was. I was so fearful that I rode my skateboard on my butt or stomach until the third grade, and I didn't take the training wheels off my bike until two of the bigger kids in my neighborhood decided it was time and did it for me. Mattias, on the other hand, is going into the fourth grade and was "dropping in" on the top of eight-foot ramps with kids four and five years older than him.

He watched with longing as they skittered up the other side of the wall to the top of the opposing on foot. Finally, he had to try it for himself. The first few times, his ride made it to the top, and his body didn't. But this didn't dissuade him. He just got back up and tried again. On the fourth try, he fell backward instead of forward, landing with his full weight on his left wrist.

The emergency room diagnosed him with both a stress fracture and something called a torus fracture, also called a "green stick" fracture. Because kids' bones are softer and more pliable, sometimes they end up with a bend rather than a full break. The doctor explained that, like a stick that dries and gets more brittle with age, so do our bones, and that he was lucky to be so resilient.

Bones and sticks aren't the only ones. How easily we forget, as individuals and as churches, the incredible value of staying green, of bending without breaking, of being open to change and to being changed along with it. One of my favorite books growing up was *Rumble Fish*, and my favorite line of all was, "Stay gold, Pony-boy." I didn't know exactly what it meant, but it sounded cool. I guess the modern-day equivalent, at least in this context, would be, "Stay green, Christians."

Prayer for the Week

God, help me stay infused with a spirit that is thirsty for change. Help me bend but not break in the face of struggle. Help me always grow and change in ways that help me understand my faith more fully.

Popping Off

Art/music/video and other cool stuff that relate to the text

Rain Man (movie, 1988)

Les Misérables (musical, 1980–; movie, 2012)

Those People

Lectionary Texts For

September 15, 2019 (Fourteenth Sunday after Pentecost)

Texts in Brief

My dog ate my Bible!

FIRST READING

Jeremiah 4:11–12, 22–28

Jeremiah offers a dire image of a scorching wind that will render everything to ruin. This is not a paring down to separate the good from the bad; rather, everything will be swept away, as it has all gone beyond redemption.

and

Exodus 32:7–14

God is distraught by the Jewish peoples' faithlessness, having created a golden calf to worship. God vows to destroy them all, but Moses implores God to offer mercy, reminding God of the covenant with Abraham, Isaac, and Jacob. God's mind is changed, and God agrees to spare them.

Psalm

Psalm 14

The psalmist decries the foolishness of claiming there is no God. All who God has created seem to have strayed from the path set before them. And yet there is hope at the end of the psalm for redemption and a return to Zion, the promised land.

and

Psalm 51:1–10

A psalm of repentance, seeking mercy from God for all of his wrongdoing. David (the psalmist) asks God to create a clean heart within him and to renew his spirit.

Second Reading

1 Timothy 1:12–17

Paul counts himself among the worst of the worst when it comes to sinners, which is why he is so crazy about sharing with others the depth of God's mercy. If he can be forgiven, after all, who can't be?

Gospel

Luke 15:1–10

Jesus tells two parables, one of the single lost sheep among the hundred, and another of the woman seeking her lost coin. He says that God is equally vigilant in pursuing and saving the lost, and that such redemption is a cause for great celebration.

Bible, Decoded
Breaking down Scripture in plain language

Sin—the Greek root of the word *sin* literally means to fall short or to miss the mark. It's easier for us to think of sin in particular terms, like murder or (the time-tested Christian favorite) sexual sin. But it might also be a sin not to live into our full potential, to fall short of what we can really be. We also need to keep in mind that there is such a thing as corporate/communal sins, not just individual sin. We contribute to inherently sinful systems by the way we live, and the first step toward reconciliation is honest confession.

Golden calf—The Israelites were rebelling in Moses's absence while he was on the mountain speaking with God, and Aaron created the idol to placate them. This represents a lapse into old ways—bad habits—as the bull was a common object of worship among non-Jewish cultures. It symbolized their abandonment of the God who had delivered them from the Egyptians. Ironically, it was likely a symbol they would have identified as having godlike status in Egypt.

Points to Ponder
First Thoughts

One message from these texts is that we all screw up. We all stray from the path. But another, more hopeful message is that God errs on the side of mercy. God has a heart that longs to be reconciled with us. There is no satisfaction, no "I told you so," for God in the suffering we bring on ourselves. And regardless of how far we stray, there is always the persistent, inexhaustible opportunity to come home, to return to the source of mercy and renewal.

We all have "those people" in our lives. Often they are the ones who help distract us from our own shortcomings. If we're honest, there's usually something about "those people" that scares us most about ourselves. Who are "those people" to you? Perhaps they're simply those who you consider to be intolerant? Or maybe there's a group of people you just can't seem to stop looking at with a less-than-compassionate heart. But like David in the psalm, God is always waiting for our call, for us to lay ourselves open, to be honest about the barriers we place between ourselves and others, and between ourselves and God. And the good news is that God gives us the tools to smash those barriers if we're willing to take them up and use them.

Digging Deeper

Mining for what really matters . . . and gold

What makes Moses and Paul such ideal leaders for God? It's certainly not because of Moses's remarkable elocution (he had a stammer) or Paul's outstanding resume (he killed Christians for a living before becoming one). It's because they find real, deep compassion for those around them, including—or maybe even especially—for "those people." They have a soft spot for the screw-ups, most likely because they've been there themselves.

We've all been a part of "those people" at one time or another. We've been on the outside of the circle of acceptability, either because of something we've done or because of who we are. Maybe we identified ourselves as one of "those people," deeming ourselves as somehow unworthy, or maybe others have pushed us to the margins.

This experience of being the so-called lost sheep usually goes one of two ways. Either the experience engenders in us a sense of humility as well as a longing to draw others in—to include them, to show them the mercy we wished for in our time of exile—or we draw new lines, placing ourselves at the center and others on the outside, making them "those people." One breaks down such barriers, while the other builds them up. One serves the coming of God's reconciling kingdom, and the other melts down our pain, our fear, our sense of false worth, and our self-centered motivations into the golden calf that becomes our new God.

Heads Up

Connecting the text to our world

While my wife, Amy, was in seminary, she and I worked together at a small church in Fort Worth. The church could not afford a full youth program by itself and had no room in the small building where we worshiped. So, we ended up partnering with two other Disciples churches in town, pooling our resources and meeting in the gym of the largest church.

Sometimes, we had as many as thirty kids come on Sunday evenings. When it was nice outside, we'd play games in the parking lot.

Through the big wrought-iron fence, we began to notice children across the street, living in the apartments, who were curiously watching us. We agreed as a group to invite them to join us.

We visited with the children's parents, explained what our group was about, and invited their children over for food, games, music, and Bible study. A few came the first week. The next week, they brought their brothers and sisters. The following week, all of them brought their friends. Within a couple months, we had as many as a hundred kids, teeming all over the gym.

It was barely contained chaos at times, but it was joyful. At first, our kids and "those kids" didn't play together much. It was "us and them."

We decided to get them playing games to help them get to know each other.

Soon, they realized some of the kids from the apartments enjoyed skateboarding and video games, just like them. Others loved sports, just like them. They had families and pets, and loved pizza and hated homework, just like them.

Over time, the differences that divided them gave way to the commonalities that united them. Older women from the church started cooking dinner for them every week, and all of the kids started calling them "Grandma." There were occasional scuffles, and prayers and study time were always wiggly, but we were growing, learning, and having fun—together.

In this Scripture from Luke, Jesus is embracing "those people," the ones of doubtful reputation, and asking us to "Rejoice with him," for they have turned to God.

It would be easy for Jesus to look at all the tax collectors and sinners as "those people." After all, there are plenty of other people who it would be easier for him to reach, right? Why make it harder than it has to be? Why bother with "those people?" Because for Jesus, they all are his brothers and sisters. There are no people who are "those people" to him.

Maybe good guys and bad guys aren't as obvious as we would like to think.

Maybe those who need finding aren't as lost as those who think they've found all the answers.

Prayer for the Week

God, I know what's it's like to be among "those people." Help me not only avoid such labels for others, whoever they are, but also empower me to tear down such false labels and divisions in the hastening of your coming kingdom of reconciliation.

Popping Off

Art/music/video and other cool stuff that relate to the text

Rudy (movie, 1993)

Lincoln (movie, 2012)

Wonder (movie, 2017)

Mutual Interest Is Self-Interest

—\/\/—

Lectionary Texts For
September 22, 2019 (Fifteenth Sunday after Pentecost)

Texts in Brief
My dog ate my Bible!

First Reading
Jeremiah 8:18–9:1

The prophet mourns over the suffering of his people. He longs for healing for those who seek it and is heartsick for those who have died among them.

and

Amos 8:4–7

Amos calls out those who are engaged in price fixing, and who exploit the poor for personal gain. In short, God is going to kick their collective asses for taking advantage of the poor and using their power for selfish means.

Psalm

Psalm 79:1–9

The psalmist speaks in no uncertain terms about how profoundly God's people have screwed up. And yet, there is a plea for mercy, a confession of sin in the faint hope that God's wrath will not endure forever.

and

Psalm 113

A song of praise to a God of justice, who raises up the suffering and marginalized and makes level the social playing field, so to speak. This God is an equalizing force, lifting up the lowly and humbling the great.

Second Reading

1 Timothy 2:1–7

Paul is urging Timothy to lead his fellow Christians in prayer, particularly for those in positions of power. He urges them not to pray for their destruction but rather for their salvation, because the God revealed by Jesus offers such healing and salvation to all.

Gospel

Luke 16:1–13

Jesus tells a story about a money manager who is being fired by his boss for mishandling the funds. In a final act of self-preservation, the manager goes to those who owe his master a debt and cuts each of them a deal so that they will be grateful to him and welcomed him into their homes. Jesus commends this kind of shrewdness and also notes that we cannot serve both God and wealth.

Bible, Decoded
Breaking down Scripture in plain language

Balm in Gilead—A healing ointment made from bushes that were plentiful in Gilead, a mountainous region east of the Jordan River. Jeremiah is speaking figuratively, calling out in desperation for relief for his suffering people.

Ephah/shekel—denomination of money; the *ephah* was a lot of money, and the *shekel* was pocket change.

Points to Ponder
First Thoughts

It is believed among the people of Israel that the drought and famine are a punishment from God because they have been worshiping false gods. At the time that Jeremiah is writing about, harvest time has come and gone with no relief, and there is no hope for salvation in sight.

It is interesting that, in looking at Amos, we see that those who controlled trade routes and the flow of currency have been manipulating the system for thousands of years. In some ways, it's reassuring to know that recent stunts like the subprime mortgage lending crisis are not a particularly new dimension of human nature. On the other hand, it seems pretty clear that the old saying about repeating history if we don't learn from it is soberingly true.

It is worth noting that the justice of God described in Psalm 113 is remarkably similar to the injustices of those in power in Amos. This is, in a sense, an example of God's restorative justice setting right all the wrongs of humanity and offering salvation to those who suffer because of the sins of others.

Digging Deeper
Mining for what really matters . . . and gold

Often times, when we find difficult texts in the prophets, Old Testament laws, or the letters from Paul, we can always fall back on a parable from or story about Jesus. This is not one of those weeks though.

Most biblical scholars would chalk this text in Luke up as the most troublesome or challenging parable included in the Gospel of Luke. It appears that Jesus is holding up a selfish man, who was acting purely out of his own self-interest, as an example from which his disciples could learn a lot. Basically, this guy is wheeling and dealing on his way out the door in order to save his own ass, hoping that the generosity he shows to the debtors (who owe his master a debt, and not him) will come back to him in the form of hospitality when he has nowhere else to go.

But it is most likely that Jesus is not holding up the self-serving nature of this money manager as the thing to emulate, but rather his shrewdness in making the best of a bad situation and in being very creative in how he will get himself invited into the homes of those who are probably not his biggest fans. Similarly, the disciples are not always met with the red-carpet treatment wherever they go, and as Jesus says in other places in the Gospel, they should be shrewd like serpents when considering how to ingratiate themselves to a foreign culture.

Also, this parable is consistent with the story of the prodigal son, as it is about a man of power and status being made humble and effectively placing himself at the feet of those he has recently had much sway. He is very savvy in finding the best way to place himself at their mercy. And ultimately, even though he is acting from a selfish place, the result is a win-win for all involved. The master gets repaid, at least most of what he is owed. The debtors are freed from their burden. The former money manager has new friends in the people who otherwise would've been his greatest adversaries.

Heads Up

Connecting the text to our world

I offer workshops around the country from time to time about realizing greater diversity in our communities, engendering cultural competency, and helping to expose otherwise invisible privilege in our midst and how to help use it for furthering the coming of God's kingdom. One of the first points that I make, early on in the day, is to remind people that "mutual interest ultimately is self-interest."

When we wrestle with ideas like making room in our midst for the "other," or better yet, in finding ourselves as being the other and having to ingratiate ourselves to an unfamiliar host, it can be pretty uncomfortable. Things might change. We might lose something important to us. We might be rejected or humiliated. Any number of things could go wrong, and of course, that is where our minds tend to go first!

Then I share a story about a church board that realized that their leadership did not fairly represent those within the congregation. In particular, they had no one representing those with so-called disabilities in a position of power. So they invited—some of them grudgingly—the only deaf woman in the congregation to take part in the board. They knew that doing this would be challenging, as they would have to accommodate her special needs, and they also would have to make room on the board by someone else stepping down.

But before long, the woman presented them with an idea. She knew of dozens of people in the community like herself who did not go to church, even though they wanted to, because no one was offering sign language throughout the entire worship service. Why didn't she try signing for a few weeks, just to see how it went?

Less than a year later, the church had a vibrant deaf ministry, with more than forty new members who attended faithfully and brought refreshing new experiences, stories, and perspectives to the congregation. It has been a blessing to an otherwise struggling faith community, and while serving as a much-needed ministry to a historically marginalized group of people, it has also brought new life and opportunity to the church.

Sometimes, in order for God to do the work that needs to be done in our lives, all we have to do is carve out the room and be open to the possibility that someone or something different than ourselves might actually make us that much better by sharing a seat at the table.

Prayer for the Week

God, help me to be shrewd for all the right reasons. Help inspire in me a creative imagination that raises everyone up and helps transcend the fear of loss that we all experience when we are facing difficult change.

Popping Off

Art/music/video and other cool stuff that relate to the text

Big (movie, 1988)

Charlie and the Chocolate Factory, by Roald Dahl (book, 1964; movie, 2005)

Willy Wonka and the Chocolate Factory (movie, 1971)

Rich People Suck

Lectionary Texts For
September 29, 2019 (Sixteenth Sunday after Pentecost)

Texts in Brief
My dog ate my Bible!

First Reading
Jeremiah 32:1–3a, 6–15

The prophet Jeremiah writes from jail about a command from God to purchase some land in Judah, even as it is under siege by the Babylonian military, which is threatening to bring it under their control.

and

Amos 6:1a, 4–7

Amos offers a grave warning for those who live the easy life, while not mourning the ruin of the people descended from Joseph, who will be the first to suffer in exile for their indifference.

Psalm

Psalm 91:1–6, 14–16

A song about God's protection and salvation for those who seek shelter in God.

and

Psalm 146

A warning not to place too much trust in human leadership, which will fade away, falter, or die, but rather to trust in the God of Jacob. This is the true God who sets right the world's wrongs, liberates the oppressed, and brings the wicked to their knees.

Second Reading

1 Timothy 6:6–19

Paul explains to Timothy that the godly path is not in the pursuit of material wealth but rather in the pursuit of contentment with our present circumstances. Love of money is at the root of much evil, he warns, and he charges Timothy with the challenge of pushing the rich not to focus on keeping what they have or getting more but rather in bearing the social responsibility they have of helping others who have less.

Gospel

Luke 16:19–31

Jesus tells a parable of the rich man, who ignores the poor, and suffering Lazarus, who sleeps at his gates. When they both die, Lazarus joins Abraham in paradise, and the rich man goes to Hades to suffer. Though

Abraham explains there is no hope for him now, he begs to have Lazarus sent back to warn his brothers of what awaits them if they don't repent. But Abraham notes that if they're too stubborn to learn from the teachings they already have, a warning from the dead won't change their hearts.

Bible, Decoded

Breaking down Scripture in plain language

King Zedekiah—The king ruling in the land of Judah who placed Jeremiah under arrest for his prophecies, criticized the leaders in Judah, and predicted their fall at the hands of the Babylonians. Interestingly, even as it is clear this prediction is coming to full fruition, Zedekiah still hasn't freed Jeremiah from prison.

Field—The image of the field in Jeremiah is important because it's not just an issue of territory, wealth, or sustenance; it is a symbol of a birthright. When land is owned by a father, it is, by right, handed down to the children. As such, Jeremiah is prophesying (even as the city is about to fall into the hands of Babylon) that this land is still by all rights endowed to the people of Israel. Though they will be exiled, they will return to this place someday.

Hades—This was an image from Greek mythology, which Jesus referred to from time to time throughout his ministry. In the traditional Jewish belief, *Sheol* was the only place of rest for the dead, and it didn't separate the good from the bad or submit people to suffering. But Jesus pulls from Greek theology as a stark example of somewhere you don't want to end up.

Points to Ponder

First Thoughts

It is easy for us to vilify the wealthy in our social circles now, sometimes even citing choice passages from Scripture to make our case. But this week, we see that it is not having wealth per se that leads to a great fall. Rather, it is focusing on getting more or keeping what we have while others suffer without our help that is at the root of the sin. So really, the greater transgression is indifference or a lack of empathy that emerges when we are so far removed from the suffering of others that it's all too easy to look the other way.

It is worth noting that Jeremiah, the same one who has been issuing fiery words of judgment, warning, and condemnation to the people of Israel, now offers an image of hope, even as they are on the verge of destruction and exile. Clearly, he doesn't rejoice in being right about the Babylonians coming in to sack the city and drive them out, and even though he writes this from jail (where he was put by the king of Judah, his own people), he spends no time with "I told you so." As a true prophet does, he looks ahead and offers a different image of the future than what appears to be possible in the present.

This parable from Luke is a continuation of the "great reversal" theme found throughout this Gospel. Once again, the lowly are elevated, and the mighty are humbled. And Jesus offers no good news for the wealthy who don't learn from the wisdom they already have in their midst.

Digging Deeper

Mining for what really matters . . . and gold

There are a few interesting things in this week's texts when considered side by side.

First, compare the vision cast by Jeremiah to that in the parable offered by Jesus. In the midst of the direst circumstances, Jeremiah offers nothing but hope, while Jesus tells the rich man he's pretty much screwed for not heeding the wisdom found in Scripture when he had a chance. And he won't even indulge the man's requests to send a messenger from the afterlife to warn his brothers! This Jesus is pretty harsh, don't you think?

Also worth noting is how many times Paul quotes Jesus in his letter to Timothy. First, he cites Jesus's claim in Mark that love of money is at the root of human evil. Then he notes the claim also made by Jesus that wherever our treasures are stored up, that's where we'll also find our hearts. Clearly Paul knows his Gospels, but more important, he keeps pointing away from himself and toward Jesus. He is simply passing on wisdom that is already there for them, which is what Jesus says in the Luke story to the rich man.

We focus so often on the money aspects of these texts, and it's easy to do because it keeps the focus off of us. We can talk more about how evil money is (though this isn't what Jesus or Paul say) and how rich people are going to hell. But the true sin is indifference, or a willful turning away from our brothers and sisters who are suffering. It's in willful ignorance about what we already know is right because of the wisdom of Scriptures, or because it is etched on our hearts.

I have a spoken-word piece that I share in worship sometimes called "Six Degrees." Toward the end, there's a line that keeps resonating for me within the context of this study. It says, "Comfort kills the will to change." When we talk of Jesus or the prophets afflicting the comfortable, it's not so much a punishment, perhaps, as it is the necessary irritant to wake us up from our own self-imposed slumber. Open your eyes! Pay attention to the needs of the world around you. Not tomorrow—*right now!*

And as for Jesus being harsh, keep in mind that this is a parable he's telling people who are still alive. This is really their divinely inspired wakeup call. Like a loving parent, he's being a little hard on them ultimately because he cares so much. But he also knows that he can't make them change their ways. We each have to come to that conclusion on our own, regardless of how much wisdom surrounds us.

Heads Up

Connecting the text to our world

Rich people are jerks. They're greedy and selfish, and they don't care about anyone else. That computer software guy might be the antichrist. Money is just plain evil.

I've heard statements about the evils of wealth and the corruption of people of means. Sometimes people quote Scripture to support their case. Often, the exclamation point at the end of the polemic is about how money is the root of all evil. Read it. It's right there in your Bible.

Actually it isn't. Though Paul does say that the *love* of money is the root of all evil (a quote he takes from Jesus), money itself is amoral. It is a tool, much like a brick or a vial of nitroglycerin. The former can be used to build a hospital or crush someone's skull. The latter can help prevent heart attacks or be made into dynamite. Money is no more inherently evil than any other tool.

The power is in how we use it, and how we value it.

Some rich people really are jerks, but some are incredibly generous, faithful, and well-adjusted. I've met some pretty obnoxious poor people in my life too, and some that give of themselves as if their money would spoil tomorrow if not passed on.

Does Jesus really want the rich man to give everything away? Maybe. But at the heart of his message is this: You can follow all the rules, go to church, say all the right prayers, and study your Bible, but if you let money or *anything else of this world* get between you and God, you'll be lucky to squeeze through the gates of heaven, trying to cling to all of that baggage.

There's a Malay proverb that says, "If you have, give. If you lack, seek." Now, go live it.

Prayer for the Week

God, help me set aside those things of the world that I have allowed to come between us. Grant me the assurance that although I do not have all that I want, there is more than enough.

Popping Off
Art/music/video and other cool stuff that relate to the text

Batman/Dark Knight (movie series, 2005–2012; comic book series, 2011–2014)

King Midas (movie, 2003)

Getting Honest about Doubt

‑‑‑‑‑‑‑‑‑‑\/\/\‑‑‑

Lectionary Texts For
October 6, 2019 (Seventeenth Sunday after Pentecost)

Texts in Brief
My dog ate my Bible!

First Reading
Lamentations 1:1–6

Judah has been invaded and captured by the Babylonians. The citizens of Judah fled and abandoned the city. This is a poem personifying the city as if it were an abused and neglected woman.

3:19–26

An affirmation of the hope still found in God, despite present circumstances.

and

Habakkuk 1:1–4; 2:1–4

The oracle is crying out for relief from their captors. It seems that there is no end in sight to the suffering, and God seems far away, not answering their cries for reprieve. Finally God responds, promising that the end will come, that the faithful will prevail, and that ultimately, the proud have no ground to stand on.

Psalm
Psalm 137

The psalmist is being held captive by the Babylonian occupiers and forced to sing the songs of the people of Jerusalem for their entertainment. He vows never to forget the stories of Jerusalem or the God of that land, and rejoices in the idea that, someday, his captors will get what is coming to them.

Psalm 37:1–9

A psalm of warning not to be jealous of those who prosper by unjust means. Their days are numbered, and those who persist in their faith will find the rewards that they deserve. The psalmist also warns of lapsing into evil or vengeful thought.

Second Reading
2 Timothy 1:1–14

A letter of encouragement for Timothy from Paul, who writes with hope and courage even while in prison. Timothy seems to be struggling with a crisis of faith of some kind, and Paul is trying to help remind him of where his strength comes from: his faith in God, inherited from his parents.

Gospel
Luke 17:5–10
The disciples ask Jesus to help them strengthen their faith, to which he says they only need a miniscule amount in order for it to take root within them. Rather than worrying about growing their faith, he directs them to do what they are called to do as servants of the gospel commandments, with faith that God will take care of the rest.

Bible, Decoded
Breaking down Scripture in plain language

Mustard seed—A really tiny granule, like a piece of dust or sand.

Gospel—Literally means "good news." This is the message of Jesus about our path to liberation from the sins, desires, and struggles of this world, and the promise of something better found in a life that puts love and service of God first.

Apostle—Sometimes used interchangeably to describe the disciples, an apostle is one who is sent. It is also translated as "a messenger." Those who were sent to create and lead the early churches to whom Paul was writing were also apostles, even though they were not necessarily among the twelve disciples named as the original followers of Jesus.

Points to Ponder

First Thoughts

It is particularly interesting that, in our first psalm reading, the author rejoices in the idea of his captor's children being murdered in an act of revenge. However, in the second psalm reading, we see a word of warning about harboring such vengeful, violent thoughts against those who oppress us. On the one hand, those who seek to embrace the theology of retribution could use this first reading to justify themselves. On the other hand, perhaps this is a window into the utter humanity of those who authored the Bible.

We see Paul at his best in this letter to Timothy. Even while he seems to have no hope for his own future, he is the one offering hope and courage to those on the outside who are struggling. And rather than focusing on the downfall of those who hold him captive, he puts his energy into the affirmation of the faith of those who have committed their lives to the gospel.

The book of Lamentations is so beautifully written, and it offers such a stark contrast to these two readings between the seeming hopelessness of the current situation and the green of promise the author still embraces at the core of his faith.

Digging Deeper

Mining for what really matters . . . and gold

The texts this week are all about clinging to our faith when everything else turns to crap. The people of Judah are either an occupied people or exiles from their city. Their minstrels are forced to entertain their captors with the cultural songs of their ancestors. Our beloved psalmist wants to smash baby heads against rocks in an act of revenge. Timothy seems to be losing his grip is a leader of the early church. And the disciples—those who are closest to Jesus himself—seem to be wrestling with some crisis of faith.

What hope is there for us if these, our examples, can't seem to remain steadfast in their efforts to keep God at the center of their lives? What hope do we have of replacing our petty human notions of retributive justice with something that looks more like the kingdom of God, even if the authors of our sacred texts seem to want to justify vengeful violence? How can we possibly believe in a Messiah from two thousand years ago when those who followed him and witnessed his miraculous deeds every day still struggled to wrap their minds and hearts around the gospel?

Personally, there is assurance knowing that my occasional crises of faith find plenty of good company in the Bible. Frederick Buechner says that we should ask ourselves every day when we wake up if we can believe it all over again. But before giving an answer, we should read the news and consider the brokenness of the world around us. If after that, our answer every day is still "yes," then we probably really don't know what it means to believe.

About half of the time, Buechner says, the answer should be "no," if we are truly being honest with ourselves. But then, on those days when the answer is "yes," then it should be an affirmation filled with confession, laughter, and great joy, because that truly is something to celebrate.

Heads Up

Connecting the text to our world

A friend of mine was a pastor at a church, and she admitted to me that her congregation had different ideas about what faith looked like than she did. For them, the mark of true faith was a steadfast certainty that did not change from day to day. For her, on the other hand, the practice of faith was more like a journey to brilliant mountaintops followed by journeys into deep, dark valleys of doubt.

One time, after she brought a prominent speaker who not only gave people permission to explore their doubt but affirmed it as a necessary part of the practice of faith, the leaders of the church sat her down.

"We need to know what you really believe about Jesus," they said sternly. "Can you honestly tell us, here and now, that you believe that Jesus is the son of God?"

"I knew my answer was going to cost me my job," she told me, "but I simply couldn't look them in the eye and lie." She told them that although she desperately wanted to believe this every day of her life, there were days when she admittedly had her doubts about what this meant and whether she could claim such a faith with all of her heart.

Not long afterward, the church board convened and resolved to ask her to step down from her position as minister of the church. It was heartbreaking, but at the same time, she found some strange freedom in her own confession.

"I had a choice," she said. "I could continue collecting a paycheck and doing 'ministry' to people who wanted me to pretend to be something I was not. Or I could free myself from that dishonesty to explore what it is that I really believe, why believe it, and where—if it all—I might find a place where I could serve others who were on a similar path."

Does Jesus require certainty or mustard seeds? Is God enduring enough to withstand our doubts? Is there really no room in the Christian faith for questions, for hard days, for those moments when we feel so far from God that we wonder if we can really believe any of it?

At least we find honorable company in our struggles to remain faithful. It may not be as comforting as the illusion of certitude, but at least it's more honest. And not nearly as lonely.

Prayer for the Week

God, I want to believe; help me in my unbelief.

Popping Off

Art/music/video and other cool stuff that relate to the text

The Apostle (movie, 1997)

"Barbara Kruger's Artwork Speaks Truth to Power," from Smithsonian.com (article, 2012): https://tinyurl.com/y8nwjgcl

Hamlet (movie, 1996)

The Return of Ansel Gibbs, by Frederick Buechner (book, 1958)

A Leper's Messiah

Lectionary Texts For

October 13, 2019 (Eighteenth Sunday after Pentecost)

Texts in Brief

My dog ate my Bible!

FIRST READING

Jeremiah 29:1, 4–7

Jeremiah advises the exiles from Jerusalem to Babylon to go on with their lives while in exile, and even to pray for the welfare of their occupiers, since their well-being and the exiles' well-being are married together.

2 Kings 5:1–3, 7–15c

Story of Naaman

Naaman is a great warrior for King Aram, but he suffers from leprosy. Elisha invites Naaman to his house in order to be healed. When Naaman gets there,

Elisha sends a servant who tells him to bathe himself seven times in the Jordan River. Naaman is offended that Elisha doesn't come out in person and almost goes home. But his servant convinces him to follow through on what Elisha has told him to do, and he is healed.

PSALM
Psalm 66:1–12

A song of praise for a God who not only is with God's people through times of hardship and trial, but who also delivers those same people into liberation.

and

Psalm 111

A poem reinforcing the idea that God keeps God's promises. For the psalmist, the beginning of wisdom is found in respecting what is expected of us by God in our covenants with God.

SECOND READING
2 Timothy 2:8–15

Although Paul is imprisoned, he offers confidence to Timothy that the Word of God cannot be similarly restrained. His followers are called to endurance and faithfulness, and Timothy himself is emboldened by Paul to present himself as an authoritative leader, whose teaching supersedes the bickering about interpretation of Scripture that the early Christians under his care might otherwise engage in.

Luke 17:11–19

Jesus offers healing to ten lepers. He orders them to go to the temple to show the priests that they have been healed, and along the way, they realize the healing has taken place. Only one of the ten returns to Jesus to offer him praise. Jesus notes that only this "foreigner" has demonstrated the kind of faith that truly will make him well.

Bible, Decoded

Breaking down Scripture in plain language

Leprosy—A disease of the skin that was highly unattractive and a very contagious. Leprosy would be the equivalent of what AIDS was for us in the not-too-distant past. There were all kinds of social stigmas attached to having the disease, and generally they were sent to live in exile with "their own," apart from the rest of society.

Babylonians—The most recent occupiers of Jerusalem. As the Egyptians enslaved the Jewish people and took many of them to work in the Egyptian homeland, so did the Babylonians after taking over Jerusalem. And of course, given the words of the prophets throughout the Old Testament, we can assume that they believe this Babylonian occupation is the natural consequence of the people of Israel breaking their covenant with their God.

Points to Ponder

First Thoughts

There is always an interesting balance of reprimand and hope offered in the words of the prophets. Clearly, they draw direct connections between the hardships of the people of Israel and their failure to honor their covenant with God. However, it is difficult to know with many of these prophetic writings how many of them were actually written down by the prophets themselves before the hardships came upon the people of Israel, and how many of them were written after the fact and attributed to the respective prophets. I am curious how, if at all, these two perspectives change our understanding of the texts.

There is an important theme throughout these texts that God is faithful to us, even when we are not equally faithful to God. It is worth noting, I think, that although only one of the lepers healed in the Gospel of Luke returns to thank and praise Jesus, Jesus does not remove the gift of healing from the other nine. However, he does reinforce the statement he makes so often, "Your faith has made you well." This seems to suggest a deeper level of spiritual or existential healing that the others will not enjoy, not because Jesus withheld it, but because they did not see and embrace it when it was right in front of them.

Digging Deeper

Mining for what really matters . . . and gold

Everyone has something that seems to get between them and their ability to fully honor their covenant of faith with God. For Naaman, it seems that his pride and ego almost keep him from taking advantage of the gift of healing that was presented to him.

For the people of Jerusalem, there seems to be some historical amnesia when it comes to history repeating itself in a series of rather unfortunate ways. Like Naaman, they begin to turn to self-reliance and self-aggrandizement rather than the humility called for in their faith.

For Paul to take the time to write this letter to Timothy, encouraging him in healing divisions manifesting themselves within his young Christian community, Timothy is likely at risk of losing heart that he is the right man for the job. Basically, Paul seems to suggest that the tendency of the people within that community to depend on their own wisdom and knowledge, rather than the wisdom and knowledge revealed to them or their leader, is causing the strife and division he is observing. But as it says in Proverbs 3:5–6, we are not to lean too heavily on our own human understanding but rather to trust that God's faith, grace, and love are big enough—even for us and all of our doubts, flaws, and conflicts.

In this story from Luke, once again Jesus notes that the one person who truly seems to "get it" is a foreigner: an outsider. So not only was this person plagued by the socially alienating disease of leprosy, but he also apparently got the double dose of the burden of being one of the "others." It is interesting how often it seems to take this sort of outsider status in order for people to really stop and recognize what God is doing in their lives.

Perhaps this is why Jeremiah admonishes the people of Jerusalem to pray for their captors and the homeland to which they have been taken. They are now the outsiders. They are the outcasts, the "less than," the inferior people. They are the lepers of the Babylonian culture. But if these are the moments in which God seems to reveal God's self in ways we can most readily see it, perhaps this is why Jeremiah shares the hope that many other prophets have seemed to echo at one time or another that, in their times of greatest struggle and trial, God waits expectantly for us to reconcile ourselves to God.

Heads Up

Connecting the text to our world

It may seem strange to be referencing the show *Breaking Bad* in a Bible study. After all, how can we glean any sort of gospel wisdom from a methamphetamine-cooking high-school teacher turned international drug lord?

The thing about this show is that over five seasons, we watch what seems to be a basically good guy succumb to small temptations and compromises that he works diligently to reconcile with whatever choices he is making at the time in his life. None of it happens overnight; it's not like the typical "good guy gone bad" dramatic turn we see in most movies. It is subtle, gradual, and incremental, and somehow there is always some sort of seemingly virtuous justification for the less-than-virtuous conclusions at which he arrives.

He is a dying man. He has nothing to lose. He has a responsibility to his family. Ultimately, all of this is done out of love and concern for those he cares about. And yet, we look back after five years and realize the massive carnage he has left in his wake. His friends are either dead or have disappeared. His own brother-in-law was the unfortunate victim of his selfish decisions. And the very family he claimed to be the reason for all of his nefarious choices has fallen apart, turned their back on him. They are terrified of him and want nothing to do with him.

What's more, he has even lost control of most of the money he had amassed to care for his family. All of these compromises, these minor divergences from the path of what is right in his life, have led him toward a reality that is little more than an illusion. It is lonely, isolated, and without hope. It is much like I expect Timothy feels, surrounded by a broken and fractious church, or the people of Jerusalem under the oppressive thumb of the Babylonian Empire.

We compromise so much for what we think we want, and then when we get it, so often we realize not only that it wasn't what we wanted after all but that the things we gave up to get there really were the things that had true value to begin with. But just like in these Bible stories, and like in our lives, there is at least a glimmer of hope for redemption in *Breaking Bad*—even for good old Walter White.

In the end, Walter is faced with an opportunity to do something truly selfless. He throws himself on top of his old friend, Jesse, saving him from a hail of bullets tearing through the house of the professional assassins in which they find themselves. Yes, Walter has done many, many bad things. He is not a good man, and the ripple effects of his choices will extend outward and affect so many lives for years to come. But even in the midst of all of that darkness, hopelessness, and bloodshed, and despite all of the greed and compromised morals, there was still a tiny little spark left of the heart of such a broken man.

And if, in the end, there is hope for Walter White, I have to hold out hope that there is even a chance for a guy like me.

Prayer for the Week

God, please don't give up on me, even when I seem to have given up on you or on myself. Help reveal in me the potential for good even when I try to hide it. I am grateful, for your faith in me is sometimes enough to make up for my own lack of faith.

Popping Off

Art/music/video and other cool stuff that relate to the text

"Felina," from *Breaking Bad*, season 5, episode 16 (TV series, 2008–2013)

Liar Liar (movie, 1997)

Be Annoying
for God

Lectionary Texts For

October 20, 2019 (Nineteenth Sunday after Pentecost)

Texts in Brief

My dog ate my Bible!

FIRST READING

Jeremiah 31:27–34

God is preparing to spiritually clean house with the people of Israel. Although they broke the covenant with God that had been made before their time in Egypt, God will infuse this new covenant within them, on their hearts, so they cannot forsake it. All former sins will be forgiven, and there will be a new beginning.

and

Genesis 32:22–31

Jacob wrestles with a man in a place he names "Peniel" after the experience he had there. He claims to have seen

God face to face that night and refuses to let the man go without being blessed. The man ultimately blesses him (renaming him "Israel") but also strikes him on the hip joint, which explains his off-balance walk.

Psalm
Psalm 119:97–104
A song of praise for God's law, which keeps the psalmist on the path of righteousness and away from evil.

and

Psalm 121
A psalm beseeching those who hear it to trust in the God of Israel for both protection and guidance throughout their lives. Theirs is a God who can be trusted.

Second Reading
2 Timothy 3:14–4:5
Paul encourages Timothy to hang in there, and to cling to the teachings of the ancient sacred texts and from the Gospels that he has depended on his whole life. He notes that there will be times when people will stray from proper teaching and will seek out religious leaders who say what they'd rather hear. But Timothy's mandate, per Paul, is not to buckle under the pressure or criticism but rather to stay true to what he's been taught.

Gospel
Luke 18:1–8
Jesus tells a parable about persistence. A woman annoys a judge who holds no regard for God or other

people until he imparts to her the justice she seeks, if for no other reason than to get her to shut up about it. Jesus's point is that part of our job in being faithful is to be persistent in asking for the justice we seek for ourselves and the world. Rest assured God will provide it, undoubtedly more immediately than some judge who is only interested in picking up a paycheck.

Bible, Decoded
Breaking down Scripture in plain language

Peniel—A place on the east of the Jordan River and north of the Jabbok River. It is called "Peniel" by Jacob, meaning "face of God," because he "saw God face to face, and yet my life was spared."

Israel—Means "triumphant with God," or "one who prevails with God," which is a reference to Jacob wrestling all night with what the Scripture says is a man, others interpret as an angel, and still others suggest actually was God.

Points to Ponder
First Thoughts

I can relate to Jacob in this text where he wrestles with God—or maybe an angel—all night long. How many of us have fought with our faith, sometimes for what seems like forever, only to come out a little bit beaten up on the other side? Our faith is not one that is passive, benign, or always perfect. It's a struggle, which draws some parallel with the true Muslim understanding of the word *jihad,* which literally means "holy struggle." The good news is that if Jacob can enter into a *jihad* and come out of it with a divine blessing, maybe all of this wrestling is worth it after all.

If this text in Timothy doesn't cause every Bible study teacher a moment of pause, they're not paying attention! We'd all like to think that we're getting at the heart of the texts, but what if we're the ones Paul is warning Timothy about? I think the only way to know is to search our own hearts for that covenant inscribed deep within us by God. No, it's not another set of rules or some magical key to unlock universal truth. Rather it's a deep sense of knowing, an assuredness that when we seek with earnestness the voice and path of God, we will find it.

I don't know about you, but I'm incredibly impatient. This idea of having to struggle day and night for a blessing, or to be a holy pest to get the justice we seek in this world is . . . well . . . exhausting. "Give me peace and patience, God," we say, "and give it to me now!" But that's not really how it works. If the world is a stone, perhaps our prayers are the water. Sometimes it may not seem like we're getting anywhere, but as we all know in that scenario, the water ultimately prevails.

Digging Deeper

Mining for what really matters . . . and gold

What makes a prophet? Is it someone who is clairvoyant? Can they gaze into the equivalent of their crystal ball, listen for some hot tips from God, and share tidbits from the future with the rest of us? Or is it someone who can hold two seemingly disparate realities in tension at the same time? Someone who can see and name the brokenness of the world as it presently is while also holding onto an inspired vision of what God calls us toward?

If we met Jeremiah today, we might diagnose him with multiple personality disorder. In one moment he's breathing fiery judgment down on the people of Israel for straying from the path of righteousness. But then, only verses later, he's offering hope and encouragement to those same lost souls.

A prophet is someone who is not swayed by trends, the convenient teachings of the latest hip speaker, or bestselling books. This isn't to say they reject present culture out of hand, but rather everything has to be framed within a larger context—one in which God's vision for us is at the center of our imagination.

We're so easily distracted by superficial fascinations, self-serving messages, or even the hardships that cause us to sit back and shake our heads in despair. But there is something bigger going on. Something new is being made in the midst of the old. Something is waiting to be born, even while surrounded by all of this death.

It's the stuff that dreams are made of, and not just the kinds that fade to our subconscious once we wake up. These dreams haunt our waking hours, consume us, and put everything else into a healthier perspective.

Heads Up
Connecting the text to our world

Kids can be annoying. I know; I have two of them. The other day, my son saw an ad on TV for some flying thing that, although he didn't know existed thirty seconds before, he absolutely could not live without now.

"Dad," he hollered. "I've got to have an X-27 Hyper Jet!"

"No," I said, almost reflexively. This is my default answer, especially when the sentences preceding my "no" began with "Dad, I want . . ."

"But dad, it has twin rotors!"

"Do you know what rotors are?"

"No," he sighed, "but it's got two of them, and it looks awesome."

"You already have three flying toys you don't play with," I said.

"Dad, the helicopter won't charge, and the other two are broken."

"Answer's still no, buddy."

"But Dad . . ."

"Nope."

"But I. . ."

"I said no."

"But I really, really, *really* want . . ."

"No."

He stomped off to the other room, whispering under his breath about the new thing that had become the center of his universe in no more than a minute and a half.

We can learn from this, actually.

How often do we offer up halfhearted prayers, maybe while driving to work or as we drift off to sleep? How often do we not even bother to pray, resigning ourselves to cynicism over the state of our government, the Middle East, or even our own lives?

The difference between that and the obsessive nature of a kid is that the thing they are consumed with takes over their lives. It overwhelms them, causing everything else to shrink into the background.

I'm not suggesting that we get equally obsessed about the latest gadget we see, the car we want, the spouse we long for, or the neighbor's life we covet. The Scriptures call us to be persistent and tireless in our seeking of justice. We are to demonstrate a childlike obsession with seeking rest for the weary, wholeness for the broken, and hope for those in despair.

Such persistence despite present circumstances, or even in spite of what seems to be common sense, is a sign of hope. It is the byproduct of a faith that believes, regardless of how bad things get, that love, wholeness, and reconciliation prevail.

Granted, conventional wisdom tells us this is naive, a waste of time. And skeptics may be right in suggesting that things won't always get better today, tomorrow, or even in our lifetime. But for a people whose collective prayer is, "Thy kingdom come, thy will be done, on earth as it is in heaven," we claim such an idealistic, counterintuitive hope.

The question is: how deeply do we believe it? No need to give an answer. Our lives, and how we choose to live them, are response enough.

Prayer for the Week

God, sometimes I lose sight of the bigger picture, getting caught up in present struggles and the discouraging news cycles of the day. Help renew me with a childlike hope so that I can summon the will to be annoyingly persistent in my pursuit of your kingdom on earth.

Popping Off
Art/music/video and other cool stuff that relate to the text

Into Thin Air, by Jon Krakauer (book, 1997)

127 Hours (movie, 2010)

Being Bad
at Doing Good

Lectionary Texts For

October 27, 2019 (Twentieth Sunday after Pentecost)

Texts in Brief

My dog ate my Bible!

First Reading

Joel 2:23–32

Respite from the droughts and plagues of locusts has finally arrived. Rains have returned, and the earth is yielding food in abundance. The time of judgment is over, and God's people are now entering a time of restoration and plenty.

and

Jeremiah 14:7–10, 19–22

Jeremiah is doing two things in this text. First, he offers a prayer of confession for the sinfulness of the people of Israel. He speaks on their behalf to God and begs for mercy. Then, Jeremiah basically calls God out, holding God to God's own covenant with Israel. He prays for God not to break this promise and even suggests that, within the persistence of suffering of his people, perhaps God has abandoned them. And yet Jeremiah holds out hope.

PSALM
Psalm 65
A song of praise to God for God's provision in great abundance and for God's tireless mercy when we stray from the path of righteousness.

and

Psalm 84:1–7
The psalmist longs so deeply for communion with God that they are enraptured by the very thought. It notes that even the least of God's creatures are cared for, which is a testament to God's care for all creation.

SECOND READING
2 Timothy 4:6–8, 16–18
In his letter to Timothy, Paul indicates that his days on earth are numbered. He likens the conclusion of his life to the pouring out of a cup as an offering of communion. He notes that, when he was on trial, no one came to advocate for him. And yet, he prays that God will not hold this against any of them. Even in his imprisonment, Paul has found the strength to testify about his faith to those who hold him captive. He trusts that God will care for him until his final day.

GOSPEL

Luke 18:9–14

Jesus tells a parable to those who hold themselves in higher regard over others. He compares a religious leader to a tax collector; the latter would be reviled in his community, and the first revered. But when the religious leader prays, he only thanks God that he is better than everyone else, whereas the tax collector seeks forgiveness and humility.

Bible, Decoded

Breaking down Scripture in plain language

Mount Zion—This is the site where it is believed that Abraham took Isaac to sacrifice him to God. It is the hill outside of the old city in Jerusalem where the famous Jewish temple was built.

Baca—An ancient name for what we now know as Mecca, the holy city of Islam. In our text, it is a place of many freshwater springs, and therefore it represents abundance and provision.

Points to Ponder

First Thoughts

The section in Joel that says the people of Israel will prophesy, see visions, and dream dreams is often connected to the occurrences written about later at Pentecost. In this one all of those disciples present are caught up in the Holy Spirit and begin to speak in the various tongues of the cultures around them, to whom they will be commissioned to share the gospel.

We see another of Luke's "great reversals" in this Gospel text. This time, Jesus claims that those who think highly of themselves will be humbled before God, and those who come to God with humility will be raised up and exalted. This reflects much about how the author of Luke understands justice in the kingdom of God: a flipping of the order of things as they are on earth to set them right.

Digging Deeper

Mining for what really matters . . . and gold

It may be a little bit of a challenge to see the connection between the Old Testament prophet texts this week and the New Testament letter and Gospel texts. But we have to remember with the people of Israel had been going through in the last few weeks of our studies.

This all began with the people of Israel deciding they could go it alone without God. They had become particularly full of themselves and had placed themselves at the center of things rather than God. What followed was an epic period of divine judgment, but from that came profound confession and humility. This, it seems, is what allows them to be reconciled to God, rather than them having paid a sufficient price for their transgressions.

In Luke, Jesus is making a compelling point to those who try to earn good standing with God by doing all the right things with a selfish and self-centered heart. Granted, the Pharisee has the respect of the people, holds great religious wisdom, and even honors the covenants commanded by Scripture. But in the end, he's pretty much a jerk and seems to be doing all of this with a tremendous sense of superiority.

If the Pharisee is the "before" picture of the people of Jerusalem, then the tax collector is the "after" image. He represents someone whose pretenses and pride had been broken down, and who recognizes that nothing he does makes him worthy to be in God's gracious presence. But in acknowledging this, he actually justifies himself, whereas the other man—by all accounts a "holy man" in the eyes of his community—was not justified in any of his actions in the eyes of God because of his motivation for it all.

And then we have Paul. Here is a man who has given his entire life, including his own personal welfare and well-being, in service to God. At this point, he really has nothing to lose, as he is on his way out. Even as he has given so much to those around him, they have not returned the favor and have abandoned him in his time of greatest need, just like Jesus was abandoned by his followers. But like Jesus, Paul begs for forgiveness on their behalf.

It seems to suggest that whatever issues we may have with some of the writings of Paul, he has, in the end, adopted the heart of Christ. He gets it. He lives it. And as such, he is able to live out the final days of his life with a sense of peace that he has done all that he has been called to do.

Heads Up

Connecting the text to our world

I spend a lot of time talking to people about what it means to be a Christian. Of course, there are the conventional notions of what it means, like asking Jesus into your heart, being baptized, and proclaiming him as your personal Lord and Savior in front of a congregation of Christian peers. But the thing that lots of people observe, and rightly so, is that after people undergo these rituals, often times they seem to become real jerks. Maybe they were jerks to begin with, and maybe not. But bathing in the light of Christ certainly didn't de-jerk-ify them.

Often times this seems to come from what I call a Christendom mentality. Basically, we Christians are now on the side of light, and we can rejoice in being among God's chosen. Meanwhile, those poor lost souls on the other side of the line should be grateful that they have us to help direct them to the path of righteousness and salvation.

Now, if you're already skeptical about the whole Christianity thing to begin with, how in the hell will someone with this sort of attitude help convince you that this is something worth committing your life to?

Sure, they may give to charity, work one night a week at the food bank, and even dedicate the weekend every once in a while to a local mission trip. They go to church, and man, they let you know it. There seems to be no ounce of humility in their actions or attitudes. In fact, if anything, it seems that being a Christian has made them even more arrogant.

This is exactly what Jesus is warning about in the Gospel of Luke. We can go through all the proper motions, say all the flowery prayers, and even convince those around us that we are the holiest of the holy. But God wants much more from us than for us to do a few good things. Yes, the actions matter. But the heart of the person behind those actions matters even more.

We have a habit of doing good pretty badly. We find a way to make it about us, to get praise or attention for our good deeds. Or we just do it for a sense of personal satisfaction and superiority. But if Paul is praying on behalf of those who abandon him at his most vulnerable moment (and mind you, he is not praying for them to change, but rather for their forgiveness), why is it that we seem so bent on what others need to change about themselves, all the while being so very blind to what is still left undone within ourselves?

Prayer for the Week

God, even when I try to do good, I have a habit of doing it badly. I'm sorry. Help me approach every task with a pure and selfless heart, acting as a humble servant rather than as one who is trying to impress others or racking up credits in a heavenly bank account.

Popping Off

Art/music/video and other cool stuff that relate to the text

"The Selfish Act of Kindness," from *Psychology Today* (article, 2009): tinyurl.com/yav4aqoq

"Is There Such a Thing as a Selfless Act of Kindness?" (discussion thread on TED Talks, 2012): tinyurl.com/y9dqz2p6

"The Problem with Charity" scene from *About a Boy* (movie, 2002): tinyurl.com/ybz6a4oq

Show Your Cheeks for Jesus

Lectionary Texts For

November 1, 2019 (All Saints Day)

(To be used in place of Proper 26 (31) texts on November 3)

Texts in Brief

My dog ate my Bible!

First Reading

Daniel 7:1–3, 15–18

Daniel has a dream of four beasts rising from the ocean. His dream interpreter explains to him that these beasts represent four kings who will rule over the land but also that the one true king (God) will prevail over all earthly authority.

Psalm

Psalm 149

A curious song of praise that also serves as a rallying cry to battle for the people of Israel. First, it calls them to joyful praise of God at every moment in the day and to humility in all that they do. Then, there is the image of the two-edged sword, which they are to wield against all other nations and punish them for their godlessness.

SECOND READING
Ephesians 1:11–23

In his letter to the church in Ephesus, Paul exhorts them to remember that they are inheritors of God's kingdom by putting their faith in Jesus. He prays for them to have a spirit of wisdom and revelation about them, so that when they themselves pray, it will be revealed to them what God intends for them to do. Finally, he asserts the primacy of Jesus as the singular godhead figure to which all eyes and hearts should be oriented.

GOSPEL
Luke 6:20–31

In Luke's version of this speech, the ones who are to be blessed are the poor, the hungry, and those who are hated and marginalized. Immediately, Jesus contrasts this with a judgment on those who are rich, have a full stomach, or who are held up in high regard in society. He warns those listening to repay hate with love and violence with peace. When struck, we are advised to turn the other cheek. And if someone bags from something from us, we are to give it with no exception and no expectation of getting it back.

Bible, Decoded

Breaking down Scripture in plain language

Blessing/blessed—In general, to be blessed in the Bible means to be held within the favor of God. There are many other traditions that have similar notions, such as Anglo-Saxon and German pagan traditions, in which receiving a blessing means particularly to be marked with blood. This, too, shows elevated or favored status.

Holy Spirit—In the Old Testament, the concept of the Holy Spirit is only introduced three times and is different in meaning than the frequent references to it throughout the New Testament. In ancient Judaism the notion of a Holy Spirit was more of a divine, mystical attribute of the one God, whereas many Christian traditions (particularly those who ascribe to a trinitarian understanding of God) understand the Holy Spirit to be more personified. Here, the Holy Spirit is one of three manifestations of God: God the Father, Jesus the Son, and the Holy Spirit.

Points to Ponder

First Thoughts

Whereas in most of the book of Daniel, the prophet is an interpreter of dreams for others, this is the first one where he is the one having the prophetic dreams. It is also the only truly apocalyptic piece of literature in the Old Testament.

It is significant that the beasts in Daniel are rising from the ocean. First, they draw a dramatic parallel to a four-part statue he describes five chapters earlier in

Daniel. However, having these beasts emerge from the waters pulls from Eastern mythology, which suggests that everything that emerges from the seas brings chaos with it. This is certainly a dark and ominous foretelling.

A shorter version of the so-called beatitudes listed in Matthew is what is often called the "Sermon on the Mount." In Luke, this is often called "The Sermon on the Plain." Not only is Luke's version shorter and less poetic than the one in Matthew, it is very specific and direct in contrasting those who are blessed and those who are cursed, which is consistent with the "great reversals" throughout Luke.

Digging Deeper

Mining for what really matters . . . and gold

It is an interesting time in the lectionary to have many of these texts come up. Several of them (aside from the Gospel text) seem to focus on the supremacy of the God of Israel over all other earthly and non-earthly forces and authorities. There are predictions of doom and gloom for those who do not believe in God, for those who believe in the wrong God, and for those who place their faith in earthly leaders. Pretty much the only ones it works out well for are those who are on the sides of the authors.

These texts—and especially the Psalm—stand in stark contrast to the commandment by Jesus to love those who hate and persecute us. He deconstructs the idea that those who were faithful will receive a just reward in this life. Though they may earn God's favor and blessing, they may still be reviled, hungry, and poor.

He goes further by explaining precisely what we should do when struck by another person. He says that all acts of hate, violence, aggression, and injustice should be repaid with an equal measure of love, compassion, and patience. But it is important to understand why Jesus is asking us to do what he is asking of us. He doesn't just want us to be meek and mild punching bags, the proverbial doormats of the world, upon whom everyone will wipe their feet in disdain and run over at every turn.

Keep in mind that Luke in particular is fascinated with paradigm-shattering reversals. He wants to see the life and teaching of Jesus flip the entire world order on its head. And how can this possibly be achieved if we keep doing what we have always done?

It is clear to the authors of the Gospels and to Jesus that the old ways, though perhaps understandable and even scripturally justified, have not necessarily gotten us closer to realizing God's kingdom on earth. For this to happen, the entire system of human behavior, from economics and politics to family dynamics and even religion, must be challenged and often subverted.

To this point, order has been maintained through force. The rulers may have changed, but for the most part, the rules have not. One oppressor defeats and replaces another, and one sword is smashed by another, which then is then wielded over those it has defeated.

But Jesus wants more for us. He wants wholeness, not just victory. The true blessing that we seek from God is not simply to be better than the other but rather for all to coexist within a reality that affords no one any power or status over another. Can the simple turn of a cheek really achieve this? Can one man's life, innocently lost through crucifixion, really make any difference? For each of us, this is a question that must be answered through prayerful reflection and study. But once we have arrived at our conclusion, we're to live as if our lives depend on it.

Heads Up

Connecting the text to our world

One of our favorite consequences in our home when our kids are not getting along is to make them sit together, holding hands. You would think that the other one was radioactive, given the cringes and groans of misery that we hear when they are forced to engage in such an arduous task.

When do they get to let go of each other? As soon as they also let go of the idea that one of them has to be right-er than the other. Usually when they fight, it is because they are both convinced that the other one is an idiot. And rather than sorting that out for them and leaving one to gloat over the other, we prefer to focus on making the point that reconciliation is a far greater virtue than self-righteousness.

Imagine if you were made to hold hands with every person in your life that drives you crazy: your in-laws, Democrats/Republicans, the guy who wanders into worship late, always smelling of alcohol and urine, or someone who reminds you so much of yourself that you can hardly stand it. How long would it take for the two of you to work it out? How much pride would you have to swallow in order to come to agreeable terms with your enemy?

Unfortunately, these days we leave all of our conflict resolution to third parties. That's why lawyers live in bigger houses than us. The fact is, Jesus wants us to work it out face to face. If we do as the Gospels command us, there is no need for judge or jury to sort out our conflicts and differences. We are to wrestle together with their problems until we come to the realization that our shared humanity and our shared divinity are far more precious the satisfaction of being right or better.

And aside from being consistent with the teachings of Jesus, you get the extra satisfaction of putting a trial lawyer out of business. Talk about a win-win!

Prayer for the Week

God, help remind me to value the wholeness and reconciliation of all of your people more than my own need to be right or superior. Help me turn the other cheek. Help me to love those who hate me.

Popping Off

Art/music/video and other cool stuff that relate to the text

Twins (movie, 1988)

The Quick and the Dead (movie, 1995)

The Faith Needed
to Fail

Lectionary Texts For

November 10, 2019 (Twenty-Second Sunday after Pentecost)

Texts in Brief

My dog ate my Bible!

FIRST READING

Haggai 1:15b–2:9

Haggai is trying to rally the Jewish faithful to restore the temple to its former glory. At the moment they are very discouraged by the fact that it is sitting in utter ruin from the previous siege. The prophet assures them that prosperity and honor will return to them as a people soon enough, and he reminds them that the state of the temple is symbolic of their relationship with God.

and

Job 19:23–27a

Job is making a proclamation of his enduring faith, despite the dire present circumstances of his life. He believes, as all of his earthly being fades away and dies, he will come face-to-face with God.

PSALM

Psalm 145:1–5, 17–21; or Psalm 98

A song of praise to God for honoring God's covenant with the people of Israel. There is a longing for the time in the future when God will come and judge the earth with equity and righteousness. Those who have been wronged will be vindicated, and all will be restored to its proper order.

and

Psalm 17:1–9

King David is feeling threatened from all sides. He cries out to God for protection and vindication and claims openly that he has done all that God has asked of him. He even urges God to search his life over thoroughly, and that he will find no transgression.

SECOND READING

2 Thessalonians 2:1–5, 13–17

The members of the early church in Thessalonica are clearly discouraged. They are being persecuted for their faith, and some of them may be straying from the practices that Paul has taught them. He reminds them both that they are lucky to have been chosen to carry God's Word to the world, and also that he warned them from the outset that this journey would not be easy. Paul encourages them to stay the course despite present circumstances.

Gospel
Luke 20:27–38

The Sadducees, trying once again to make Jesus look like an idiot, pose a question about resurrection to him. It's important to note, though, that the Sadducees do not believe in resurrection after death. So they asked Jesus about a hypothetical woman who marries seven brothers, one after another, after the previous one dies. If she has no children with any of them, none of them seems to have special standing with her in the afterlife, so they ask which of the brothers will be married to her in heaven. Jesus basically blows them off, suggesting that the very question is senseless since such earthly covenants do not compare to the covenant that God makes with God's people. All are children of God, and all will be reconciled to God.

Bible, Decoded
Breaking down Scripture in plain language

Sadducees—This was a Jewish subset that came to prominence after the second reconstruction of the temple on the mount. They were among the social and economic elite, and one of their roles was to care for the temple. In our particular Gospel text, the fact that the author of Luke notes they do not believe in resurrection is an indication that he does not believe the Sadducees are a legitimate part of God's chosen people.

Haggai—As you probably already figured out by now, Haggai was a prophet who taught the people of Israel during the period of the second construction of the temple. So he and the Sadducees probably would've bumped into each other now and again. One of his primary roles was that of encourager of the people rebuilding the temple, as is noted in this first reading for the week.

Points to Ponder

First Thoughts

Things are pretty crappy for a lot of people in our texts this week. Job has been screwed from every possible direction, the Jews have had their land and their sacred temple sacked once again, and the early Christians in Thessalonica are freaking out because of the pressure of persecution they are under. But the primary theme this week is "hope despite present circumstances." Obviously, it is easy to feel hopeful when things are going well, but a truer sense of the integrity of our faith is how it performs when everything seems to be going south on us.

The reconstruction of the temple reminds me, in some ways, of our approach to the aftermath of 9/11. We knew as a society that we simply couldn't do nothing. It also didn't seem right just to rebuild what was already there without any acknowledgment of what had happened in the past. Those scars, and the pain that they represent, will never go away and should not be forgotten. One has to wonder how the temple builders commemorated the hardship that they and their people had been through to get to this point.

It is important to note that God doesn't need this temple. Rather, the Jewish people need it for several reasons. First it is a symbol of their faithfulness in the midst of adversity. Second, it is a project around which they can all rally and in which they can find hope. Its reconstruction suggests that no matter how many times they are torn down, they can get back up. And perhaps more important, God will meet them there.

Digging Deeper

Mining for what really matters . . . and gold

This is not the first time the temple in Jerusalem has been rebuilt. And unfortunately, it is not the last time that it will be torn down. It seems kind of pointless, really, to keep building something up only to have it crumble all around you. It would be easy to lose hope. No one could blame them really, especially after all they have been through.

But one thing that we see time and again, both in the Gospels and in the Old Testament stories, is that God/Jesus seems to connect with people in the most meaningful and profound ways when they are at their lowest points. Is it because God is testing us, seeing if we can hang in there long enough until he calls a heavenly timeout? Is it because he finally feels sorry for us? Or is it all because we need to be taught a lesson?

Personally, this is not the God of my understanding. God doesn't "do things" to us. And God never withholds God's self from us either. But when we are doing well, when things are going smoothly, it is all too easy to give ourselves a little bit too much credit, to feel like we are bulletproof, maybe even immortal, or at least more puffed up and full of ourselves than the humble servants to the world that we are called to be.

It's easier to remember this when life sucks. Our egos are no longer in the way, our willingness to change is greater, and we are simply more open to life as it comes at us. Yes, we can lose heart and our faith can falter, but God is there in those desperate, disconsolate moments.

God won't rebuild our broken lives for us, but God can be the source of renewal, hope, and persistence that we require to keep on building. Toward what, we can't always say. As Dory says in the movie *Finding Nemo*, sometimes the best thing we can do is just keep swimming.

Heads Up

Connecting the text to our world

Apple's cofounder Steve Jobs was, by all accounts, a tremendous success in the fields of technology, design, and business. He was meticulous, perfectionistic, and so obsessed about the quality of his work that some found him fairly impossible to work for. But what some people don't realize is that Steve Jobs failed far more often than he ever succeeded.

For starters, Steve Jobs was a college dropout. He only made it through one semester or so of classes before calling it quits. Interestingly, he is in good company, as Microsoft founder Bill Gates and Facebook creator Mark Zuckerberg both dropped out as well.

And although he finished strong with Apple, let's not forget that he was fired by the very company he helped create. And after being let go by Apple, Jobs started a new company that, by all accounts, was a spectacular failure.

Even Apple, the modern-day picture of technological success, and one of the most valuable and successful companies in the history of the world, has had far more products fail that it has had successes.

When asked about his many challenges and struggles, and how he managed to prevail and succeed anyway, Jobs was very matter-of-fact. In the end, he didn't feel that he had any greater capacity for success than anyone else. But what he did have was a high tolerance for failure. He was willing to fail often enough and terribly enough, and yet keep going because he believed in what he was doing and who he was.

Now just imagine if Steve Jobs had been in charge of the reconstruction of the temple in Jerusalem. Do you think everyone would have been reading the Torah from iPads?

Prayer for the Week

God, please help me never to be defined by my failures, and to never let them keep me from the work and the life I am meant to live into. Remind me that failure isn't nearly as bad as hopelessness or giving up. Give me the courage to fail often, and to do it with all of my heart.

Popping Off

Art/music/video and other cool stuff that relate to the text

Rushmore (movie, 1998)

"No for an Answer" scene from *Tommy Boy* (movie, 1995): tinyurl.com/y8lctjbv

What's Old Is New . . .
and Then Old Again

Lectionary Texts For

November 17, 2019 (Twenty-Third Sunday after Pentecost)

Texts in Brief

My dog ate my Bible!

First Reading

Isaiah 65:17–25

The prophet envisions a new heaven and earth, in which life in Jerusalem will be long, prosperous, and no longer in service to occupying powers. There will be unprecedented peace, down to the wild animals, who will lie together. The only one out of luck is the serpent, who has to eat dust. Poor guy.

and

Isaiah 12

A prayer of praise and thanks to God, who is the people's strength and salvation. God forgives, gets over past anger, and makes for a fresh start.

and

Malachi 4:1–2a

A new day is coming, in which those who are evil will be consumed by fire, and the pains of the righteous will all be healed by God.

Psalm

Psalm 98

A call for all of creation to join in a new song of praise to God. This is an anticipation of the coming judgment of God, which will be fair and just.

Second Reading

2 Thessalonians 3:6–13

A warning from Paul for all Christians to follow his example, earn their keep, and not take advantage of anyone's hospitality. Always operate from a place of humility and leave no opportunity for others to believe you have something you didn't work for and don't deserve.

Gospel

Luke 21:5–19

Jesus predicts the fall of the temple in Jerusalem again. There will come a time first, however, when wars, famines, and persecution will challenge the people of Israel. They will be captured and imprisoned for their faith, and he warns them not to make excuses, but rather to trust that God will look out for them. God will also use their persecution as a means to show others the conviction they have in what they believe.

Bible, Decoded

Breaking down Scripture in plain language

Malachi—The name of the last book in the Old Testament and the name attributed to the author of the text. It is estimated that this book was written about four hundred years before Jesus's birth. It doesn't mention the predicted restoration of the temple, which many other Old Testament prophets do, and it is possible that "Malachi" isn't actually a person's name; it translates simply as "messenger of God."

Serpent—We often equate biblical images of serpents with the garden of Eden story, assuming that all serpent references refer to evil, the devil, and so on. However, it was also a symbol in the ancient Near East of fortune-telling or divination of spirits. This was considered not of God, and so Jeremiah may be warning people not to succumb to the words of false prophets but to leave them in their proper place in the lowly dirt.

Points to Ponder

First Thoughts

It seems that Malachi and Isaiah need to get together and get their prophecies straight. Whereas Isaiah speaks here of peace among all—both oppressors and oppressed, predators and prey—Malachi is all about the bad guys getting crushed and burned to cinders. This seems to speak to two very distinct visions of what a hopeful future for the people of Israel looks like.

It seems, from Paul's letter here, that the Christians in Thessalonica are getting a little bit lazy. Part of his warning for them to get off their asses seems to be a matter of personal discipline. They should earn their place in society. But the other is a matter of appearances, of setting an example for others, as he has tried to do for them. He doesn't want people's impression of Christians to be that they are shiftless and unmotivated and take advantage of the generosity of others. They should be people in society to whom others look for an example.

Digging Deeper

Mining for what really matters . . . and gold

I recently attended a lecture by a sociologist who suggested that our tendency to see history as both linear and progressive is a symptom of our modernist, Western way of thinking. We tend always to presume that things will generally improve over time, and that we're headed toward something better than the present offers us. This is very evident in the surveys conducted of Americans, who have been found to be some of the most optimistic people on the planet. It may not be a realistic conception of the future, but it's also fueled innovation and ongoing investment at times, despite what seems to be common sense that should suggest quite the opposite.

And while we could debate night and day about whether this is a positive cultural trait, or if it simply is a byproduct of imperialist privilege (manifest destiny, will the future to be what you want it to be), it's important to consider that not all cultures in all times have though this way about the world.

It would be easy to imagine that the people of Israel would get discouraged after so many centuries of captivity, liberation, and more captivity, as well as building up, only to get torn down, and then start the cycle again. They keep building the temple up, and occupying forces knock it down. They live free for a while, and then they get exiled or imprisoned again.

Some cultures understand history to be more cyclical rather than linear. And if you think about it, this is more consistent with the patterns we see in nature. Birth, growth, attrition, death, renewal . . . and the cycle starts again. This helps explain why, when things have been pretty crappy for the Israelites, the prophets offer a message of hope.

But then again, when things are going pretty well, Jesus reminds them that everything has its season. Don't get too comfortable and too used to the good life. Enjoy it, yes, but also be realistic about what is to come.

For some, this would be an unnecessarily pessimistic or even nihilist worldview. But because we are called to be open to the wisdom of Paul, Jesus, and the other prophets, we should recognize that this is not just an inevitable part of the culture in which they lived; it's the example that we are called to live into.

Heads Up

Connecting the text to our world

One of my favorite cartoon characters growing up was a guy named Glum. No matter how well things were going to him and his companions, Glum would offer some dire prediction: *We're doomed. We'll never make it.*

Yes, having a guy like Glum around would be annoying (some of us may have a few Glums hanging around work or at church, reminding us how much worse things could—and probably will—be), but they're also a necessary reminder that life isn't perfect, that struggle and suffering are a part of it, and that this also is part of what makes it all so precious and beautiful.

I'm reminded of a quote by Frederick Buechner from his book *Whistling in the Dark*, where he talks about why the trappings and false happiness of Christmas is so, well ... annoying. It's because it's not real, he says. It's a façade we put on, trying to convince ourselves that it'll all be great and that this is, in fact, reality.

But it's not. And if it were, that would just be boring and tedious, to be honest. Here, Buechner points to the delicate balance of beauty, vulnerability, light, and dark, all wrapped up within the true story of the coming of Jesus:

> The Word become flesh. Ultimate Mystery born with a skull you could crush one-handed. Incarnation. It is not tame. It is not touching. It is not beautiful. It is uninhabitable terror. It is unthinkable darkness riven with unbearable light. Agonized laboring led to it, vast upheavals of intergalactic space/time split apart, a wrenching and tearing of the very sinews of reality itself. You can only cover your eyes and shudder before it, before this: "God of God, Light of Light, very God of very God ... who for us and for our salvation," as the Nicene Creed puts it, "came down from heaven."

Came down. Only then do we dare uncover our eyes and see what we can see. It is the Resurrection and the Life she holds in her arms. It is the bitterness of death he takes at her breast.

Prayer for the Week

God, help me recognize the difference between true hope and false, superficial optimism. Help me see the world both as it really is and as it could someday be, at the same time.

Popping Off

Art/music/video and other cool stuff that relate to the text

Whistling in the Dark, by Frederick Buechner (book, 1993)

How the Grinch Stole Christmas, by Dr. Seuss (book, 1957; movie, 1992, 2000)

12 Years a Slave (movie, 2013)

It's Not What It Looks Like!

———⟍╱╲╱⟍———

Lectionary Texts For

November 24, 2019 (Twenty-Fourth Sunday after Pentecost)

Texts in Brief

My dog ate my Bible!

First Reading

Jeremiah 23:1–6

The prophet, speaking for God, condemns the failure of previous Jewish leaders to protect their people from outside forces, while also offering a promise to reconcile those exiled together, once again.

Psalm

Psalm 46

A song of the power of God to preserve the city of David (Zion), and also to end all war and conflict for all times, in every corner of the earth. It is a call to hope and faith even when present circumstances are dire and seem to offer no positive future.

Second Reading
Colossians 1:11–20

Paul is praying on behalf of the church in Colossae for endurance for them. He reminds them also that their God has already delivered them from darkness before, which suggests they are in the midst of dark times now.

Gospel
Luke 1:68–79

A song of praise offered by Zechariah, husband to Elizabeth, both of whom are very old and unable to bear children. However, God has provided them with a son, whose name would be John. He will become known in adulthood as John the Baptist.

Bible, Decoded
Breaking down Scripture in plain language

Psalm—A psalm is really just a song, generally given up to God as a musical gift offering. Although the majority of psalms are collected in the book of the Bible of the same name, there are psalms throughout the Bible, such as this one sung by Zechariah in thanks and praise to God for him and Elizabeth being given a son. Sometimes Paul's letters read as poetically as psalms as well, though they were not specifically written as such.

Shepherd—This is a phrase used in many contexts in Scripture. In this case, in Jeremiah, it's referring to the kings of Israel and Judah. But of course, Jesus also is referred to as the shepherd, connoting that he is re-establishing the order of leadership among God's people.

Points to Ponder

First Thoughts

The theme in all our texts this week certainly is "hope beyond current circumstances." In some cases, it's hope for a particular change of situation. In others, it's prayers of thanks for things that have already happened that were unexpected. Still others are reflections on past graces to offer courage for the future. But it's worth taking the time to consider what we mean by hope. Is it hope in a particular outcome? Or is hope simply hope in and of itself? Can we remain filled with divinely inspired hope, even when things never seem to turn around?

I explore this further in the "heads up" section below, but this set of texts is a good sort of preamble to Advent, a time of open-ended expectancy as opposed to narrow-minded, proscribed expectations. There's a big difference: one leaves room for God, for the mystery of "perhaps," and the other one is little more than a wish list we hand over to Santa.

Digging Deeper

Mining for what really matters . . . and gold

Why do they keep going? What compels the people of Israel to persist after being enslaved by the Egyptians, exiled into the desert for forty years, and besieged by the Assyrians and the Babylonians? Why keep rebuilding, coming back, and sticking together when time after time, it leads to pain and heartbreak?

I can't say for sure, but one argument that can be made is that there's far more at stake than simply surviving and prospering as a single nation. Not that the Jews living back then could have possibly known what the Jewish and Christian faiths would look like today, or that Abraham's lineage would give rise to the three most dominant religions in modern history. And it's not so much about that either, but rather about understanding that hope calls us forward and through the hard stuff, no matter what.

Thank goodness God offers words of encouragement, vision, and guidance from people like Jeremiah, Paul, David, and Jesus. These are "big picture" people, if you will, who have a gift for looking past the present toward a much bigger context, in which we're all a part.

Thy kingdom come, thy will be done, on earth as it is in heaven.

That's really an impossible dream, isn't it? I mean, look around. Are we really living out the kingdom of God? Some days it feels more like two steps forward, three giant leaps back. But we need our prophets, our sure and steady shepherd, to help us look out beyond the horizon and to say, "There, that's where we are headed."

We want to know what happens when we get there. Give us the plan, the specific roadmap, and be sure to mark all the potholes and landmines. But competent shepherds have their flock's bet interest at heart, and it's the job of the flock to trust that.

We can't all be shepherds. Not all of the time. Sometimes we need to remind ourselves how to be better at just being part of the fold.

Heads Up

Connecting the text to our world

Situation comedies are the worst. You know the ones; they're always thirty minutes long, usually filmed on a soundstage with a live audience, and feature the worn out, pre-recorded laugh track in the background to let you know when something is supposed to be funny. They've gotten better in recent years, but most of them still seem to recreate the same tired scenarios over and over again.

One of my least favorite situations is when a character gets caught up in a hopelessly compromising position, only to have his significant other walk in at the absolute worst time.

"It's not what you think!" he says, inevitably, although we all know it is *precisely* what she thinks.

In our most recent lectionary texts, we have a lot of these kinds of situations. We seem to have a pattern going on wherein people will assume things are one way, and then God (or one of God's emissaries) suggests it's not actually as it appears to be. With the people of Israel and Judah, they've been dominated by the Assyrians, scattered to the four corners, and now the Babylonians are threatening. But despite what seems to be an impossible situation, Jeremiah assures them that God will restore them and all that is theirs.

Zechariah and Elizabeth are sure their chances for childbearing are dried up, and then—*poof*—she's pregnant. David's psalm recalls the many times God has remained faithful when prospects were dim, and Paul assures the church in Colossae that they're looked after.

It's actually a great theme to help us prepare for Advent.

Something is coming. Nature may be in retreat, and the days getting shorter. We may seem to be shrouded in darkness, and yet, I bring good news of great joy . . .

The thing we have to be careful about when it comes to God is cashing in one existing set of assumptions for another. Yes, we may see no way out of a situation, but that also doesn't mean just because we pray that God will magically make everything go our way. Just like we read in last week's Gospel text, Jesus reminds his followers that for their faithfulness they'll be jailed, abandoned, persecuted, tortured, and even killed. What a blessing, right?

But In holding fast to our faith that God is in all things, even the bad things, we can begin to see glimmers of hope, wisdom, and growth in the most miserable circumstances. We begin to be able to imagine what the world might look like if the brokenness and suffering were, once and for all, transcended. We can start to share with others this inspired vision that calls us toward a reality far greater than the present circumstances.

Will it turn out the way we want? Maybe, and maybe not. Jesus certainly wasn't what lots of people expected or wanted. But advent is a time of expectancy rather than expectation. One is hope-filled, open to mystery and possibility, while the other is dead set on a particular outcome. Time and again, people don't get what they want in the Bible, and yet things tend to turn out as they should. So for this coming advent season, let's try to replace some of our many expectations with the more open-ended expectancy that asks, "What's next?"

Then, let's go forward and find out together.

Prayer for the Week

God, help me stop trying so hard to always be the shepherd. Help me remember that it's part of my job to trust, to be part of the flock, and to follow in faith.

Popping Off

Art/music/video and other cool stuff that relate to the text

"The Purpose of Training" scene from *The Karate Kid* (movie, 1984): tinyurl.com/yd67uqrm

"88 Miles per Hour" scene from *Back to the Future* (movie, 1985): tinyurl.com/ybtex328